The Red River Campaign

Civil War Campaigns and Commanders Series

Battle in the Wilderness: Grant Meets Lee by Grady McWhiney

Death in September: The Antietam Campaign by Perry D. Jamieson

Texans in the Confederate Cavalry by Anne J. Bailey

Sam Bell Maxey and the Confederate Indians by John C. Waugh

The Saltville Massacre by Thomas D. Mays

General James Longstreet in the West: A Monumental Failure
    by Judith Lee Hallock

The Battle of the Crater by Jeff Kinard

*Cottonclads! The Battle of Galveston and the Defense of the Texas
    Coast* by Donald S. Frazier

A Deep Steady Thunder: The Battle of Chickamauga
    by Steven E. Woodworth

The Texas Overland Expedition of 1863 by Richard Lowe

Raphael Semmes and the Alabama by Spencer C. Tucker

War in the West: Pea Ridge and Prairie Grove by William L. Shea

Iron and Heavy Guns: Duel Between the Monitor and Merrimac
    by Gene A. Smith

The Emergence of Total War by Daniel E. Sutherland

John Bell Hood and the Struggle for Atlanta by David Coffey

*The Most Promising Young Man of the South: James Johnston
    Pettigrew and His Men at Gettysburg* by Clyde N. Wilson

Vicksburg: Fall of the Confederate Gibraltar by Terrence J. Winschel

This Grand Spectacle: The Battle of Chattanooga
    by Steven E. Woodworth

Rutherford B. Hayes: "One of the Good Colonels" by Ari Hoogenboom

Jefferson Davis's Greatest General: Albert Sidney Johnston
    by Charles P. Roland

Unconditional Surrender: The Capture of Forts Henry and Donelson
    by Spencer C. Tucker

Last Stand at Mobile by John C. Waugh

George Gordon Meade and the War in the East by Ethan S. Rafuse

Winfield Scott Hancock: Gettysburg Hero by Perry D. Jamieson

The Last Stronghold: The Campaign for Fort Fisher
    by Richard B. McCaslin

Sherman's March to the Sea by John F. Marszalek

Campaign for Corinth: Blood in Mississippi
    by Steven Nathaniel Dossman

Campaign for Wilson's Creek: The Fight for Missouri Begins
    by Jeffrey L. Patrick

The Red River Campaign

The Union's Final Attempt to Invade Texas

Gary D. Joiner

State House Press

Buffalo Gap, Texas

To Ludwell Johnson and Grady McWhiney

Library of Congress Cataloging-in-Publication Data

Joiner, Gary D.
The Red River Campaign: The Unions Last Attempt to Invade Texas
Gary D. Joiner
     p. cm. (Civil War Campaign and Commander Series)
Includes Bibliographical references and index.
ISBN- 978-1-933337-60-9 (pbk. alk. paper)
ISBN- 933337-60-5 (pbk. alk. paper)
1. History United States 2. History / Civil War 3. United States: History-19th
century. 4. Texas History / Civil War, Texas
This paper meets the requirements of ANSI/NISO, Z39.48-1992(permanence
of paper) Binding materials have been chosen for durability ∞
I. Title.

"Cataloging-in-Publication Data available from the Library of Congress"

Manufactured in the United States
Copyright 2013, State House Press
All Rights Reserved
First Edition

State House Press
P.O. Box 818
Buffalo Gap, Texas 79508
325-572-3974 · 325-572-3991 (fax)
www.tfhcc.com

Printed in the United States of America
Distributed by Texas A&M University Press Consortium
800-826-8911
www.tamupress.com

ISBN-13: 978-1-933337-60-9
ISBN-10: 1-933337-60-5

Book Design by Rosenbohm Graphic Design

Contents

Biographical Sketches, Maps, Illustrations, and Major Players   vii

Preface   xi

1   Origins of the Red River Campaign   1

2   The Confederates Prepare   15

3   Union Plans to Take Louisiana   35

4   The Union Advances   49

5   The Battle of Mansfield   65

6   The Battle of Pleasant Hill   81

7   The Camden Campaign   93

8   The Navy   117

9   Union Retreat   137

Appendixes   157

Notes   177

Selected Bibliography   195

Index   203

CAMPAIGNS AND COMMANDERS SERIES

Map Key

Geography

 Trees

Marsh

 Fields

Strategic Elevations

Rivers

Tactical Elevations

 Fords

Orchards

———————— Political Boundaries

Human Construction

)(Bridges

+++++++++ Railroads

 Tactical Towns

● ○ Strategic Towns

□ ■ Buildings

✝ Church

✕ Roads

Military

  Union Infantry

  Confederate Infantry

 Cavalry

ılı Artillery

Headquarters

Encampments

Fortifications

Permanant Works

Hasty Works

Obstructions

Engagements

Warships

Gunboats

Casemate Ironclad

Monitor

Tactical Movements

Strategic Movements

Biographical Sketches

Nathaniel P. Banks	10
Edmund Kirby Smith	16
William R. Boggs	19
John Bankhead Magruder	27
Andrew Jackson Smith	39
William B. Franklin	55
Albert L. Lee	59
Richard Taylor	66
Thomas E. G. Ransom	72
John G. Walker	74
Camille Armand Jules Marie, Prince de Polignac	75
Frederick Steele	96
Sterling Price	98
John S. Marmaduke	101
James F. Fagan	108
David Dixon Porter	118
Thomas O. Selfridge, Jr.	122
Seth Ledyard Phelps	124
Joseph Bailey	132

Maps

Louisiana in 1861   2

Trans-Mississippi Region   7

Shreveport in 1864   24

Tone's Bayou Forts   26

Banks' Plan of Invasion   43

Red River Campaign Battles   61

Battle of Mansfield   76

Battle of Pleasant Hill Opening Positions   86

Battle of Pleasant Hill Final Positions   87

Red River Campaign and Camden Campaign   94

Battle of Poison Spring   105

Battle of Jenkins' Ferry Opening Positions   111

Battle of Jenkins' Ferry Final Positions   113

Steele's Campaign in Arkansas   115

Battle of Blair's Landing   121

Cane River Island   140

Battle of Monett's Ferry   142

Battle of Mansura   149

Battle of Yellow Bayou Early Afternoon   151

Battle of Yellow Bayou Late Afternoon   152

Polignac's Attack   153

Photographs

Fort DeRussy Raft	21
Confederate Engineers at Shreveport	29
Detail of the Raft at Shreveport	31
Raft at Shreveport	32
USS *Eastport*	45
Brigadier General Joseph A. Mower	50
Fort DeRussy	51
Colonel James Hamilton Beard	67
Brigadier General Jean Jacques Alexandre Alfred Mouton	73
Brigadier General Thomas Churchill	84
Brigadier General John M. Thayer	99
Colonel Horace Randal	112
Brigadier General William R. Scurry	114
USS *Osage*	123
USS *Cricket*	126
USS *Signal*	129
USS *Neosho*	130
Portion of the Union Fleet Trapped above Alexandria	133
Bailey's Dam	135
Bridge of Boats at the Atchafalaya River	154

Major Players

Joseph Bailey	US Colonel, Engineer, Nineteenth Army Corps
Nathaniel P. Banks	US Major General, Commander of the Department of the Gulf
James Hamilton Beard	CSA Colonel, Consolidated Crescent Regiment
William R. Boggs	CSA Brigadier General, Chief of Staff, Department of the Trans-Mississippi
William H. Emory	US Brigadier General, Commander of the First Division, Nineteenth Army Corps
William B. Franklin	US Major General, Commander, Nineteenth Army Corps
Ulysses S. Grant	US Lieutenant General, Commander of all Union armies
Tom Green	CSA Major General (Brevet), Commander of the Texas Cavalry Corps
Henry Halleck	US Major General, Union General-in-Chief
Albert L. Lee	US Brigadier General, Commander, Cavalry Division, Nineteenth Army Corps
John Magruder	CSA Major General, Commander, District of Texas
John S. Marmaduke	CSA Brigadier General, Commander, Cavalry Division in Arkansas
Jean Jacque Alexandre Alfred	CSA Brigadier General, Commander, Louisiana Division
Joseph Mower	US Brigadier General, Brigade Commander
Seth Ledyard Phelps	US Lieutenant Commander, Captain, USS *Eastport*
Camille A. J. M. Polignac	CSA Brigadier General, Brigade Commander
David Dixon Porter	US Rear Admiral, Commander, Mississippi Squadron
Sterling Price	CSA Major General, Commander, District of Missouri and Arkansas
Thomas E. G. Ransom	US Brigadier General, Commander, Provisional Division, Thirteenth Army Corps
Thomas O. Selfridge, Jr.	US Lieutenant Commander, Captain, USS *Osage*
Andrew Jackson Smith	US Brigadier General, Commander, Sixteenth Army Corps
Edmund Kirby Smith	CSA Lieutenant General, Commander, Department of the Trans-Mississippi
Frederick Steele	US Major General, Commander, District of Arkansas
Richard Taylor	CSA Major General, Commander. District of Western Louisiana
John G. Walker	CSA Major General, Commander Texas Division

Preface

The body of publications written about the Civil War over the past 150 years is enormous. From biographies to battle account monographs, the fondness for both writers and the reading public has been insatiable. There is one geographic area that, until the past decade, has not seen as much scrutiny. This is the vast region of the Trans-Mississippi. The name illustrates its origin. I almost titled one of my books *Too Far from Virginia to Matter Much*, but the publisher thought that it was too negative. Perhaps it was. The campaigns in the Trans-Mississippi are largely misunderstood by Eastern and Midwestern historians of the Civil War. The distances are huge, the battlegrounds are far flung, and the units, at least on the Southern side, were unorthodox. One logistical problem in the telling of these sagas is that reporters following the armies were rare. It was often weeks before they could get their stories out and the news was then stale. Official reports were often written later and were not of the best quality.

The focus of this book is the Red River Campaign of 1864. It was the largest combined arms effort by the Union west of the Mississippi River during the war. The Union forces consisted of more than 42,500 soldiers, sailors, and marines. The Navy brought almost all of the Mississippi Squadron, at least 108 vessels, up the shallow, tortuous, and fickle Red River in a grand effort to accomplish two objectives. The first was the capture and occupation of Shreveport, Louisiana. Shreveport was the Confederate capital of Louisiana, the home of a burgeoning naval facility, the command center for the Army of the Trans-Mississippi (also known as the Army of Western Louisiana), and the nexus for a far-flung military procurement operation that stretched into Texas as far as Houston and into southwestern Arkansas, as well as most of northern Louisiana. The second objective was to invade Texas and plant the US flag at some viable place from which to declare a free-soil Texas state. To do this, Union forces would converge by moving up the Red River to Alexandria, march across southern Louisiana to near Opelousas and then march northeast to Alexandria, and a third column would descend on Shreveport from Arkansas. The latter force would begin in Little Rock and Fort Smith, join at Arkadelphia, and then drive the final distance together.

Opposing them would be the much smaller Army of the Trans-Mississippi. This widely scattered force was composed of units from Texas, Louisiana, Arkansas, Missouri, and the Indian Territory (Oklahoma). It was never able to amass more than twelve thousand men on the field at one time. Led by Major General Richard Taylor, the small army finished the war without surrendering. The greatest battle of the campaign was fought three miles southeast of the town of Mansfield. It would be the last major Southern victory in the war. This is the story of battles lost and battles won and of leaders on both sides with giant egos or tempered brilliance. It is a story too often ignored. For those of us who live in the Trans-Mississippi, it is our story, our past, and the events that shaped our civilization.

Several historians have dedicated all or large portions of their careers to this theater of operations. It is to these professionals that the author considers among his dearest friends and comrades. He would be remiss to recount all of them for fear of leaving someone out. You know who you are. Two people must be singled out for their contributions, and it is to these individuals that this modest work is dedicated. First is Ludwell Johnson, the dean of Red River Campaign studies. His book, *Red River Campaign: Politics and Cotton in the Civil War*, was first published in 1958. This work was a groundbreaking analysis of both the military and the economic backgrounds to the campaign. All historians following him have used this book as point of departure. Second is the late Grady McWhiney. McWhiney was a renaissance man in the truest sense. He authored fourteen books, many articles, and was a lightning rod for his beliefs. He was an expert on Celtic ways and Southern life. He carried this knowledge to new realms of thought. McWhiney once said that "Southerners lost the Civil War because they were too Celtic and their opponents were too English." Among the best and brightest of the Civil War scholars found in this region were either graduate students of McWhiney or taught by them.

The author would also like to thank Thomas A. Pressly III M.D. of Shreveport, a good historian in his own right, for the kind permission of the use of his image of Thomas E.G. Ransom in the biographical sketches.

Finally, the author must thank two important individuals: Donald S. Frazier, President and Chief Executive Officer of the McWhiney History Education Group, and Scott Clowdus, Director of Operations of the McWhiney History Education Group. Frazier not only runs the McWhiney group, but he was also one of those graduate students referenced previously. He is a fine author, a great cartographer, a terrific speaker, and an essential co-investigator in all things Civil War in the West. Clowdus is one of the best people to work with in the publishing business. He is diligent, kind, and a consummate professional. This work would not appear without them.

Gary D. Joiner, Ph.D.
Chair, Department of History and Social Sciences
Louisiana State University–Shreveport
February 2014

1
ORIGINS OF THE
RED RIVER CAMPAIGN

As 1864 began the Union armies focused on two major axes: Tennessee to Georgia and movements toward Richmond in Virginia.[1] The only major campaign that year not part of these efforts was one far removed from them. The Red River Campaign in Louisiana, and a companion campaign in Arkansas, went terribly wrong for the Union.

The Red River Campaign was a pivotal combined arms operation between the Union army and navy during the Civil War. The expedition up the Red River in the spring of 1864 saw the greatest concentration of inland naval vessels operating in concert during the entire conflict.

Following the falls of Vicksburg and Port Hudson in July 1863, the US Navy's Mississippi Squadron, commanded by Rear Admiral David Dixon Porter, patrolled the Mississippi River with a vast array of heavily armed vessels. Porter's hold on the Mississippi and its tributaries was absolute with the exception of the Red River. He consolidated Union control of the Mississippi River as Ulysses S. Grant moved into Tennessee and raised the siege of Chattanooga.

In March 1864, Grant was promoted to lieutenant general and general-in-chief of the army and moved his headquarters to Virginia. The

Louisiana on the eve of the Civil War, 1861. Cartography by Gary D. Joiner.

Mississippi Squadron continued to patrol the waters of the Mississippi Valley until it was called on to assist Major General Nathaniel P. Banks in an attack on Shreveport.

When the Red River Campaign was proffered as an operation in early 1864, Major General William T. Sherman wanted to lead the expedition and Porter jumped at the chance to work with his old friend. When Sherman was forced to bow out to command the Atlanta Campaign, Porter was stuck. The admiral expected to work with his old comrade, but his enthusiasm cooled when he found that he would be cooperating with Banks. Despite his concerns, Porter was a naval officer who had signed on to the mission, and he needed to carry through with it, but he did not trust Banks. Both Grant and Sherman disliked the political general and Porter was well aware of his lack of success through both personal contact and the communications with the admiral's foster brother, Admiral David Glascow Farragut. The air of mistrust emanating from Porter, Grant, and Sherman extended up and down the chain of command. Their opinions sowed the seeds of discord during the campaign. Sherman's men were western veterans and their views were typically those of their leader; they held little regard for political generals. The naval officers held the same attitudes.

Economic and political considerations played a key role in planning campaigns after the fall of Vicksburg and this was particularly true for operations in the Trans-Mississippi. Cotton was not simply an economic boon to the Confederacy, but it was also a great economic attraction for the North, particularly the textile mills of New England that were starving for the raw material of their businesses. The existence of tremendous amounts of quality Red River Valley cotton was without a doubt the key factor in Shreveport being added to the Union High Command's target list.

In 1864, Shreveport's local economy was much healthier than her small population in 1860 might have indicated and its importance as a war center had become assured. Its location near the northern limits of navigable waters on the Red River made it a safe haven for those fleeing the war. In late 1863, Union military planners were prosecuting the war in Tennessee and Virginia, planning to move into Georgia, and the concept of an attack on Texas via the Red River Valley in Louisiana was being formed.

So, why Shreveport? A major reason is certainly the presence of a field army that had been largely unchallenged. A Rebel state capital was located in the town; Austin, the capital of Texas, was in close proximity; and two Confederate capitals-in-exile were nearby and unmolested (Missouri's at Marshall and Arkansas's at Old Washington, both within sixty miles of Shreveport). But the overriding reason for the campaign was the existence of cotton.

The Confederates termed the area west of the Mississippi River the "Department of the Trans-Mississippi," which extended westward to the present border between California and Arizona, and northward into the Indian Territory that is present-day Oklahoma. Shreveport was its headquarters. The town also served as the capital of Confederate Louisiana and as the nexus for the rudimentary military-industrial complex west of the Mississippi. In addition it was the primary cotton-exporting and trans-shipment point north of New Orleans. Shreveport was the most important trading center in the Red River Valley.

The lower Red River Valley served as a dividing line between Catholic southern Louisiana and Protestant northern Louisiana. Settlers migrating from the east with Scottish, Irish, and English heritage populated the river valley.[2] Shreveport was situated near the northwest corner of the state. It had been incorporated for less than thirty years. As such, it was still developing its own culture and identity. One thing was certain, though. Its location on the Red River and its proximity to Texas and Arkansas made it the economic center of a region that encompassed northwest Louisiana, northeast Texas, and southwest Arkansas.

The town was the northernmost point on the Red River open to navigation. Its location placed it at the head of the Texas Trail, the cattle and immigrant road that led livestock and migrating pioneers to south and west Texas. The trail was the major route of goods and supplies coming from Mexico. Before the annexation of Texas into the Union in 1845, the towns of Shreveport, Greenwood, and Logansport had been the westernmost in the United States. Shreveport occupied an approximately one-mile square diamond-shaped plateau. With the exception of Grand Ecore in Natchitoches Parish, about 60 miles downstream, the Shreveport hill terraces on the west side of the river were the last high ground on the Red River before it emptied into the Mississippi River, some 230 river miles downstream.[3]

In 1860 the population of Shreveport had been just 2,190.[4] But by 1864, this number had swollen to more than 12,000 as war refugees flooded in from southern Louisiana, Arkansas, and Missouri.[5] Many of the refugees were family members of men serving in the area; others were from places nearer the front lines.[6] Although some of these people found work in war-related industries, many were destitute and required aid from the military and local government.[7] Those who found jobs did so because Shreveport and Caddo Parish had become an important trading center. It was the primary trans-shipment complex for north Louisiana and east

Texas cotton. Situated at the end of the Texas Trail, it was a shipping point for cattle being sent down river. In 1860, Caddo Parish was fourth in the state of Louisiana in the total number of business establishments and second in the state in the annual value of products manufactured (on a per-parish basis), providing even more opportunities.[8] The economic vitality of the area and Shreveport's location at a crossroads for trade and navigation made it an ideal center for a military complex.

The Red River Valley in Louisiana, southwest Arkansas, and deep east Texas had taken the nickname, the "Upper Cotton Kingdom," with good reason. This was the greatest cotton-producing area in the Confederacy. The rich, deep, sandy alluvial soil of the Red River was one of the most perfect in North America for growing cotton. The weather in 1863 had been kind, rainy at the beginning of the growing season, but not too wet. It cleared as the cotton plants matured for harvest, and the dry spell ensured a bumper crop.[9] By late winter of 1863–1864, tens of thousands of cotton bales, the "white gold," had been harvested by the cotton plantation slaves and processed into bales at hundreds of gins in the region. The bales were then moved by wagons to steamboat landings and were sitting on the banks of the Red River and its associated streams ready for shipment southward. Late cotton crops were still growing and had not yet been harvested.[10]

Beginning in March 1863, Shreveport became the focal point for a vast array of defenses on and near the Red River. The town was the hub of a vital war industry with a naval yard, factories, foundries, arsenals, powder mills, and other facilities that reached into other states. The outlying facilities directed from Shreveport were located in Texas at Houston, Tyler, Marshall, and Jefferson. Confederate military units in Louisiana, Texas, Arkansas, and the Indian Territories of Oklahoma, New Mexico, and Arizona all answered to Shreveport. The war-related industries at these locations armed, clothed, and sustained Confederate forces west of the Mississippi River. Of course, blockade runners brought goods into Texas ports and there was significant trade across the Rio Grande from Mexico as well.

Shreveport was well fortified with a series of forts, walls, and artillery emplacements. Near the mouth of Cross Bayou was a construction yard for a fledgling riverine naval force, the nexus of a thriving small-scale military-industrial complex.[11]

Shreveport's position at the head of the Texas Trail and its status as a military, political, and economic center ensured this position. However, it became an important military target almost by accident. Union military planners conceived the Red River Campaign as a result of political pressure. Military necessity played a secondary role. Once the primary target was chosen and the principal military units were identified, preparations for the expedition proceeded rapidly. Union commanders allocated huge numbers of men and boats to the mission, but from the beginning, they used flawed logic.

The year before the Red River Campaign began brought many changes in the course of the war. During the first half of 1863, the Confederates maintained their viability as nation, though they were pressured militarily. The Union army had suffered several failures or costly tactical ties in major battles by the middle of the year. Then the tide of war began to change on both the eastern and western fronts. Union successes following the great twin victories in July 1863 at Vicksburg and Gettysburg fueled a common opinion that the end of the war was near. The South was not ready to admit defeat, but Union pessimism turned into an air of overconfidence. On January 17, 1864, the Union General-in-Chief, Major General Henry Halleck, wrote to his protégé, and soon-to-be General-in-Chief, Major General Grant that "people . . . are acting in the mistaken supposition that the war is nearly ended, and that we shall hereafter have to contend only with fragments of broken and demoralized rebel armies. Such is the tone of the public press and the debates in Congress."[12]

On the other side, the Confederacy was hard-pressed but still possessed strong field armies, although they were shrinking as a result of attrition. West of the Mississippi River, the situation was more optimistic. The vital supply lines from the Texas coast and Rio Grande,

The Trans-Mississippi

KANSAS
Lawrence
Lexington
Fort Scott
St. Louis
MISSOURI
Baxter Springs
Springfield

Fort Union
INDIAN TERR.
Fort Gibson
Santa Fe
Albuquerque
NEW MEXICO TERR
Fort Cobb
Fort Arbuckle
Boggy Depot
Doaksville
Fort Smith
ARKANSAS
Little Rock
Fort Hindman
Camden
Fort Craig
ARIZONA TERR.
Paris
Fort Bliss
Dallas
Tyler
Shreveport
TEXAS
LOUISIANA
Alexandria
Fort DeRussy
Fort Davis
Fort Lancaster
Austin
Baton Rouge
New Orleans
Niblett's Bluff
Houston
New Iberia
Fort Clark
San Antonio
Galveston

Brownsville

into the heartland of Texas, Louisiana, and Arkansas, supplied the Trans-Mississippi units. Ranchers and farmers, with their huge quantities of cattle, grain, and that most important trading commodity, cotton, to a large extent, created a self-contained economy. Trade and supply chains between the Confederate areas east and west of the Mississippi River were mutual with more arms coming from the east to the west.[13]

The grandiose-sounding Confederate Department of the Trans-Mississippi was largely cut off from the east and the Mississippi River once it came under Union control. The Union navy heavily patrolled the great river, at times allowing only limited contact between Confederate forces on either side. Guns, powder, and other items necessary to keep armies running were either manufactured in northwest Louisiana and east Texas or smuggled up from Mexico, but they could not be consistently shipped across the Mississippi River to assist the eastern armies.

Confederate troops west of the Mississippi River were scattered across northern Louisiana, southwest Arkansas, and throughout east Texas. On paper the number of Confederate cavalry available, particularly in Texas cavalry regiments, appeared huge. In fact, most of these western units were dismounted and fought as infantry.

The Union believed that Confederate troops were spread so thinly on both banks of the Mississippi River that only guerrilla raiders operated against the vastly numerically superior Union forces in hit-and-run attacks. In fact, although Admiral Porter believed that only bushwhackers operated on the Louisiana side of the river, the autumn and winter of 1863–1864 saw Major General John G. Walker's Texas Division all but shut down the Mississippi to military traffic for several weeks.[14] Union Major General Sherman, posing an obvious threat and taunting the Confederates, marched his forces out of Vicksburg and crossed the state to attack Meridian near the Alabama border. He met almost no opposition on his march.

Cotton, particularly the lack of it in New England mills, played a key role in the early planning of the Red River Campaign. The Union invasion of the Lower Mississippi in 1862 had several objectives. The closing of the Mississippi River to the Confederates and the capture of New Orleans, the largest city in the South, were certainly priorities, but the chance to capture a huge supply of cotton and bring the New England mills back online offered tremendous political and economic opportunities.[15] President Abraham Lincoln needed New England for the 1864 elections. The region's political general favorite sons, Benjamin Butler and Banks, both major generals, were the senior-ranking field officers in the Union army and both were politically ambitious and well aware of the needs of their textile mill benefactors.

President Lincoln realized he had to keep New England pacified, alleviate the cotton shortage, and carry on the business of ending the rebellion. The primary source for cotton to operate the textile mills was the South and the war had cut off this source. The textile industry was a major component of the New England economy, and the lack of cotton had created massive layoffs. Before the war, almost five million spindles operated in the mills in New England.[16] In 1862, only 25 percent were operating.[17] The capture of New Orleans had yielded only twenty-seven thousand bales, a drastic reduction from the two million bales processed by the port before the invasion.[18] New Orleans was the receiving point, not the producing center, for cotton from the Mississippi Valley and its tributaries. The lack of cotton available at the port of New Orleans came as a tremendous shock to the Union strategists. Cotton must be obtained, and the general who procured it would reap tremendous political rewards.

President Lincoln had been led to believe—incorrectly as was demonstrated by later events—that the German immigrant farmers of the hill country of central Texas near Austin were pro-Union and would stage a revolt against their Confederate leaders if the opportunity arose.[19] New England needed cotton desperately, and bankers and mill owners were lobbying hard for relief. Liberating cotton-producing areas and bringing them back into the Union fold could achieve this. Butler suggested an amphibious invasion at some point along the Texas coast, at which time the anticipated counter-revolution by the German patriots would occur in the Texas hill country.[20]

Banks was identified as the replacement of General Butler, who had run afoul of the command staff in Washington and the citizens of New Orleans. Banks was rakishly handsome, a fastidious dresser, and a political heavyweight. He was honest but authoritarian, with no tolerance for those questioning his judgment, even career military officers. To his discredit, he was vain and at times showed exquisitely timed poor judgment.[21] Pressure was placed on Banks, as it was on his predecessor, to plant the flag in Texas, and now events outside the control of Washington or New Orleans began to spin affairs in a new direction.[22] Even before Vicksburg fell, French troops landed in Mexico and quickly installed Maximilian as the Emperor of Mexico on June 7, 1863. There were renewed fears in Washington that the French, and perhaps the British, would enter

Nathaniel P. Banks

Born in Massachusetts in 1816, Banks received little formal education. He was admitted to the bar in 1829; entered Massachusetts legislature, rising to speaker of the house; presided over the state's 1853 Constitutional Convention and was elected to the US House of Representatives that same year. During his tenure, he was elected  speaker of the House in 1856 and then was elected governor of Massachusetts in 1858, serving until 1861. At the outbreak of the Civil War, he offered his services to the Union and was appointed major general US Volunteers by President Abraham Lincoln. Banks headed the Department of Annapolis before assuming command of the Department of the Shenandoah. He was prevented from reinforcing General George B. McClellan on the peninsula by the aggressive actions of General Thomas J. Jackson's Confederates in the Shenandoah Valley. He later defeated Jackson at Kernstown, Virginia, in March 1862 but fared poorly in subsequent actions. Banks was assigned to command the Second Corps in General John Pope's newly formed Army of Virginia but was defeated by Jackson at Cedar Mountain during the Second Bull Run Campaign in August 1862. After Pope's army was dismantled, Banks headed briefly the Military District of Washington before assuming command of the Department of the Gulf. He conducted a costly operation against Port Hudson, which fell only after Vicksburg's capture left it untenable and directed the marginally successful Bayou Teche Expedition in the fall of 1863. Following the failure of his Red River Expedition in 1864, Banks was relieved by General E. R. S. Canby; he received the thanks of Congress for Port Hudson and mustered out of volunteer service in 1865. Banks returned to Congress where he served six more terms (not consecutively); declining health forced his retirement from Congress in 1890. He died in Massachusetts in 1894. General Banks was among the most active of the higher-ranking "political" generals. He was consistently placed in command positions that were beyond his abilities; his personal courage, devotion, and tenacity could not overcome his lack of military training.

into open cooperation with and perhaps even formal recognition of the Confederacy.[23] Planting the US flag on Texas soil became a political necessity, not simply a presidential wish. Once the Mississippi River was open to federal navigation, President Lincoln and communiqués from General-in-Chief Henry Halleck instructed Banks to move forward.

Halleck had proposed an attack up the Red River, but Banks countered that an attack on Sabine Pass at the mouth of the Sabine River that formed the boundary between Louisiana and Texas, would serve as a better base to attack Houston and from there to advance into deep east Texas.[24] On August 31, 1863, Banks ordered Major General William B. Franklin to load one brigade from the First Division of the Nineteenth Corps onto transports, and with the accompaniment of naval gunboats, land at and secure Sabine Pass.[25] The small fleet arrived at the pass on September 7 and was met by a force of some fifty men with five guns dug in at a mud fort. The small contingent neutralized two of the gunboats, and the remainder was forced to retire. The transports never had a chance to deploy their soldiers on the mud flats, and the entire expeditionary force was compelled to return to New Orleans.[26] Banks blamed the fiasco on the navy.[27] Neither the army nor navy was blameless. Neither invested adequate time in planning this foray. Banks' vocal accusations of the navy caused a rift between him and Farragut and Porter. The distrust created would only increase in the following months.

In late October, Banks sent Franklin on another invasion attempt; this one even less thoroughly planned than the first. His idea was a march overland through the Bayou Teche country and into the prairies of southwest Louisiana to a point somewhere on the Sabine River where the expedition could ford or otherwise cross into Texas. Franklin picked his way across south central Louisiana, which was at that time sparsely populated. The region supplied almost no ability to forage for needed supplies. The column made it to Opelousas in St. Landry Parish and then turned around, unsure what to do.[28] The navy approached Alexandria, but reversed course when no contact with the army was made.

Simultaneously with Franklin's expedition, other actions were taken. During this trek, the navy sent units up the Ouachita and Red Rivers to divert attention from Franklin's column. The gunboats did little damage. Action was also seen in southern Louisiana in St. Mary Parish. In conjunction with these disparate movements, an amphibious force landed at several points along the lower Texas coast. Banks reported to his superiors that "the flag of the Union floated over Texas to-day at meridian precisely" when it was planted into the sand dunes at Brazos Santiago.[29] Landings were also successful at Brownsville, Matagorda Bay, Aransas Pass, and at Rio Grande City.[30] In reality, the flag of the Union flew over uninhabited sand dunes on barrier islands. The total effect on the Confederate state of Texas was inconsequential, but Banks, the commander of the Department of the Gulf was pleased with himself.[31]

Halleck fired off a letter to Banks on December 7, 1863, detailing his displeasure, and thus forcing Banks to reevaluate his position.[32] Halleck then wrote letters to Sherman, who at the time was engaged in wreaking havoc in eastern Mississippi, and Major General Frederick Steele, the newly appointed commander of the Department of Arkansas, to solicit their opinions about a Red River expedition.[33] Steele's department adjoined the target area and Sherman was enthusiastic. Sherman wanted to command the force personally and operated for a time under the assumption that he would do so. Sherman had spent some eighteen months before the hostilities as the superintendent of the Louisiana Seminary of Learning and Military Institute in Pineville, across the Red River from Alexandria.[34] Of all the officers involved in the campaign, Sherman knew more about the area than anyone else and provided much valuable information, particularly to the navy.

Once these opinions were solicited, Halleck approached Grant, flush with victory at Chattanooga.[35] Grant and Banks at this time were both in favor of a move on Mobile, and Grant was formulating what would become Sherman's campaign against Atlanta. Banks foresaw what the capture of a city of Mobile's stature would do for his presidential hopes. Halleck's letter to Grant was forceful in explaining that President Lincoln believed a Red River expedition was more politically important than the capture of Mobile. He also implied that Banks' coastal positions in Texas were part of the grand scheme to recover Texas. President Lincoln wrote Banks a congratulatory letter on Christmas Eve 1863, perhaps at the urging of Halleck.[36] Grant tried to lobby for the Mobile campaign over a Red River expedition by circumventing Halleck but he failed to secure support.[37]

Grant could also clearly see the negative side of a Red River campaign.[38] The troops would be heading in the opposite direction of his plans for attack. If the campaign became mired, he would lose their usefulness in the East where he needed them most. Sherman wanted to command the Red River expedition, but Grant wanted Sherman to rip up Georgia. Even if the campaign were a success, the troops would be hard-pressed to join their parent units in time for the Atlanta Campaign. Last, Grant could not help but see a major drawback to this Louisiana foray. What was the goal? If the expedition reached Shreveport and the Confederates did not come out and fight, where would the climax come? If the Rebels decided to fight in the pine hills of Texas east of the Sabine River, how would the army pursue them? How would the lines of supply be configured? Where would supply bases be established and would they be safe? What if tens of thousands of men were strung out deep in enemy territory and were cut off? Where would the blame be leveled?

Finally Banks received several letters from Lincoln urging him to bring about elections in the free part of the state.[39] Lincoln wanted a congressional delegation loyal to him from Louisiana in the next elections. Banks could see that a successful campaign under his command up the Red River would be more helpful to him in the upcoming election than it would be to Lincoln. He conceived a grandiose, but overly complex scheme and by the third week of January 1864, and he turned his boundless enthusiasm to accomplishing Lincoln's wishes for a new Louisiana political order, a rejuvenation of the New England textile industry, and preparation for his bid for the presidency.

2
THE CONFEDERATES PREPARE

From March 1863 until the campaign began in March 1864, the Confederate commanders in the Department of the Trans-Mississippi worked at a feverish pace to prepare for an anticipated invasion up the Red River. Their efforts were astounding considering the limitations of time and manpower. At the same time, events in the war moved farther away from this theater, but political and economic needs of the New England states and the politicians wooing them forced the Union focus back to the Rebel territory west of the great river. The preparations for the campaign by both the Union and Confederacy illustrate a scene of fragmented purposes, conflicting strategic and tactical goals, and vastly differing levels of experience and command style. The efforts made by the Confederates also show remarkable ingenuity.

The Confederate government reorganized its western military districts early in 1863. The areas under its control west of the Mississippi River were placed in a separate command or "department." During the twelve months between March 1863 and March 1864, the new command made impressive progress in preparing for a possible invasion of the Red River Valley. The command was hampered, though, by conflicting ideas among the leaders as to the best means of defending the region, and it was particularly concerned about the rapidly deteriorating Confederate

Edmund Kirby Smith

Born in Florida in 1824, Kirby Smith graduated from the US Military Academy in 1845, twenty-fifth in his class of forty-one. He was commissioned second lieutenant of infantry and earned brevets to first lieutenant and captain in the Mexican–American War. He taught mathematics at West Point from 1849 to 1852 and was promoted to first lieutenant and captain before joining the newly formed Second Cavalry in 1855. As a major in this elite regiment, he resigned his commission in 1861 to enter Confederate service. He was commissioned colonel and served on General J. E. Johnston's staff in the Shenandoah Valley. He was promoted to brigadier general June 1861 and led troops and was wounded at First Manassas. He was elevated to major general in October 1861 and was assigned to command the Department of East Tennessee in March 1862. In conjunction with General Braxton Bragg, Kirby Smith invaded Kentucky in the summer of 1862. After his victory at Richmond, the campaign ended after Bragg's inconclusive actions at Perryville. Kirby Smith was promoted to lieutenant general in October 1862 and was ordered to the Trans-Mississippi Department. He assumed command there in February; however, the fall of Vicksburg in July

1863 left the Trans-Mississippi cut off from the rest of the Confederacy. The isolated department became known as "Kirby Smithdom" in which the general exercised virtually independent command for the balance of the war. He promoted to full general in February 1864, and in the spring of that year, the federals launched the ambitious Red River Campaign to capture Shreveport, Louisiana. General Richard Taylor directed the repulse of federal General Nathaniel P. Banks' approach at Mansfield and Pleasant Hill while Kirby Smith repulsed General Frederick Steele's advance in Arkansas. Taylor, angered by Kirby Smith's handling of the campaign, asked to be relieved and was later reassigned. Owing to his isolation from the Confederate capital, Kirby Smith promoted several generals on his own authority, only a few of which were ever approved and confirmed by President Jefferson Davis and the Confederate Senate. With the collapse of the Confederacy, Kirby Smith surrendered the last organized Confederate force to General E. R. S. Canby at Galveston, Texas, in June 1865. Fearing arrest, Kirby Smith fled to Mexico, returning to the United States several months later. After failing in business, he became president of the University of Nashville, and in 1875, he joined the faculty of the University of the South at Sewanee, Tennessee. The last survivor of the eight Confederate generals of full rank, Kirby Smith died at Sewanee in 1893.

positions east of the Mississippi River. The fall of Vicksburg on July 4, 1863, almost completely halted the movement of supplies flowing from Louisiana and Texas to the armies in the east. Even before Vicksburg's fall, the Confederate command west of the Mississippi River began repositioning forces to counter an ever-increasing Union threat. The Rebel commanders were not in agreement as to how this was to be done.

Lieutenant General Edmund Kirby Smith, commanding general of the grandiose-sounding "Confederate Department of the Trans-Mississippi" and Major General Richard Taylor, his head of the District of Western Louisiana, kept a close watch on Union movements in late 1863 and early 1864. Taylor's spies in New Orleans and Confederate reports elsewhere led both men to believe that either Union major generals William T. Sherman or Nathaniel P. Banks would make a thrust up the Red River when the spring rains made the river rise.[1]

Taylor and Kirby Smith were constantly at odds, and their frustration at each other's style is evident in reports at the time and in postwar correspondence. In his memoir *Destruction and Reconstruction*, Taylor referred to Kirby Smith and his large headquarters staff as "[the] Hydrocephalus at Shreveport."[2] Taylor, following in the manner of his training under General Thomas J. "Stonewall" Jackson, wanted fast-paced movement and a measure of finesse to meet the enemy.[3] He was experienced in masking his movements to keep his opponent off balance. Kirby Smith wanted elaborate plans using strong points to defend his department. Among these, approximately nineteen miles south of the original site of Shreveport, was located a man-made water channel, which is today called Tone's Bayou. This feature was approximately thirty-one miles south of the town by river in 1864.

By the spring of 1864 Shreveport had a thriving war-based industry.[4] With little or no help coming from east of the Mississippi River, it had to be self-sufficient. Fortunately the region's ample natural resources and antebellum infrastructure allowed this to happen. Outlying military installations, including several in east Texas, were also directly linked to the army command in Shreveport. Arsenals, foundries, a powder mill, and magazine were created in Marshall, Texas, and a powder house and warehouses in Jefferson, Texas. Tyler, Texas, housed an ammunition factory and ordnance works were found in Houston and San Antonio.[5] Shreveport was the location of at least one foundry, a powder house, an arsenal, two saw mills, and corn storage sheds, all of which were located along the south bank of the Red River or near Cross Bayou.[6]

This industrial base served two purposes. First, of course, was to support the Confederate army in the region. The second was to support the naval construction and repair yard.[7] The Confederates built the ironclad CSS *Missouri* here. The iron armor for the *Missouri* was obtained by ripping up the rails from a segment of the prewar Southern Pacific Railroad tracks that had been laid west of Shreveport.[8]

The Union navy had limited knowledge of the naval facilities and of some of the vessels built and stationed there. The primary questions concern the extent of their knowledge and when and how this information was discovered. The most secret operation at the Shreveport navy yard was the construction of five submarines for the defense of the Red River. The subs were never used in battle, but the Union navy certainly knew about them from naval and army correspondence and orders issued during 1864–1865.[9] It is certain that Union spies operated in Shreveport from January 1864 and periodically thereafter to the end of hostilities. They often had great difficulties in sending their information across the battle lines. It is uncertain whether the US navy knew about the submarines prior to the campaign.

On March 7, 1863, Kirby Smith arrived in Alexandria, about 112 miles downstream from Shreveport, and took over formal command of the Confederate Trans-Mississippi Department.[10] The location of the headquarters in Alexandria soon proved to be untenable, and it was moved to Shreveport in May 1863, when General Banks threatened Alexandria.[11] The move was reasonable because Shreveport's remote location provided a longer distance from a Union invasion from the south; however, it would also provide for shorter response time in the event that a Union operation originated at Little Rock. Taylor had

William R. Boggs

Born in Augusta, Georgia, on March 29, 1821, Boggs studied at Augusta Academy as a youth. He entered the US Military Academy in July 1849, excelling in math and science. He finished fourth in his class in 1853. Among his classmates were James B. McPherson, Philip Sheridan, and John Bell Hood. Being in the top 10 percent of his class, he had his choice of career track in the army. He chose engineering and received the rank of second lieutenant in the Topographical Bureau. He worked on the Pacific Railroad surveys. Boggs transferred to the Ordinance Corps in 1854 and was second in command at the arsenal in Troy, New York. He was promoted to first lieutenant in 1856. The following year, Boggs was transferred to the federal arsenal in Baton Rouge, Louisiana. In 1859, he was assigned as the inspector of ordinance at Point Isabel, Texas. When the Civil War broke out, Boggs was assigned to the Alleghany Arsenal at Pittsburg, Pennsylvania.

Boggs resigned from US Army service the same day Georgia adopted its secession ordinance. He was appointed by the governor of Georgia to be the purchasing agent to assemble supplies for Georgia troops. He became an engineer and ordinance officer on the staff of General Braxton Bragg. He never led troops in battle during the war but served with distinction as an engineer and chief of staff, particularly in the Trans-Mississippi Theatre under General Edmund Kirby Smith. Boggs served under Kirby Smith from the time of Kirby Smith's operations in Kentucky until the end of combat in 1865.

Kirby Smith ordered Boggs, now a Brigadier General, to create the Confederate defenses in the Red River and Ouachita River valleys. Boggs spent a year from March 1863 to March 1864 preparing for the expected Union invasion of upper Louisiana. His defensive positions were often massive and reflected his West Point training. After the Red River Campaign, Boggs had a falling out with Kirby Smith. He enlisted for military service in Mexico to assist Emperor Maximilian, but returned to Confederate service. He withdrew to Houston, Texas, with Kirby Smith and participated in the surrender of the Confederate forces in June 1865.

Following the war, Boggs became a professor of mechanics at Virginia Polytechnic Institute in Blacksburg, Virginia. Later, he moved to Winston-Salem, North Carolina, where he lived until his death at the age of eighty-two. He is buried in Salem Cemetery.

suggested Shreveport as a suitable site from the beginning of his tenure in Louisiana, but General Kirby Smith had opposed it, preferring the central location of Alexandria.[12]

Kirby Smith brought Brigadier General William R. Boggs with him as chief of staff. Boggs was a graduate, fourth in his class, of the US Military Academy at West Point, Class of 1853. Once in Louisiana, Kirby Smith gave Boggs the task of creating a defense of the Red River Valley and its tributaries, especially the Ouachita and its lower portions known as the Black River. He made an inspection trip to determine possible positions and methods of defense. With Boggs' evident support, Smith began to consider bringing slave labor both into public works projects and into the army as early as September, 1863.[13]

Boggs determined that several measures should be undertaken. With the brief scare of a thrust up the Red and Ouachita Rivers in the spring of 1863 as a major distraction, he began to lay out his ideas. To protect the Ouachita he built a fort at Trinity near Harrisonburg. This emplacement was known as Fort Beauregard. He also began the entrenchment and fortifications of the high bluffs at the village of Grand Ecore, which served as the port town of Natchitoches, four miles to the southwest.[14]

Boggs selected a position near the town of Marksville in Avoyelles Parish for a lower Red River fortification. This was named Fort DeRussy for the engineer (Colonel L. G. DeRussy) who constructed it. The Confederates had previously begun work at this location but had abandoned the effort. Taylor agreed with Kirby Smith that Fort DeRussy should be strengthened in some manner to counter any naval invading force, but believed that in its current state it might be untenable.[15] The site was located on a hairpin turn in the river, and if properly armed and manned, it could thwart gunboats. Boggs designed the fort with forty-foot-thick walls of packed earth that stood twelve feet high, with the entire structure surrounded by a deep, wide ditch.[16] This fort and its outlying works became the southern anchor of the Confederate defenses on the Red River. The fortification was to be augmented with a division of infantry, consisting of three to

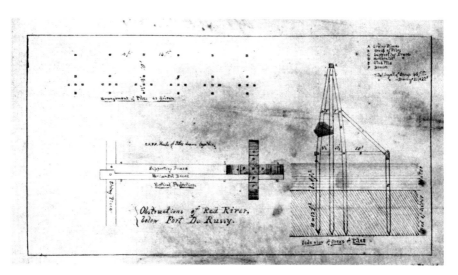

Confederate Engineers' sketch of the Fort DeRussy raft obstruction. Major Richard Venable, 1864. Jeremy Francis Gilmer Papers, Southern Historical Collection, University of North Carolina, Chapel Hill.

five thousand men, who were to operate in the vicinity but not be garrisoned at the site.[17]

Boggs established sites for four small forward defensive positions close to the town of Simmesport near the mouth of the Red River. The largest of these was named Fort Humbug, and known to the Union soldiers as Fort Scurry, after one of the Texas Division brigade commanders, Brigadier General William R. Scurry. These small defensive positions are known collectively as the Yellow Bayou forts.

Taylor wanted to build an obstruction that would allow the Great Raft, the giant logjam on the Red River, to recreate itself. He hoped to build this structure near Fort DeRussy, thinking that only a complete jamming of the river would stop the Union Navy. Throughout 1863 and the first half of 1864, Taylor openly disagreed with Kirby Smith over defensive strategy. Later he would contemptuously call the fort "our Red River Gibraltar."[18] Taylor's dissatisfaction with the fort was evident in his refusal to man the structure fully, although he had a full division of Texas troops in the vicinity.

Taylor ordered Boggs to build the obstruction below the fort in the fall of 1863, and it appeared to be formidable. It was built of heavy wooden pilings created from trees felled from around the site and driven into the streambed completely across the river.[19] To these was added a second line constructed shorter in height. These two lines were braced together and strengthened with cross-banded ties. Attached to this structure was a raft of trees and timber, which rested on the floor of the stream.[20] In addition, the Confederates had cut down "a forest of trees" upstream and piled them up above the structure. They also drove pilings into the riverbed downstream from this dam, extending two hundred yards at what appeared to be close but random intervals.[21]

With Fort DeRussy and the obstruction near completion, Boggs focused on the defenses upstream by scouting and preparing positions. There were no defensible positions between Fort DeRussy and north of Alexandria. In fact, no fortifications were prepared in Alexandria until after the 1864 expedition. Boggs gambled on Fort DeRussy and ample land forces under General Taylor to save the central Louisiana town. His primary mission, of course, was to protect Shreveport.

The first truly high ground encountered coming up the river from Alexandria was the high bluff at Grand Ecore. Boggs was not the first military engineer to see the value of this site. The hill and bluff complex had been the site of a military camp and fortification during the Mexican War. It had been one emplacement in a vital line of fortifications both guarding the Red River from the Mexicans in Texas and serving as a marshaling point for the forces of General Zachary Taylor (the future president of the United States and father of General Richard Taylor). A portion of the hill structure was used for Fort Salubrity during that war. Among the young officers who had served in the complex was Ulysses S. Grant.[22] The bluffs at Grand Ecore were 120 feet high. Boggs began fortifying the hills and bluffs with his usual vigor, an action Kirby Smith supported.[23]

North of Grand Ecore and extending upstream to the bluffs south of Shreveport, the river narrowed and the currents were swifter. At various points, the banks were elevated from the surrounding land, but there was no place to create a commanding fortified position using elevation as the central feature. The Red River Valley with its great looping meanders, obscured parallel channels, distributaries, and ox-bow lakes would become the next segment in Boggs' master plan.

It was located near the southernmost bend of Scopini Island, the piece of ground formed between Scopini's Cut Off and Tone's Bayou. To guard this vital dam, Boggs built two fortifications, one on either end of Scopini Island.[24] The southern structure is a long artillery battery. It overlooked the Hotchkiss dam and had clear field of fire across open ground to the next downstream meander of the Red River. The battery was approximately 570 feet in length and shaped like a giant, elongated *E*. The northern anchor is a pond that may have been a borrow pit or a gun emplacement.[25] Lying behind this emplacement was a large infantry camp, Camp Morgan, designed to provide garrison for the forts.[26] The northern structure was a square star fortress with a causeway and apparently a water battery. It resembled Fort DeRussy in design, though perhaps not in scale.[27] This emplacement guarded Scopini's Cut Off and was designed to provide enfilade fire for the southern battery. The winding river would allow either fortification to assist the other with covering fire. With Bayou Pierre on one side and the Red River on the other, a landing force encountering fire from either battery would have disembarked troops and headed over land. Because of the level of the ground and the cut-in bank nature of the old river surrounding Scopini Island, the troops would have marched up to an all but impenetrable river with a swift current and into the face of heavy artillery and infantry. The open field objective, the narrow marching front, and almost nonexistent flanking opportunities are reminiscent of the Rodriguez Canal, which was the fortification line for General Andrew Jackson at the Battle of New Orleans in the War of 1812. If the Union army had followed the Summer Road up the west bank of the Red River instead of invading inland, Taylor would have had the opportunity to marshal his forces behind this line. A portion of the artillery from the defenses in Shreveport as well as all his field artillery would have been available to him.

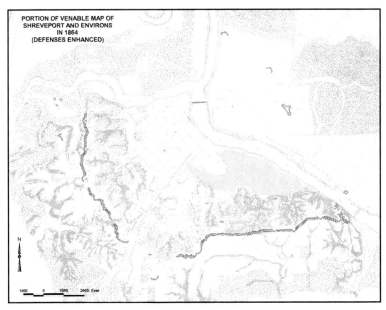

Shreveport and its inner defenses, 1864. Map by CSA Major Richard Venable.

Boggs was not satisfied with having this Tone's Bayou defensive system stand alone. His intent was to slow the fleet down first. He knew that if the river level dropped significantly, the Union navy could not bring its heavier draft ships up through the narrows. (He was correct as the history of the 1864 campaign was played out.) He asked for and received permission to sink one of the Confederate defense fleet vessels below Tone's Bayou. The vessel was the *New Falls City*, which was at anchor in or near the mouth of Coushatta Chute. *Ways Packet Directory* lists her as being an 880-ton sidewheel packet with a wooden hull, having a length of 301.3 feet and a beam of 39.7 feet with a draft of 7.6 feet.[28] The great vessel was possibly the largest vessel to navigate the Red River up until that time and certainly one of the largest ever to do so. Not only was it to be sunk, the sidewheeler was be wedged across the stream creating a sand bar beneath it. This would halt the Union warships until the hulk could be removed. Kirby Smith, through Boggs' suggestion, ordered the vessel to be taken from Coushatta Chute (Bayou Coushatta) and placed at the foot of Scopini's Cut-Off.[29]

There are only two sources that describe or directly mention the Tone's Bayou complex. David French Boyd, while in captivity at Grand Ecore during the campaign, tried to smuggle a letter to Taylor. He told his commander to "Move heaven and earth to close up Scopini's Cut-Off!" to remove the remainder of the river. The second is the Lavender Soil Survey map of 1906, which portrays the forts and dam.[30]

Boggs also deployed a chain across the Red River at some point near his trap above the wreck of the *New Falls City*. The chain was forged at a plantation near Loggy Bayou on the Bossier Parish side of the river.[31] This complex of forts, dams, chains, and a steamboat became the most important part of the Confederate defenses on the river during the campaign, although the Union naval force had firsthand information only about the *New Falls City*. General Boggs was also commanded to create an extensive defensive complex to protect Shreveport directly.

The works were indeed impressive based on the amount of time it took to construct them, the amount of labor available, and the fact that their designer was also working on various other major fortification projects at different points all along the Red River, even several hundred river miles away.

Boggs chose the highest hills, ridges, and bluffs as anchor points for the defensive system.[32] The complex extended across the Red River to cover the eastern approaches in Bossier Parish. On the Caddo Parish side, the anchor forts were linked by defensive walls that resembled levees.[33] At hill, ridge, or bluff tops, which were too small for large fortifications, Boggs placed artillery batteries. The large forts were combinations of construction types typical of Dennis Hart Mahan's textbook.[34] They made full use of the hill lines and interior routes of communication.[35] Boggs did not build his line on the central plateau of the town itself. He extended his defenses to adjacent ridges. There were three large anchor forts on the Caddo side and one on the Bossier side.

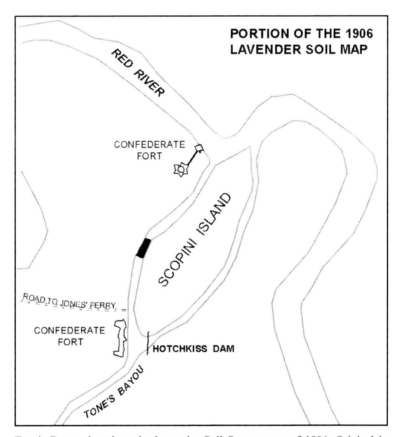

Tone's Bayou, based on the Lavender Soil Survey map of 1906. Original in Archives and Special Collections, Noel Memorial Library, Louisiana State University, Shreveport. Additional cartography by Gary D. Joiner.

Beginning at the eastern anchor on the Caddo side, Boggs established a large fort on the first high ground north of Grand Ecore, known as Coate's Bluff. This fort was named Fort Turnbull, but the local name, attributed to General John Magruder, was Fort Humbug. He called it a "humbug" because of the use of "Quaker guns" (tree trunks blackened to look like cannon and mounted on wagon wheels). These were interspersed with real ordinance to give the impression of an impregnable position. The river in 1864 came up to the foot of the bluffs on which the fort was built. It was a large complex and covered several interior bluff lines.

John Bankhead Magruder

Born in Virginia in 1807, Magruder graduated from the US Military Academy in 1830, fifteenth in his class of forty-two. Commissioned second lieutenant and posted to infantry, he soon transferred to the First Artillery. Promoted to first lieutenant in 1836, he served in the Seminole Wars and in Texas, and he distinguished himself in the Mexican War, earning brevets for Palo Alto, Cerro Gordo, and Chapultepec. Magruder was promoted to captain in 1846, served on the frontier, and commanded the post at Newport, Rhode Island. With the secession of Virginia, he resigned his commission to enter Confederate service, in which he commissioned a colonel. He rose quickly through the ranks, gaining promotion to brigadier general in June 1861 and major general in October. Magruder was placed in command of rebel troops on the Virginia Peninsula and fought and won the first battle in that state at Big Bethel in June 1861. Because of his flamboyant manner and dress, he earned the sobriquet "Prince John." In the spring of 1862, he masterfully deceived the federals during the early stages of the Peninsular Campaign by creating the impression that his force was much larger than it  actually was, but during the Seven Days' Battles, Magruder buckled under the strain, prompting accusations of drunkenness. He was sent to the Trans-Mississippi shortly thereafter and took command of the District of Texas, New Mexico, and Arizona—a position he held until the end of the war and discharged with great energy. In January 1863, he directed the recapture of Galveston and, in the spring of 1864, dispatched the bulk of his command to assist General Richard Taylor in Louisiana during the Red River Expedition. Throughout Magruder's tenure, Texas remained relatively untouched by the federals. Refusing to surrender at the close of the Civil War, he fled to Mexico, where he became a general in the service of Emperor Maximilian. After the fall of Maximilian in 1867, he returned to the United States, making a living as a lecturer. Magruder died in Houston, Texas, in 1871; he remains among the war's most colorful characters.

Radiating from this fort were several artillery batteries. To the north was a battery that was to provide cross fire for a position across the river (Battery Ewell).[36] Due south of Fort Turnbull was Battery I, located on the southernmost rise of the bluff structure. West and somewhat north of this was Battery II, located on the west side of the bluff complex. Next in line were batteries III and IV. Battery III was located on an extension of the bluff and was positioned so that it could cover the area to the south of the defensive line or be turned to the north to fire at targets in the river. Battery IV was placed close to the Confederate hospital on the high ground above it. These batteries would most likely have been under the direct control of Fort Turnbull.

Battery V was located on a high hill behind the defensive line where it could offer fire to either the south or be turned to the east and cover targets in the river. Battery VI and two unnumbered batteries faced south and were to provide support for the next anchor fort, Fort Jenkins. This fort was positioned outside the defensive ring and occupied the highest topographic elevation in Caddo Parish. The line then proceeded westward to Battery VII, located at the southwest corner of the ridge line extending westward from the river at Coate's Bluff. Between this bluff and the town of Shreveport was Silver Lake, a shallow bog overflow from the Red River. Only one road entered the town from the south and Fort Jenkins provided a frowning battlement to guard it.

From Battery VII, the defensive line extended to the northwest. Connecting to another ridge, this one aligned north to south. Behind this ridge lay the marsh and the Bottoms. Batteries VIII, IX, X, XI, and XII were all located on this ridge. Battery XII was located on the extreme northern tip of this ridge. Behind it and to the east was a spectacular view of the town; to the north was Cross Bayou. Any attempt to ford the stream below this point would have been difficult at best because of the stream's depth and open position.

On the ridge running parallel and west to the one just discussed, Boggs built Fort Albert Sidney Johnston. This was a long fort designed to cover Cross Bayou to its north and to prevent any attempt to attack Shreveport from the west. Any skirmish line formed west of this ridge would have met with fire from the fort. Attackers from the west would have been forced to cross an opposing parallel ridge line and then descend into a densely wooded stream bottom before rising

The engineers of the Trans-Mississippi Department who served under General William Roberston Boggs. *Standing, left to right:* David French Boyd, major of engineers; D. C. Proctor, First Louisiana Engineers; unidentified; and William Freret. *Seated, left to right:* Richard M. Venable, chief topographic engineer; H. T. Douglas, colonel of engineers; and Octave Hopkins, First Louisiana Engineers. From Francis Trevelyan Miller et al., eds., *The Photographic History of the Civil War in Ten Volumes* (New York: Review of Reviews Co., 1912), 1:105.

to the fort's ramparts atop a high ridge. This entire line radiates out like the rim of a wheel from the town of Shreveport, extending from one to three miles in a broad arc. Inside this defensive line was the center for the military industrial complex of the Trans-Mississippi west, the naval yard, a major infantry compound, and the Confederate government of Louisiana.[37]

To cover the Confederate capital from the east, General Boggs designed a series of four fortifications with one being an anchor. This was a triangular star fort named in honor of Kirby Smith. It was aligned to protect from an attack to the east, north, or southeast. South of this was a smaller square fort named Battery Ewell. Northwest of Fort Kirby Smith was Battery Price, which was formed as a large lunette facing northeast. To the west-northwest of Battery Price was another large lunette, Battery Walker, located on the river and facing north. The three northernmost Bossier-side emplacements could provide enfilade fire for each other. The southern fort, Battery Ewell, was designed to protect Fort Kirby Smith, provide fire coverage against riverine targets, and offer enfilade fire for Fort Turnbull and its north battery.

The entire defensive ring was well laid out. Forces in place within Shreveport or in the defensive works could have gotten where they were needed the most within a minimum amount of time. This would include crossing troops from the Shreveport/Caddo side to the Bossier side. This was facilitated by a pontoon bridge, located near the mouth of Cross Bayou.[38]

Boggs and his engineers created a final significant structure on the Red River just below Shreveport and guarded by Fort Turnbull and Battery Ewell. This structure appears on the Venable Map of the defenses of Shreveport as a thick line labeled "Raft."[39] Two Confederate engineers' drawings exist that explain the significance of this structure. They are from a set of maps, surveys, and drawings prepared by Confederate Major Richard Venable, and the only copies exist are those that were sent to Richmond. These were spirited away and the end of the war and now a portion of the Southern Historical Collection at the University of North Carolina at Chapel Hill.

The plan of the raft shows an ingeniously constructed floating dam made of wood. It spans the river and is held in place by ships' anchors. Both sides are secured by heavy supports that appear to be tower bases. The distance below water from the base of the structure to bed of the river channel is approximately twenty feet. This would allow the submarines to leave the safety of the harbor and move downstream undetected. The vessels could foray under the raft and prying eyes would have great difficulty in seeing them. In the center of the dam and directly over the flow channel of the river was located a large trapezoidal shaped plug. This device was held in place by the current of the river. It could be

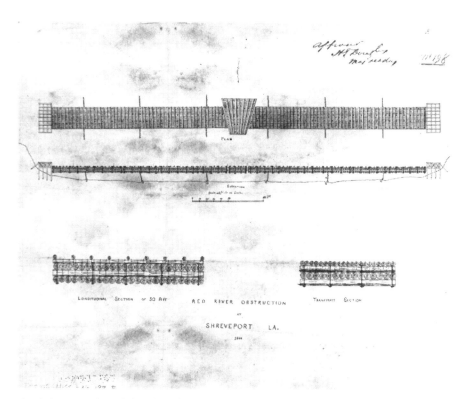

Confederate Engineers' drawing of the raft at Shreveport. Jeremy Francis Gilmer Papers, Southern Historical Collection, Wilson Library, University of North Carolina, Chapel Hill.

pulled back upstream and to the side when vessels needed to either enter the Shreveport safe harbor or be deployed to the south. The flow of the river was unimpeded by the raft whether the plug was open or closed. The second engineering drawing describes the system by which the plug was opened and returned to the closed position. The raft was placed near Fort Turnbull, the largest of the defensive positions, for obvious reasons. Battery Ewell, slightly upstream and on the eastern bank of the river would be in position to provide enfilade fire. Additionally the north battery of Fort Turnbull and Battery III could provide additional covering fire if needed. The thick construction of the raft would have made ramming difficult at best and covering fire provided by the elevated fort

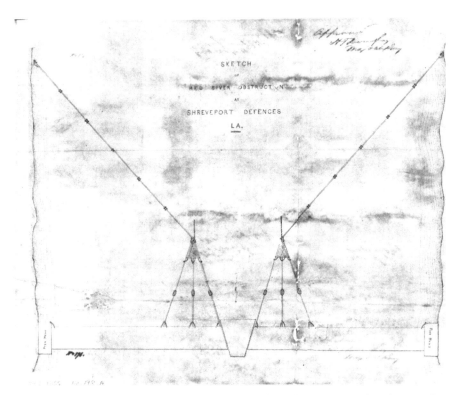

Confederate Engineers' drawing of the raft at Shreveport showing the operating mechanism. Jeremy Francis Gilmer Papers, Southern Historical Collection, Wilson Library, University of North Carolina, Chapel Hill.

and batteries on the west bank and the river level battery on the eastern bank would have made an attack by the river or land an extraordinarily complex maneuver.

As the winter of 1863–1864 progressed, news arrived of Sherman's Meridian expedition and both Kirby Smith and Taylor began to think that perhaps Mobile was the next target, but Banks' men were still poised in New Orleans. Taylor believed Banks would not move from the Bayou Teche area without Sherman's support.[40] All hopes of a reprieve seemed to evaporate as news came in from reliable sources in both New Orleans and Vicksburg of a huge naval build-up at Vicksburg and massing of infantry and support troops at both Vicksburg and near New Orleans.[41]

Kirby Smith ordered his widely scattered troops into new concentration areas in early March.

As usual his orders were carried out with varied degrees of urgency, with Major General John Magruder's Texas-based troops the last to be released to Louisiana soil.[42] Kirby Smith ordered these units, consisting primarily of cavalry regiments, to gather in Alexandria.[43] He also ordered Taylor to reposition his forces. The brigade of Texans under the French Prince and Confederate Brigadier General Camille Armand Jules Marie de Polignac was ordered from Trinity, near Harrisonburg on the Ouachita River, to join the brigade of Louisiana troops led by Colonel Henry Gray at Alexandria. Major General John G. Walker's division of Texans was to operate in the prairie near the mouth of the Red River.[44] This area, between Marksville and Simmesport, offered good maneuvering room, assuming the troops did not find themselves trapped in the winding courses of Bayou de Glaize and other streams. The bayous and streams that sliced through the region made organized marches all but impossible without the constant assistance of engineers.[45] At this stage of planning, only Louisiana and Texas troops were repositioned.

3
UNION PLANS TO TAKE LOUISIANA

While the Confederates worked on their defensive strategies for slightly more than a year before the campaign began, the Union commander, Major General Nathaniel P. Banks had just a few months to prepare his plan. Although Major General Richard Taylor's ideas were bold in the manner of Thomas J. "Stonewall" Jackson and Lieutenant General Edmund Kirby Smith's plans were rooted in the solid military foundations taught at West Point, Banks brought little of this acumen to Union planning procedures. He was sent by President Abraham Lincoln to replace Major General Benjamin Butler in Louisiana in December 1862.[1]

Once in Louisiana, Banks participated in the Vicksburg Campaign (although Banks would argue that this was a separate campaign) with operations culminating in the siege of Port Hudson. The Confederate bastion was located just upriver from Baton Rouge. Although Banks made several spirited attacks, the Rebels held out until after the fall of Vicksburg, denying him his great battlefield victory, although he certainly won the contest.[2]

Lincoln next directed Banks to invade Texas to accomplish two goals. The immediate need was to thwart the ambitions of the French puppet ruler of Mexico, Maximilian of Austria. The president believed that Napoleon III of France wanted Mexico to regain its former holdings, including Texas. Aid to the South from both England and France was still an issue at that time, and goods were pouring across the Texas–Mexico border. The other goal was to bring Texas back into the Union by creating an area of pro-Union sentiment.[3] This was a continuation of the president's reconstruction policy begun with the taking of New Orleans the previous year. Lincoln trusted Banks to do this. Although he was a potential rival, Lincoln believed he was the ideal man for the job.[4]

Banks' attempt to invade Texas was poorly conceived and resulted in a botched attempt to land forces at the mouth of the Sabine River on the Louisiana–Texas border.[5] Shortly after this failure, Banks sent his newly formed Nineteenth Corps across southern Louisiana in a move to invade Texas. Banks' nemesis in the Shenandoah Valley, Taylor, newly promoted to the rank of major general, had just arrived in Louisiana as the commander of the District of Western Louisiana. He fought the federal forces at Bisland in St. Mary Parish in what has been called the Teche Campaign. Union Major General William B. Franklin, commander of the Nineteenth Corps had been given no clear orders as to how he should invade Texas or what he should do once he arrived. He turned his men around in south central Louisiana, reaching no farther than Opelousas in October 1863.[6]

Banks' military career to this point provides insight into the general's character, successes, and failures. Although a major political rival of Lincoln's, Banks was loyal to the president's administration and he exhibited characteristics of a capable administrator. Lincoln held the Massachusetts general in high regard, although not as a military commander, and he appreciated Banks' adherence to the administration's plans for reconstruction. Banks was personally courageous, but he did not inspire loyalty among his soldiers. He trusted his staff implicitly, even when they were obviously giving him bad advice. Finally, his total lack of military training derailed his attempts to gain glory on the battlefield at almost every turn.

From late 1863 through January 1864, Banks changed his opinion about the best line of attack into Texas and pursued a new venture of an attack up Red River with his usual boundless enthusiasm.[7] He solicited advice from Major General Henry Halleck, the army's general-in-chief, who wanted this expedition to begin. Halleck wrote letters to show his support of a Red River expedition and to outline his intentions to Lincoln, Lieutenant General Ulysses S. Grant, Major General William T. Sherman, and other officers.[8] Halleck told these commanders that the president wanted Texas invaded via the Red River and that he (Halleck) intended to support the effort in every possible manner. Banks described his plans to his allies in New England, telling them of the possibilities of reopening their textile mills with newly acquired Louisiana cotton from the Red River Valley. They consequently made offers of support in securing cotton if the expedition was undertaken.[9] Banks also corresponded with Sherman, Grant, Rear Admiral David Dixon Porter, and Major General Frederick Steele, his counterpart in Little Rock, Arkansas.[10] His letters and telegrams to each individual varied according to what he wanted and what he expected from them.

The political landscape was changing in Washington. For at least eighteen months, President Lincoln had wanted the Union to mount a campaign to plant the flag on Texas soil. With Banks in Louisiana, Lincoln thought he had removed his most visible Republican rival for the 1864 election from the politically charged air of Washington. Banks' friends, New England bankers and textile mill owners, would be all too happy to put pressure on their congressional delegations to support the expedition. President Lincoln needed them if he was to succeed in his run for reelection in the fall.

Grant, Sherman, and Porter were all close friends and allies. Their cooperation in large-scale projects proved successful in several operations, particularly at Vicksburg. Sherman had a burning desire to lead an expedition up Red River because he had lived at Pineville, which is on the river opposite Alexandria, before the war. He lobbied Grant to put him in charge of the campaign. His friend and superior was reluctant even to consider the operation, but Halleck was pushing for it to begin and the president desperately needed it.[11] At that time Grant was in the early process of planning the capture of Mobile. He certainly felt that he could not spare Sherman from these plans. Grant, however, lacked the authority to countermand Halleck's orders and thinly veiled suggestions. He acquiesced, therefore, in the use of a portion of Sherman's troops, but not Sherman himself.

By the end of January, Sherman had begun his Meridian Campaign, limiting the time he could contribute to the planning of the Red River Campaign. Halleck was writing to Sherman directly and intimating that both he and Banks would lead the expedition when he was finished tearing up Meridian. Grant was kept out of this loop and was not told what troops, if any, from east of the Mississippi would be used. Porter had offered his full support to Sherman if the expedition were carried out. No doubt he thought that Sherman would lead the campaign and that it would be a great opportunity to work with his friend.[12]

Still thinking that Halleck might order him to be the expedition's senior field commander, Sherman agreed to meet with Banks in New Orleans. He arrived in New Orleans on March 2 and found Banks in a whirl of activity, but not—in Sherman's opinion—activities to support the pressing problems at hand. Although he had completed his planning for the upcoming campaign, Banks could not devote much time to explain his ideas to Sherman. Banks urged Sherman to remain in the city for an extra two days to attend the grand inauguration of the new Union governor of Louisiana, Michael Hahn. Sherman was disgusted and later wrote in his memoirs that Banks wanted him to participate in the ceremonies and festivities of the great occasion. "General Banks urged me [Sherman] to remain over the 4th of March to participate in the ceremonies, which he explained would include the performance of the 'Anvil Chorus' by all the bands of his army and during the performance, church-bells were to be rung, and cannons were to be fired by electricity. I regarded all such ceremonies as out of place at a time when it seemed to me every hour and minute were due to the war."[13]

Andrew Jackson Smith

Born in Pennsylvania in 1815, Smith graduated from the US Military Academy in 1838, thirty-sixth in his class of forty-five. Commissioned second lieutenant and posted to the First Dragoons, he saw service on the western frontier and in the Mexican War. He was promoted to first lieutenant 1845, captain in 1847, major 1861, and colonel and chief of cavalry to Major General Henry Halleck during his advance on Corinth, Mississippi, in 1862. As brigadier general of US Volunteers in 1862, he commanded a division in Major General William T. Sherman's attack on Chickasaw Bluffs and throughout the Vicksburg Campaign of 1863. He was detached to support Major General Nathaniel P. Banks' Red River Expedition in the spring of 1864. Smith defeated Confederates at Pleasant Hill, Louisiana, but was angered by the campaign's overall failure and Banks' ineffectiveness. He was promoted to major general US Volunteers in May 1864. Still detached, he won an independent action at Tupelo, Mississippi, before moving into Missouri and finally Tennessee. Smith joined Major General George Thomas' command in the rout of General John B. Hood's force at Nashville in December 1864. He led the Sixteenth Corps  in the operations against Mobile in 1865 and was breveted brigadier general US Army for Pleasant Hill and major general for Nashville. Continuing in the service after the war, he became colonel of the Seventh US Cavalry. He resigned his commission 1869 and then was in the civil service in St. Louis. He was placed on the retired list in 1889 by the Army with the rank of colonel of cavalry. Smith died in St. Louis in 1897. Although not as recognized as many of his contemporaries, Smith was nonetheless one of the most capable officers to serve the Union. He proved as equally effective in a subordinate role or in independent action. His soldiers were among the hardest marchers and toughest fighters on either side during the war.

Banks told the great field commander that he, not Sherman, would be the overall field commander. This was so much hyperbole because Halleck had not and never would give Banks sole authority over the expedition. Halleck confided to Sherman in April, "General Banks is not competent, and there are so many political objections in superseding him by Steele that it would be useless to ask the President to do it."[14] Sherman wrote to his wife, "I wanted to go up Red River, but as Banks was to command in person I thought it best not to go."[15] Because Banks was inducted into the army with the rank of major general, he and his predecessor, Butler, outranked not only Sherman, but also Grant and every officer serving in the field at that stage of the war. Banks' rank forced Halleck and Grant to treat him differently from any of their field commanders. This had been evident in the Vicksburg campaign and carried through now.

Sherman, after conferring with Grant, backed out of personally leading troops up the Red River. He also realized that Porter's fleet would be in jeopardy if Banks impulsively left them at some point without protection. Porter had already committed himself to the campaign. Sherman, with his typical insightfulness, loaned Porter ten thousand of his most trusted veterans under the capable Brigadier General Andrew Jackson Smith.[16] The troops were an independent command added to assist Banks but not under his direct control. They had their own transport vessels and were to accompany the fleet.

Sherman placed some severe limits on their use and the extent of their cooperation. They could operate directly with Banks, but at no time during the campaign were they to abandon the fleet entirely for land operations. General Smith and his men were to accompany Porter, not Banks. They were not to be used in a thrust further than Shreveport, and most importantly, because of Grant's upcoming projects, they were to be returned to Vicksburg no later than April 15.[17]

In March, Grant was promoted to lieutenant general and Halleck suggested that Grant be made general-in-chief. Grant was given superior rank and operated in the field, leaving Halleck dealing with politics.[18] Halleck was maneuvering for troops other than those assigned to Banks to be used in the campaign. Grant protested and told Sherman that if he did not personally lead his Western troops, they would probably be lost permanently from his command.[19] By March 12, the day Grant was made general-in-chief, the forces were moving into position. Grant made no attempt to halt the operation.

These limitations irritated Banks as did the qualities of the troops loaned to him. They were westerners, veterans, and hard fighters to be sure, but they disregarded proper military behavior, such as keeping their uniforms neat and clean. Banks felt they were too unruly and unkempt, and he displayed open disdain for them, calling them "gorillas." His easterners of the Nineteenth Corps and westerners of the Thirteenth Corps were more to his liking, cutting fine figures in parades and showing proper discipline on the march. Most of them were not battle-tested, nearly to the extent of the troops from Sherman's command, but they looked like soldiers should look and that meant a great deal to Banks.[20]

The regional differences between the two groups of soldiers were stark. The United States had existed for less than one hundred years, but the attitudes of its inhabitants east of the Appalachian Mountains were generally more refined. These descendants of the early colonists who remained between the mountains and the Atlantic Ocean often believed they were more civilized than their western counterparts. The western troops, steeped in traditions of Western expansion and rugged individualism, often believed they were tougher than the easterners and derided them. Of course, many of these men were urbanites and did not fit the mold of the frontiersmen.[21] Nevertheless, General Smith, commander of Sherman's contingent, added to this regional banter by often criticizing Banks and his staff.[22] One of Smith's men referred to the easterners as "undependable holiday soldiers, paper collar and white glove gents, who could neither shoot nor forage." An easterner responded that Smith's men were "gorillas, coarse, uncouth, ill-dressed braggarts and chicken thieves."[23]

Banks also chafed against Sherman's requirement that the troops accompany the navy, but at least this meant he would not have to put up with them. He was also bothered by the fact that March had arrived and Sherman ordered the return of these unruly westerners by the middle of April. Banks often repeated to anyone who listened that he believed the Rebels would not fight him before Shreveport, if then. He believed he would fight his big battle in Texas, and by that time, he would not need Sherman's men.[24] Sherman left New Orleans on March 3, wanting to get away from Banks and the vision of a looming fiasco. He wrote to Porter,

Grant, Halleck, and others telling them of his decisions and warning Porter to be careful.[25]

Union Major General Steele had recently been placed in command of the District of Arkansas based in Little Rock. Steele was reluctant to participate in the Louisiana campaign and was wary of the concept of the plan. He attempted to separate his forces from the proposed operation in all planning discussions. If any major Union commander in the Red River expedition was a reluctant pawn, it was Steele. He tried to commit to only a feint or demonstration to draw the Confederates away from Banks, citing, among other things, the need to monitor elections in Little Rock.[26] All of Steele's protests were cast aside, and when Grant became general-in-chief of the army, he ordered Steele to participate fully in the operation. On March 15, Grant telegraphed Steele in Little Rock, "Move your force in full cooperation with General N.P. Banks' attack on Shreveport" and added that "a mere demonstration will not be sufficient."[27]

Banks fired off several questions to Halleck concerning overall command of the operation.[28] He wanted a clear decision from the president and the general staff as to his own authority. Halleck played the part of concertmaster, writing all senior commanders who would have a part in the operation, asking the extent of their intended cooperation, while Banks was conducting his letter-writing campaign. Halleck also informed Lincoln of the communication between himself and Banks, slanted of course, to Halleck's point of view.[29] Other than his misgivings about Banks, Halleck faced the almost impossible task of assigning an overall commander for the expedition because the component units spanned three departments (Gulf, Arkansas, and Army of the Tennessee in Mississippi), the US Navy's Mississippi Squadron, the army's Quartermaster Corps's transport boats, and the independent Marine Brigade. Halleck's answer to this Gordian knot of independent command structures was not to assign an overall commander. He did move mountains to get the campaign organized.

On paper, the campaign appeared to be a sure-fire proposition. It combined overwhelming numerical superiority of infantry and cavalry

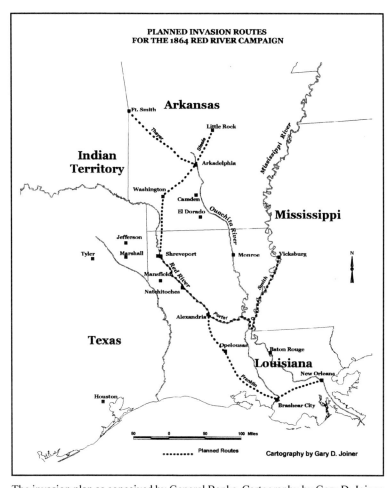

The invasion plan as conceived by General Banks. Cartography by Gary D. Joiner.

troops, a huge naval contingent, more than adequate logistical support, plus the blessings of the president, the cabinet, and the chief of staff of the army. The expedition would consist of three pincer movements. The two southern legs would meet at Alexandria, a major road and river junction in the center of the state. Union navy vessels had reconnoitered the river as far as that town the previous year. The combined force would then proceed north to Shreveport. The northern leg was to sweep down from Little Rock and approach Shreveport from the north. This plan effectively forced a battle or siege with no clear route of escape, with the possible exception of flight to the west for the Confederate army and the hapless civilians caught in the trap.

The first group was to travel via navy and army vessels up the Red River to Alexandria. Porter, commanding the Mississippi Squadron, was to bring almost all of his naval assets into the Red River. This was a precursor to modern force projection theory to supply overwhelming fire support for infantry attacking a series of fortifications located on a river or shore. Porter boasted that he would strip the inland fleet of available hulls and guns for the expedition and the total of 210 large ordnance pieces loaded on Porter's flotilla lent credence to his word. He had promised his old friend Sherman that he would ascend the Red River "with every ironclad vessel in the fleet."[30]

The fleet Porter took up the river was a powerful mixture of ironclads, monitors, tinclads, a timberclad, several high-speed rams, and supply vessels. Ironclads were vessels that were covered with at least one inch of armor plating. Tinclads were lightly armored vessels that were at least partially covered with one-quarter to one-half inch of iron plating. Monitors were hybrid vessels created during the Civil War. They were technically ironclads, but were outfitted with rotating turrets. Monitors had decks that barely cleared the water when the vessel was fully loaded with ammunition and supplies and had shallow drafts, making them ideal to work in rivers. Timberclads were created at the beginning of the war. They relied on thick laminated wooden beams for armor. Rams had little or no armor, but contained massive amounts of laminated wood at the bow to support an iron ram. The iron beak was attached directly to the keel timber and the wood laminate acted as a shock absorber when the vessel rammed an opponent.

These were the vessels that had engaged the Confederates time after time on the Mississippi, Arkansas, and Tennessee Rivers, and many had gained fame in the Vicksburg Campaign. James Buchanan Eads, perhaps the greatest US engineer of the nineteenth century, designed several of the boats. The fleet included the great ironclads *Benton, Essex, Choctaw,*

USS *Eastport*, perhaps on Red River. Note the extremely low water and mudflats in the foreground. Archives of the Mansfield State Historic Site, Mansfield, Louisiana.

Eastport, Lafayette, Carondelet, Louisville, Mound City, Pittsburg, and *Chillicothe*; the large river monitors *Neosho* and *Osage*; the lesser river monitor *Ozark*; the large tinclads *Black Hawk* and *Ouachita*; the timberclad *Lexington*; and the tinclads *Covington, Fort Hindman, Gazelle, Cricket, Juliet, Forest Rose, Signal, St. Clair*, and *Tallahatchie*. Also included were the ram *General Sterling Price* and support vessels that included dispatch boats, tenders, tugs, and supply vessels.[31] The Army Quartermaster Corps had its own transport and supply vessels. These were to accommodate the ten thousand men under General Smith from the First and Third divisions of the Sixteenth Corps and Second (Provisional) division from the Seventeenth Corps.[32] Also accompanying the fleet were the vessels of the independent Mississippi Marine Brigade with their rams, support vessels, and a hospital boat. This force carried approximately a thousand marines. In all, the fleet consisted of 108 vessels, one of the largest congregations of inland warfare craft in the Civil War. The most impressive was the *Eastport*, a behemoth 280-foot long and 43-foot wide (beam) with a draft (depth below water line) of 6 feet, 3 inches. It carried two 100-pounder rifled cannon, four 9-inch smoothbore cannon, and two 50-pounder rifled cannon.[33]

The second major group was to travel overland. This pincer consisted of 19,000 infantry and cavalry from the Department of the Gulf. They included two divisions from the Thirteenth Corps, two from the Nineteenth Corps, and Brigadier General Albert L. Lee's cavalry division of 5,000 troopers.[34] Some 2,500 men of the US Colored Troops, the *Corps d'Afrique*, were scheduled to arrive after the main column reached Alexandria. Banks' engineers and logistics troops would move north with 32,500 combat troops (including General Smith's 10,000 and the 1,000 marines) and ninety artillery pieces.[35] This huge column was to travel across the bayou country of southern Louisiana from their bases near Brashear City and New Orleans and head west to the main north-south road at Opelousas. From there it would move to Alexandria and join Porter's fleet. The combined forces were then to proceed north along the most practicable route to Shreveport with Porter's vessels providing protection and succor for the joined forces.

The third group was to sweep southwest from Little Rock and south from Fort Smith, both in Arkansas. It was to leave its base later than the other two, giving them adequate time to approach Shreveport. The particular route was left to Steele. His first intention was to proceed southward to the Ouachita River and then descend to Monroe, Louisiana. From there he would follow the bed of the prewar proposed Southern Pacific Railroad that cut across north Louisiana from east to west. Only the bed was prepared westward to Shreveport. This segment ran almost directly due west for 110 miles and it was a straightforward approach.[36]

Steele decided against this avenue of attack and opted for a lengthier approach through Arkadelphia and the Confederate capital of Arkansas at Washington.[37] This may have been an attempt to seize the entire Confederate governmental structure in Arkansas as an additional benefit. In either case, Steele would be forced to cross the Red River either at Shreveport or north of the town, and this was no small feat. The Red River was more than one thousand feet wide at the ferry landing from the Bossier Parish side to its terminus at the wharves in Shreveport.[38] In fact, this was one of the widest points in the entire length of the river.

In spring, the current typically flowed at least as fast as the Mississippi River. Steele would have known this, and it may have been a factor in preparing for a line of attack from the north rather than the east. Also, given Steele's reluctant participation in the campaign, he may have favored an approach to the Red River, which would have allowed him to support operations but not directly engage in heavy fighting.

Steele's force would consist of two columns. A column of 3,600 men of the Frontier Division, based at Fort Smith on the Indian Territory border, was to march 170 miles to the town of Arkadelphia.[39] Steele would lead the main body of troops from Little Rock and join the Fort Smith column. This force of 6,800 consisted of the Third Division, Seventh Corps, and two cavalry brigades.[40] Steele's force added 10,400 men to Banks' force converging on Shreveport, making the total effective force complement approximately 42,900, excluding sailors and support personnel such as teamsters and garrison troops.

This grand combination of overwhelming land and naval power appeared to be a truly unstoppable force. Yet, the seeds of disaster lay in the initial plans. Timing was critical. All three prongs or pincers had to arrive at specific points at predetermined dates for the campaign to remain on schedule. The troop deadline loomed large. On April 15, ten thousand of the best troops would be returned to Sherman. The three groups would be advancing independently from the others. Communications were negligible because the distance between Steele and Banks was more than four hundred miles by the shortest method of travel. No one would know if even the initial logistics would succeed. The fleet and its attached infantry would not be able to count on Banks until they all met at Alexandria. If either of the columns or the fleet were delayed, the entire plan was in jeopardy of failure. Added to all of these factors was the open distrust and skepticism of the leaders of each pincer for the other commanders. Of the three separate groups, Porter and his loaned infantry commander, General Smith, were the only two leading officers who displayed mutual respect and were operating in their combined interest.

The operation began with each group having faith that their counterparts were acting according to schedules developed in the planning process, but none had the means to verify the actions of the others. Even worse, Banks' commanders viewed him as a lightweight and a political climber who did not have the soldiers' best interest in mind. Banks' extreme overconfidence in his own abilities and an almost total lack of understanding of the Confederate forces in the region plagued the operation from the beginning. It would soon be evident that the lack of an overall commander would lead to the problems that Sherman foresaw.

4
THE UNION ADVANCES

The campaign began on March 10 with the departure from Vicksburg of twenty-one Union steamboat troop transports packed as tightly as possible with Sherman's ten thousand men and equipment. The departure date was already three days delayed from the original timetable, creating tension.[1] Brigadier General Andrew Jackson Smith led Major General William T. Sherman's troops. Army transports with Sherman's veterans proceeded down the Mississippi River from Vicksburg to the mouth of the Red River, arriving on the evening of March 11. Rear Admiral David Dixon Porter and the Mississippi Squadron met them.[2] With the entire fleet of 108 vessels gathered at the rendezvous point, Porter and Smith confronted their first problem, how to enter the river and find the main channel. The problem was compounded by a sand bar at the river's mouth, which diverted much of its water into the Atchafalaya River.[3]

Porter and Smith decided to establish their toehold near the mouth of the Red River. Porter was worried about Confederate ironclads on the Red River, however. He led his fleet into the river with the squadron's largest ironclad, the *Eastport*, which grounded on the sandbar at the mouth of the river. The *Eastport*'s captain, Lieutenant Commander Seth Ledyard Phelps, managed to wrestle the huge ironclad over the sandbar. General Smith immediately brought his transports into Old River, an

Brigadier General Joseph A. Mower. From Francis Trevelyan Miller et al., eds., *The Photographic History of the Civil War in Ten Volumes* (New York: Review of Reviews Co., 1912), 10:191.

ancient arm of the Mississippi. Smith's men disembarked at Simmesport, just west of the mouth of the Red River, which was to be his staging point for the attack on Fort DeRussy. Porter sent some of the iron-clads up the Ouachita River to neutralize a Rebel fortification at Trinity.[4] However, the bulk of the fleet was to proceed up the Red River to address the massive water batteries guarding Fort DeRussy and "amuse the Fort until the army could land."[5] Porter was delayed for several hours while his boats and crews removed most of a "raft" or dam-like obstacle built below the fort.[6]

Confederate Major General John G. Walker was the commander of the largest infantry division operating in the Trans-Mississippi. His Texas Division, known as "Walker's Greyhounds," operated at this time between Alexandria to near the mouth of the Red River.

Walker was the first Confederate commander to hear about the thrust into his territory, and he immediately sent a dispatch to Major General Richard Taylor warning him of the incursion. Walker had only 3,800 combat troops and twelve artillery pieces.[7]

Union Brigadier General Thomas Kilby Smith, who commanded the Provisional Division of the Seventeenth Corps, began probing for Walker. He began a quick march on the Marksville road to take Fort DeRussy.[8] On March 13, Kilby Smith decided to form two brigades of the Sixteenth

Sketch of Fort DeRussy by Owen G. Long for *Harper's Weekly*. April 1864. Collection of the Author.

Corps led by Brigadier General Joseph A. Mower in line of battle on either side of the Marksville-Fort DeRussy Road.[9] As his men waited for the order to attack, artillery in the fort began pouring fire into their ranks as they maneuvered into position.[10] Adding to the cacophony, and certainly disconcerting the Union troops, the *Eastport* and its entourage arrived in front of the fort, and the *Eastport* fired one of the forward 100-pound rifle shells at the water batteries.[11] The shell burst over the heads of the Confederates within the casemates, and they abandoned the water battery.[12]

At 6 P.M. Mower charged his brigades into the breastworks. The fort's three hundred men were overwhelmed in short order. Union casualties were thirty-eight killed and wounded.[13] Porter sent his heavy monitor *Osage* to accompany Mower's transports as they prepared to take Alexandria. Lieutenant Commander Thomas O. Selfridge, Jr., commanded the warship. The *Osage* arrived in Alexandria on the afternoon of Tuesday, March 15 and received the town's surrender without firing a shot.[14]

General Taylor had no qualms about leaving Alexandria to Union forces. He sought to find a place closer to Shreveport. He had ordered his far-flung brigades to meet at predetermined places, all near supply depots. The brigade of Texans under Prince Camille de Polignac had been ordered to travel from Trinity on the Ouachita River to join the brigade of Louisiana troops led by Colonel Henry Gray operating near Alexandria. Gray and Polignac joined about twenty-five miles south of Alexandria, where they were met by Taylor. The general formed the two brigades into a small division commanded by one of his favorite lieutenants, Brigadier General Alfred Mouton of modern-day Lafayette, Louisiana.[15] The Louisiana and Texas infantry divisions combined gave Taylor seven thousand combat effectives.[16] For a short period, General Taylor outmanned the Union forces.

Taylor had no viable way of keeping track of the Union troops in Alexandria. He took his army to one of the prepared foraging depots in western Rapides Parish.[17] Upon their arrival Taylor immediately sent the Second Louisiana Cavalry Regiment north to Bayou Rapides about twelve miles north of his location and some twenty-two miles north of Alexandria at the village of Cotile.[18] General Taylor's cavalry arrived on the night of March 21 after riding hard or skirmishing for six straight days with little sleep. They encamped at Henderson's Hill, a toe-shaped ridge that rose above the confluence of Bayou Rapides and Bayou Cotile. The weather turned ugly and cold and they were pelted by rain and hail. Trying to keep dry, the Confederate pickets were not vigilant.[19]

Mower led a Union force of approximately one thousand men, including a light artillery battery and the lead elements of Banks' column. Rapidly marching twenty miles in seven and-a-half hours, Mower and his men ended their march in "knee-deep mud."[20] Mower captured 350 Confederate cavalrymen and four hundred horses while suffering no losses.[21] Taylor once more was without his eyes and ears.

Beginning in New Orleans and traveling eighty miles by railroad and then another twenty-five miles by steamboat transports, the Nineteenth Corps arrived at the assembly point for their overland trek.[22] After a day of final preparations, Banks ordered General Albert L. Lee at the head of his cavalry division to lead the great column on the roads that would take them to Alexandria.[23] He then returned to New Orleans. The Nineteenth Corps assembled at Franklin in St. Mary Parish and followed Bayou Teche.[24] The column stretched twenty miles. The Thirteenth and Nineteenth Corps continued to travel in a single column as they moved into the wider alluvial plains farther north, never bothering to examine the possibility of shortening the column or rearranging the train's components.[25]

Brigadier General Lee was Banks' chief of cavalry for the Department of the Gulf. Lee commanded 4,653 officers and troopers, excluding 350 men detailed to guard and garrison duties.[26] Interspersed with his veteran cavalrymen were recently mounted infantry operating more like dragoons than cavalry. They were new to riding and had trouble handling and tending to their horses. Lee was forced to train them on the march, a difficult task at best. When he was exasperated, Lee referred to them as his amateur equestrians. After the lead elements of the cavalry division left the town of Franklin on the morning of March 13, they finally rode into Alexandria at nine on Sunday morning seven days later. They had traversed 175 miles.[27] After a short day's rest, Colonel Nathan A. M. Dudley and his First Brigade of cavalry accompanied Mower to Henderson Hill.

Banks had his trusted deputy and commander of the Nineteenth Corps lead the infantry in the campaign. This was Major General William Buel Franklin. Banks had sent Franklin across southern Louisiana the previous year with negligible success; therefore, he was familiar with the area his fifteen thousand infantry were now traversing. He began his second campaign into the interior of Louisiana with three thousand infantry from New Orleans; the remainder had been stripped from outposts on the barrier islands of Texas. They traveled with their equipment by troop transport ships to Berwick Bay, south of Franklin, Louisiana.[28] As the roads along Bayou Teche (the planned route) dried up, the column averaged seventeen miles a day.[29] The roads had been well torn up by the cavalry's passing, so there was no way the infantry could get lost.

The column crossed over Bayou Courtableu and passed through the towns of Grand Coteau, Opelousas, and Washington. From there, the column entered the low pine hill country before reaching the Red River Valley and the rich, red, sandy, alluvial plain that produced huge amounts of cotton. Here the road led them north to Alexandria, located near the geographic center of the state.[30] The column was seven days behind schedule on March 25.[31]

Banks had not endured the hazards of the march with his infantry. He had floated into Alexandria the day before on a transport named *Black Hawk*.[32] The vessel was filled with reporters and cotton speculators and Porter was not amused. He considered Banks' choice of conveyance an insult. The admiral's flagship, the large tinclad, also named *Black Hawk*, was his pride and joy.[33] The perceived insult was not lost on the admiral or his favored captains.

Porter and his forces arrived at Alexandria on March 15 and 16. With the city's surrender in hand and no sign of Banks and his legions, he quickly became bored. Because he had time on his hands, Porter was not averse to procuring cotton. In apparent response to the wholesale theft of cotton within a few miles of Alexandria, General Taylor had his soldiers burn thousands of bales to keep them out of Union hands and pocketbooks.

Franklin's Nineteenth Corps came in on the single road from Washington to Alexandria, strung out fifteen to twenty miles.[34] It took the better part of two days to get them in and bivouacked. The last regiment marched in on March 26, eight days behind schedule.[35]

Banks finally arrived and was dismayed by what he saw in Alexandria. The navy was carrying on a bustling business in gathering, processing, and trans-shipping cotton—*legally*.[36]

Banks' idea of a leisurely movement to Shreveport, such as he had undertaken to Alexandria, had now evaporated into the sky like the pillars of smoke from burning cotton. He realized that anything short of taking the Confederate capital of Louisiana would bring him political ruin, denying his presidential aspirations. Banks became obsessed by time schedules and orders of march. He was ready; the Red River was not.

Porter had been monitoring the river levels since the day he arrived, and he did not like what he saw. General Sherman, who had previously

William B. Franklin

Born in Pennsylvania 1823, Franklin graduated from the US Military Academy 1843, first in his class of forty-three that included Ulysses S. Grant. He was brevetted second lieutenant assigned to engineers and was part of Great Lakes survey team 1843–1845. He worked with with Philip Kearney's Rocky Mountain expedition 1846 and won two brevets for Mexican War service, including one for gallantry at Buena Vista. From 1848 to 1861, he was involved in numerous engineering projects, and among these was the construction of a new dome for the national capitol. Franklin taught engineering at West Point and gained slow but steady promotions, reaching captain in 1857. At the outbreak of the Civil War he was commissioned colonel of the Twelfth US Infantry and brigadier general US Volunteers shortly thereafter. He commanded a brigade at First Bull Run and a division in the Washington defenses following that debacle. He later commanded a division and then the Sixth Corps during the Peninsular Campaign. Franklin was promoted to major general US Volunteers July 1862 and directed the Sixth Corps during the Maryland Campaign and was conspicuously involved at Crampton's Gap, South Mountain, and Antietam in September 1862. He commanded the Left Grand Division at Fredericksburg, after which he was accused by General Ambrose Burnside of failing to follow orders, and although not disciplined, his career was irreparably damaged. Franklin was sent West, and he commanded the Nineteenth Corps in General Nathaniel P. Banks' Red River Expedition during which he was twice wounded, ending his field service. Brevetted brigadier general US Army for his actions in the Peninsular Campaign and major general US Army for war service, he was retired in 1866. From then until 1888, he was an executive with Colt's Firearms Manufacturing Company; he also supervised the construction of the Connecticut state capitol and held a variety of public offices until his death at Hartford in 1903. Although he owned a relatively solid service record, General Franklin could not overcome the stigma of the disaster at Fredericksburg.

lived across the river from Alexandria, explained to him that the Red River rose every spring and that this was the only time the fleet, particularly the deep-draft gunboats, could get to Shreveport.[37] Porter watched for the anticipated rise. But instead, he saw the river falling, sometimes an inch a day, sometimes an inch per hour.[38] The admiral realized he could wait no longer and prepared to move upstream. He sent light draft vessels forward to check the channel depth at various places in and above Alexandria. Porter ordered the *Eastport* over the falls.[39] Porter's intelligence sources had improperly informed him of multiple powerful ironclads and other combatant vessels at Shreveport. The idea of a squadron of up to five ironclads similar to the CSS *Arkansas* blinded him to the obvious limitations of the giant *Eastport.*

And the river, usually full and fast in the spring, what was its mystery? The Confederates had set their defense plans in motion beginning March 18. The intricate series of defensive works that Confederate Brigadier General William R. Boggs created in mid-1863 now became critical sites. Lieutenant General Edmund Kirby Smith ordered the *New Falls City* brought up from its hiding place in Coushatta Chute (Bayou Coushatta).[40] The sidewheeler was placed at the foot of Scopini Cut Off, one meander bend south of Tone's Bayou.[41] The engineers then wedged it cross-wise in the channel, so tightly in fact that the bow and stern ran up on the banks fifteen feet on each side and a sand bar began to build upstream. They then poured mud into the hold and cracked the keel, transforming the huge sidewheeler into an instant dam.[42]

After the placement of the *New Falls City*, other Confederate engineers used black powder to blow up the Hotchkiss dam, built the previous year. The river water exited its channel into the old Tone's Bayou channel and thence flowed directly into Bayou Pierre, just as planned. The admiral watched the river fall for several days followed by a brief rise. This rise was the small portion of the flow exiting Bayou Pierre and coming back into the river. The rise gave him the encouragement to begin sending the fleet north.

Banks allowed Franklin to manage the army while he played politics and decided to ascend the river to Grand Ecore after the election on April 1. The order of march was set with General Smith's veterans at the rear of the column. Lee's cavalry left Alexandria and passed Henderson's Hill on March 26. Smith's men left on the evening of the 27th and the morning of the 28th. The length of the column at times stretched more than twenty-five miles. Smith's men marched to the steamboat landing at Cotile, about twenty-two miles north of Alexandria near Henderson's Hill. There they boarded the army quartermaster transports to accompany the war fleet.[43]

General Lee's cavalry division reached Natchitoches on March 30 and took the town simply by riding in. Franklin arrived on April 1 after marching eighty miles in four days.[44] The column set up bivouac between Natchitoches and the small village of Grand Ecore, four miles farther north on the Red River. The tiny village acted as a port for Natchitoches.

Banks steamed into Grand Ecore late in the evening of April 3, delayed once more by assisting the *Eastport*, which had grounded.[45] On arrival at Grand Ecore, the Union commanders faced the most important decision in the campaign. Banks did not believe the Confederates would offer battle before he reached Shreveport, if then. He had two choices to approach Shreveport. He could accompany the navy with its big guns or he could strike inland, away from the navy's protection and into terrain that was all but unknown to Union intelligence sources. His advisor on the latter was a riverboat pilot, Wellington W. Withenbury, who desperately wanted to keep the army away from his cotton holdings just below Shreveport.[46]

Banks listened to the pilot and then pointed the army inland, leaving the safety of the fleet behind him. He used a single road and his column was poorly constructed with cavalry and infantry separated by hundreds of supply wagons.

Banks and Porter agreed to meet at a point opposite Springfield Landing in northern DeSoto Parish on April 10.[47] Springfield Landing was located just four miles from the Red River on Bayou Pierre on a narrow channel connecting Bayou Pierre Lake and Lake Cannisnia.[48] The landing was about sixty miles by road and more than one hundred miles by river from Grand Ecore.[49] According to the plan Banks was to leave Grand Ecore on April 6 and Porter was to leave on April 7.[50] At Springfield Landing or near it, Porter's fleet and the army transport vessels would replenish Banks' supply trains and the two groups would make the final approach to Shreveport.

Porter decided to compose his final assault force with the lightest-draft gunboats. He chose six vessels, the monitors *Osage* and *Neosho*, the timberclad *Lexington*, and the tinclads *Cricket, Fort Hindman,* and *Chillicothe.*[51] The admiral made the *Cricket* his flagship. The gunboats accompanied twenty army transports loaded with supplies and General Smith's small division of about 2,300 men from the Seventeenth Corps for protection.[52]

Banks established the order of march just the way he wanted it. The cavalry would begin to form up and ride out on the morning of April 6. It would take more than a day for the entire column to be underway. Lee's cavalry was followed immediately by its three hundred wagons at Franklin's insistence so as not to delay his own supply train.[53] The wagons of the column were protected by 2,500 US Colored Troops of the Corps d'Afrique.[54] Some were with Lee, but most were with the infantry wagons. Immediately following the cavalry's wagons and the train's guards were the fifteen thousand infantry under Franklin. Banks and Franklin rode at the head of this contingent. The infantry marched in the order of the two divisions of the Thirteenth Corps, then one division of the Nineteenth Corps. The men were never able to march more than four abreast because of the narrow roads.

Behind this long line of infantry were the seven hundred wagons of their supply train.[55] When Banks had taken such care in defining the marching order, he neglected to note that three hundred wagons to the front of the main infantry column and another seven hundred wagons to their rear would effectively box them in. The infantry would have difficulty assisting the cavalry to their front and would not easily be able to fall out or retreat with such a massive train behind them. Banks' use of only one road set the stage for disaster. The fact that he did not allow his cavalry to fan out ahead and seek other routes qualifies his actions as one of the greatest blunders in the Civil War. Following the seven wagons of the supply train were General Smith's 7,500 men of the Sixteenth Corps. Relegated to eat the dust of the entire column, they did not leave Grand Ecore until the next day.[56] The column's only flankers were a single

Albert L. Lee

Born New York in 1834, Lee graduated from Union College in Schenectady, New York. In 1853, he studied law and eventually moved to Kansas, and in 1861 he became an associate justice of the Kansas Supreme Court but resigned to enter the volunteer army following the outbreak of the Civil War. Commissioned a major in the Seventh Kansas Cavalry, Lee saw limited action in Kansas and Missouri before commanding a brigade at Corinth, Mississippi, in October 1862. He led a cavalry brigade in the Army of the Tennessee in the early stages of the Vicksburg Campaign and was promoted to brigadier general, US Volunteers in April 1863 (to rank from November 1862). During the move on Vicksburg, Lee served as acting chief of staff to General John A. McClernand and, following the wounding of General Peter Osterhaus, commanded the Ninth Division, Thirteenth Corps, Army of the Tennessee, at Big Black River on May 17, 1863. Two days later, leading an infantry brigade in an assault on Vicksburg, Lee was wounded in the face and head. Returning to duty in July, he filled various division commands until selected to head the Cavalry Division of the Department of the Gulf in September. Lee fared poorly commanding the cavalry in General Nathaniel P. Banks' disastrous Red River Expedition in the spring of 1864. Although Lee retained his command for a time, his troubled relationship with Banks' successor, General E. R. S. Canby, eventually cost him his job. Ostracized by Canby, Lee resigned in May 1865. After the war, he traveled extensively in Europe and engaged in business in New York City. Lee died in New York in 1907.

brigade of cavalry under Colonel Oliver Gooding. This brigade never fanned out ahead as a screen but covered the column's rear, and, when possible, its left flank.[57] Artillery was dedicated to each of the infantry components and travelled with them.

The great column traveled the single road, which some days was dusty and on others, a muddy ditch. This column of men and matériel resembled a giant accordion, stretching out at some points, squeezing impossibly tight in others, at times not moving at all. The wagon teams slowed the entire process down and effectively set the pace. The cavalry was not allowed to move far ahead and conduct its mission. Lee was repeatedly told to protect his own wagons and was not allowed to place them with the infantry's train. Banks' "bound" had become a creep. Frustration was rampant and the terrain they entered did little to ease the men's attitudes.

The column moved westward and found the relatively easy traveling in the river valleys was behind them. Red sand was replaced by red clay. Hard when dry, when wet it was slick and stuck to everything. And when wet, the clay made movement tiring, and it made footing treacherous. The giant stretches of cotton-bearing land that the troops had grown accustomed to seeing were gone, replaced by yellow pine trees that grew so thick in places that there was no undergrowth. At times the road appeared as a long green cathedral with the road the only aisle. A Union cavalry trooper called the area a "howling wilderness."[58]

As the federal soldiers picked their way west then north, General Taylor finally began receiving some much-needed reinforcements, although not all that he needed and requested. Major General Tom Green crossed the Sabine River into Louisiana at Logansport in DeSoto Parish on April 7. Leading several regiments of Texas cavalry, the fearless Green was coming to Taylor's aid, having finally been allowed to leave Texas soil.[59] After a short rest at the village and college campus at Keachi, they joined Taylor at Pleasant Hill and then rode ahead to find the location and activities of the Union forces.

Green's arrival was critically important to Taylor. The aggressive Texan cavalrymen would perform the true task of cavalry—reconnaissance and intimidation. He could not readily identify which units he would be fighting without the cavalry's assistance. It was Green's cavalry who confirmed Banks was using only one line of approach and that he had stupidly hindered his own cavalry by forcing them stay with their train.

General Lee led the column westward from Natchitoches through the rolling red clay hills on the old Spanish Royal Road. About twelve miles west of Natchitoches they passed near the old Spanish capital of Texas at Los Adaes and then turned away to the north from the old road to Mexico City at a stagecoach road intersection.[60] Lee pushed up the road to another store at Crump's Corners where four days before, his men had

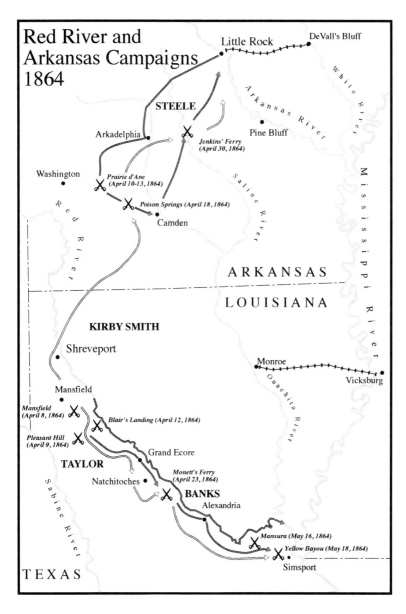

Red River and Arkansas Campaigns 1864

DeVall's Bluff

Little Rock

White River

STEELE

Arkansas River

Arkadelphia

Pine Bluff

Jenkins' Ferry (April 30, 1864)

Washington

Prairie d'Ane (April 10-13, 1864)

Saline River

Red River

Poison Springs (April 18, 1864)

Camden

ARKANSAS

Mississippi River

LOUISIANA

KIRBY SMITH

Shreveport

Monroe

Ouachita River

Vicksburg

Mansfield

Mansfield (April 8, 1864)

Blair's Landing (April 12, 1864)

Pleasant Hill (April 9, 1864)

Grand Ecore

TAYLOR

Sabine River

Natchitoches

Monett's Ferry (April 23, 1864)

BANKS

Alexandria

Mansura (May 16, 1864)

Yellow Bayou (May 18, 1864)

Simsport

TEXAS

encountered Confederate cavalry.[61] Lee halted there for the night. The next day was April 7 and the Confederates had not shown any interest in doing anything but light skirmishing.

Lee set out early with three of his four brigades; Gooding was still occupied with flanking duties. The road ran almost due north for about twelve miles with few curves and almost no homesteads. At noon Lee reached the village of Pleasant Hill. He had ten regiments of cavalry, half of which were mounted infantry, not accomplished horsemen.[62] Three miles north of the village, the column ran into four regiments of Green's cavalry at Wilson's farm.[63] Green chose to change his tactics and charged the Union cavalry. Lee could not accurately estimate their numbers. He formed his men on both sides of the road and set up his howitzers to provide support. Green charged and forced the Union right back several yards, the Rebels attacking with their customary yell. The first brigade of infantry came up and fired a volley into the Confederate ranks, which then fell back into the field. Although the battle was small compared to other actions during the campaign, it was important to the Confederates. Green forced the Union cavalry into a new mind-set. From this point, Lee was leery of every rise of ground and turn in the road.

Banks ordered a single brigade of infantry to be moved up ahead of the wagon train to support the cavalry. The brigade was under the command of Brigadier General Thomas E. G. Ransom, who commanded the Thirteenth Corps component of the expedition. Banks' mistake was not to send the entire Thirteenth Corps detachment forward with the brigade. Ransom was not sure what was expected of him and he chose to follow the order to the letter and sent only Colonel William J. Landram commanding the Fourth Division of the Thirteenth Corps and Colonel Frank Emerson's First Brigade of the Fourth Division, consisting of only about 1,200 men.[64] The cavalry moved ahead more tentatively. Lee picked his way another seven miles beyond Wilson's Farm and decided to halt for the evening. Lee posted pickets at Carroll's Mill and finally halted for the night.[65]

The next day began as a duplicate of the actions of April 7. Early in the morning of April 8, Lee moved his cavalry out with Colonel Thomas J. Lucas' First Brigade of the Cavalry Division in the lead.[66]

Almost immediately they encountered Green's Texans. Green continued his delaying tactics, trying to buy time for Taylor and determine what reaction the men in blue would have to his slow withdrawal. This constant skirmishing tired the federal troops, particularly the infantry.

Ransom began the march at 5:30 A.M. at Pleasant Hill and five hours later reached Ten Mile Bayou. He stopped as per his orders after covering ten miles. Ransom's men were moving into camp when Lee asked for relief for the exhausted infantry. Franklin ordered Ransom personally to go forward with Colonel Joseph W. Vance's Second Brigade of the Fourth Division, Nineteenth Army Corps to see what was happening and to make sure that Emerson's men came back to the main column. Franklin still did not want a large body of infantry operating with the cavalry.[67]

With constant skirmishing, Lee pushed the Confederate cavalry screen back six miles on the morning of April 8. Sometime between noon and 1 P.M. General Lee and his men found themselves at an intersection of the road on which they were traveling and one that went to a landing on the Red River. The intersection was called Sabine Crossroads. The Confederate cavalry that had been a constant menace for the last two days seemed to disappear. Lee, at the head of his column, moved another three quarters of a mile to the edge of a huge clearing, 800 yards deep and 1,200 yards across, at the slope of a ridge called Honeycutt Hill.[68] Confederate skirmishers were there in force, and as Lee and Landram moved forward, they gave way. The cavalry and infantry units moved to take the ridge. As Lee rode to the crest of the hill, he saw the bulk of the Confederate army west of the Mississippi drawn up in line of battle all across his front on both sides of the road and extending down and past his right flank.[69] Finally, Banks' belief that the Confederates were unwilling or unable to fight allowed him to lead his men into a trap as the Confederates had found their place to make a stand.

5

THE BATTLE OF MANSFIELD

Brigadier General Albert L. Lee, at the head of his cavalry column, gazed at the edge of a huge clearing, 800 yards deep and 1,200 yards across, at the slope of a ridge called Honeycutt Hill.[1] Confederate skirmishers were there in force, and as Lee and Colonel William J. Landram moved forward, they gave way. The cavalry and infantry units moved to take the ridge. As Lee rode to the crest of the hill, he saw the bulk of the Confederate army west of the Mississippi drawn up in line of battle all across his front on both sides of the road and extending down and past his right flank.[2]

Major General Richard Taylor was ready for the Union column, thanks to the time bought for him by Major General Tom Green. After a frustrating meeting with Lieutenant General Edmund Kirby Smith on April 6, Taylor seized the initiative to prepare for the coming battle. He was furious with the commanding general for not specifically allowing him to fight the battle at the time and place of his choosing and with all the forces available.[3] During early April, as Smith vacillated, Taylor wrote his commander concerning the need to do *something*, "Action, prompt, vigorous action, is required. While we are deliberating the enemy is marching. King James lost three kingdoms for a mass. We may lose three States without a battle."[4]

Richard Taylor

Born in Kentucky in 1826, Taylor was son of President and Mexican War hero Zachary Taylor and brother-in-law of Confederate President Jefferson Davis. He studied at Yale and became a successful sugar planter in Louisiana. Taylor was elected colonel of the Ninth Louisiana Infantry at the outbreak of the Civil War and went  with the regiment to Virginia, arriving too late for First Manassas. He was promoted to brigadier general 1861 and commanded the Louisiana Brigade in Major General Thomas J. "Stonewall" Jackson's Shenandoah Valley Campaign of 1862. Taylor was present but not active during the Seven Days' Battles before Richmond. He was promoted to major general and assigned to command the District of Western Louisiana in 1862. He unsuccessfully opposed Major General Nathaniel P. Banks' Bayou Teche Expedition in 1863 but turned back Banks' Red River Expedition the following spring. After a heated exchange in which he criticized his commander, General Edmund Kirby Smith, for not following up this success, he asked to be relieved; he was, however, promoted to lieutenant general and assigned to command the Department of Alabama, Mississippi, and East Louisiana. Following the disaster at Nashville, he temporarily succeeded General John B. Hood in command of the Army of Tennessee, most of which he forwarded to the Carolinas to oppose Major General William T. Sherman's advance. After the fall of Mobile, he surrendered the last remaining Confederate force east of the Mississippi to Major General E. R. S. Canby on May 4, 1865. Following the war, he was active in Democratic politics and vigorously opposed Reconstruction policies. Taylor died at New York in 1879. That year he published *Destruction and Reconstruction*, one of the finest participant memoirs to be produced. Without any formal military training, Taylor proved to be a most able commander. The Confederate repulse of the Red River Expedition, though largely overlooked, was a major achievement.

On April 7 Taylor rode south on the road to Pleasant Hill and found Green and his cavalrymen annoying the federal column. After making sure that the Union column had halted at Carroll's Mill, Taylor rode back the seventeen miles to Mansfield.[5] He told the Texan to harass the Union forces as much as possible until he met the main body of troops who would be waiting for him.[6] The next day Taylor planned to stop

Major General Nathaniel P. Banks, and chose his ground on the great field at Honeycutt Hill. This was an ideal spot because any place north of this position offered the enemy a choice of three roads to Shreveport.[7] Taylor now had to work with the terrain at hand.

After arriving in Mansfield on the evening of the April 7, Taylor began issuing orders to his commanders. He sent a courier to Keachi to summon Major General Sterling Price's men to Mansfield. The 4,400 troops had to force march twenty miles beginning at

Colonel James Hamilton Beard. Archives of the Mansfield State Historic Site, Mansfield, Louisiana.

dawn on April 8. Brigadier General John G. Walker and Brigadier General Alfred Mouton were ordered to break camp north of Mansfield and concentrate their forces at the field.[8] To cover himself, Taylor's last official act that evening was to send another courier to Kirby Smith in Shreveport at 9 P.M. Taylor wrote, "I respectfully ask to know if it accords with the views of the lieutenant-general commanding that I should hazard a general engagement at this point, and request an immediate answer, that I may receive it before daylight to-morrow morning."[9] Taylor did not expect an answer and, anticipating the battle would be fought the next day, told his friend the Prince de Polignac, "I will fight Banks if he has a million men."[10]

At 9:40 the next morning, Taylor sent another message to Shreveport declaring, "I consider this as favorable a point to engage the enemy as any other."[11] The clearing formed a giant L lying on its side with the

long axis facing east and the short axis facing south.[12] The Shreveport–
Natchitoches stagecoach road entered the clearing at the vertex and ran to
the southeast. Forests bordered the clearing on the west and north along
ridgelines. After a gentle drop to a shallow stream, the ground rose again to
a ridge forming a smaller *L* in the same configuration. The southeast side
of this ridge sloped into shallow saddle before rising gently to Honeycutt
Hill, which was mostly covered in trees. On the southeast slope of the
Honeycutt Hill was an orchard that gave way to open ground. The pasture
was bordered by a shallow stream bottom, which separated it from another
field. Southeast of this field stood a band of trees and behind these woods
was the crossroads. From the southern tip of the first ridgeline to the
stagecoach road and then continuing to the easternmost tip of the clearing,
Taylor's battle line ran more than three miles.

Taylor wanted his men with the forest to their backs. He did not want
Banks to see how many men he had. He positioned his artillery to focus
on the point at which the Union forces would exit the woods and enter
the field. He also needed the three-mile front to position his regiments.
There is no doubt that Taylor expected Banks to act rashly and to charge
his center position, at which time his two broad wings would collapse on
the Union center.[13]

On Taylor's far right, separated from the main body by several hundred
feet, were two regiments of Green's cavalry under Brigadier General
Hamilton P. Bee. To their left were two brigades of Texas infantry from
General Walker's division. Brigadier General William R. Scurry and
Brigadier General Thomas Waul led these brigades. Between them was
an artillery battery. Another battery occupied both sides of the stagecoach
road. Here the *L* turned east with the third of Walker's brigades, this one
led by Colonel Horace Randal. Next in line were the Texas and Louisiana
troops under Brigadier General Mouton. Positioned on Randal's left was
the brigade under Brigadier General Camille Polignac and to his left
was the brigade under Colonel Henry Gray. An artillery battery was
positioned in front of Mouton's troops. This battery was the closest
artillery to Honeycutt Hill. Separated by several hundred feet and to the

left of Gray, was the bulk of Green's cavalry, positioned in three tiers. They were the last to arrive and were placed to hold the most endangered flank.[14]

Taylor approached Mouton and Gray, riding up and down the line of Louisianans. He promised them they would draw first blood in honor of protecting their home state.[15] These units were battle-hardened veterans of the Eighteenth Consolidated Infantry, the Twenty-Eighth Infantry, and the Consolidated Crescent regiments. These troops would take the brunt of the initial fighting.

Price's forces were still en route and Taylor did not know when they would arrive or what shape they would be in. With Green's arrival, Taylor's force was complete. He now had approximately 5,300 infantry, 500 artillerymen, and 3,000 cavalry on the field.[16] Almost all the cavalry was to fight dismounted as infantry. An unknown quantity of other troops was also on the field for the Confederates that spring day. Taylor referred to them as "reserves" or the home guard. These were exchanged soldiers, veterans of Vicksburg, not yet legally paroled. If the Confederates had lost and these men were captured, they could have been executed by the Union forces. They were never carried on the rolls or lists of battle units, but they were there fighting for their state and their country. From diary entries and postwar compilations, they appear to have filled in the ranks of units before the battle. It is likely that there may have been from several hundred to several thousand of these reserves in the field.[17] Taylor made adjustments to the line, most notably moving Randal's brigade from its original position south of the road to north of the road.[18] With the line now in its final position, the Confederate troops saw the first Union troops come out from the woods shortly after noon.

Colonel Landram's small Fourth Division of the Thirteenth Corps had fought Green's cavalry for two days. The men were tired and wary of the Texans. As they reached the hilltop, they viewed massed Confederate regiments drawn up in line of battle across their front and to their right. Lee estimated that Taylor had between fifteen and twenty thousand troops.

The almost constant starting and stopping of the column annoyed General Banks who rode forward to see what General Lee and his amateur equestrians were doing. He found his forward infantry and cavalry units skirmishing with Confederates. Banks sent for Lee and asked him to describe the situation to their front. Lee described how he had his men deployed and Banks approved. He then told Lee that he would order the infantry to move forward.

Banks then sent George Drake, his assistant adjutant general back down the column to General Franklin. Another message followed almost immediately, this one telling Franklin to begin moving his men forward as quickly as possible. Landram's second brigade arrived on the hill about 3:30 P.M. He now had 2,400 infantry in place.[19] Lee placed his men in a smaller replica of the Confederate line shaped in an *L* configuration. He positioned Colonel Ormand Nims' artillery battery on the stagecoach road with Emerson's infantry brigade protecting them. Landram's Second Brigade took up positions behind a rail fence perpendicular to Emerson. Lee then placed Colonel Thomas Lucas' cavalry brigade on his right flank facing Green's cavalry and Colonel Nathan A. M. "Gold Lace" Dudley's small cavalry brigade on the left flank. Lee ordered the Chicago Mercantile Battery and the First Indiana battery to set up at a residence called the Fincher House, located behind and down the slope from the infantry and cavalry.[20] There they would be able to provide fire support for either the federal front or right flank. As these units came into place, the cavalry's wagon train pulled up to the crossroads about one-half mile behind the front line. The train, their teamsters, and guards from the Corps d'Afrique halted. Once again, the three hundred wagons blocked the road.[21]

About 4 P.M. Lee rode back to the crest of the hill after conferring with Banks. Thinking the infantry he requested would soon arrive, he was given an order by one of Banks' staff aides to move immediately on Mansfield. Lee was incredulous and said there must be a mistake in the order. He immediately rode over to Banks, who confirmed the order was correct. Lee later explained, "I told him we could not advance ten minutes without a general engagement, in which we should be most gloriously flogged, I did not want to do it."[22] Banks agreed to delay the advance and sent a courier to Franklin ordering the infantry up. This was the second message Franklin received.

General Taylor watched the sun sink lower into the western sky, knowing that he had only about three hours of daylight left. He had counted on Banks being impetuous, and acting rashly, but this was not happening. As his men watched, more Union regiments were arriving, and their line was getting stronger by the hour. The Confederates had to act or they would lose the initiative. There is some question as to whether Taylor ordered Mouton to attack or told him they would soon attack. The reason for the confusion is the order in which the Confederate units began their charge. Rather than having the entire line moving in unison, Mouton advanced his regiments in echelon, staggering their lines. This resulted in high casualty rates from the Union troops focusing on specific regiments as they came close to their positions. This was not a tactic that Taylor usually employed. Mouton's men had been waiting for their chance for most of the day, and their charge was magnificent as recorded by both sides.[23] The division's officers rode their horses for their men to more easily see them, and this act of bravery led to catastrophic results.

On Honeycutt Hill General Thomas E. G. Ransom had now joined Generals Lee and Landram. When Mouton's men moved forward, Ransom ordered his five infantry regiments facing the Louisianans to leave the fence and engage them in the field. The two sides met at close range and fired volleys.[24] Losses were heavy, and Mouton's attack faltered. The Union infantry began picking off the mounted officers with Mouton mortally wounded at the end of the charge. The commanders of the Eighteenth Louisiana Infantry, Twenty-Eighth Louisiana Infantry, and the Consolidated Crescent regiments were also killed. One-third of Mouton's men were killed or wounded in the attack.[25] Mouton was shot in the back several times while ordering his men to stop firing on Union troops who were trying to surrender. Some of the Union infantrymen picked up their guns and fired at the general. Mouton's men then fell on

Thomas E. G. Ransom

Born on November 29, 1834, in Norwich, Vermont, Ransom's father, Truman B. Ransom, was a colonel in the Mexican War and was killed on the assault of Chapultepec Palace when Ransom was fourteen years old. Ransom was admitted to Norwich University in 1848, attended for three years, and then moved to Illinois. He

studied topographic engineering. He became an employee of the Union Pacific Railroad and lived in Fayette County, Illinois. At the beginning of the Civil War, Ransom raised a company of soldiers, which became Company E, of the Eleventh Illinois Infantry Regiment. He was elected captain of the company in April 1861. By June that year, he rose to lieutenant colonel of the regiment. He served under and with W. H. L. Wallace. He was promoted to colonel on February 15, 1862, and then brigadier general on November 9, 1862. He became a brigade commander under Brigadier General John MacArthur's Sixth Division in the Seventeenth Army Corps.

Ransom was brave under fire and always led from the front. He was wounded several times. The first was at a small action at Charleston, Missouri, in August 1861. He received a second wound during the attack on Fort Donelson, Tennessee, in February 1862. His third wound, this one to the head, occurred during the battle of on the first day of fighting on April 6, 1863. His fourth, the most serious of his wounds, occurred at the Battle of Mansfield, Louisiana, on April 8, 1864. He was hit in the knee early in the battle; it was an incapacitating injury. He was evacuated to Chicago for treatment. Following recuperation in Chicago, he returned to action with General William T. Sherman during the Atlanta Campaign. He fell ill with dysentery and commanded until he was too weak to continue at Rome, Georgia, in October 1864. When the corps surgeons told him he had a short time to live, he responded to them: "I am not afraid to die; I have met death too often to be afraid of it now."

Ransom was considered to be one of the best Union commanders during the war. General Sherman said of him during the Atlanta Campaign, "Do you know that young man? That is General Ransom, rising man, rising man; one of the best officers in the service; been shot all to pieces, but it doesn't hurt him." Sherman kept a portrait of Ransom in his office for twenty years after the war and then donated it to the GAR post named in Ransom's honor. According to Edward Longacre, General Ulysses S. Grant wept on hearing of Ransom's death.

During his career, Ransom commanded divisions in the Thirteenth, Sixteenth, and Seventeenth Army Corps. He was awarded a promotion to brevet major general in September 1864, a few weeks before his death. He is buried in Rosehill Cemetery in Chicago, Illinois.

the blue regimental line with a vengeance. The Confederate line stalled, and the accurate Union fire pushed the Confederates back to about two hundred yards from Ransom's right flank.[26] Within minutes of the beginning of the assault, Green was the senior Confederate officer on Taylor's left wing.[27]

Brigadier General Jean Jacques Alexandre Alfred Mouton. Carte de Visite in the collection of the Mansfield State Historic Site, Mansfield, Louisiana.

To Mouton's left, the Texan cavalry made their entry on foot. This placed the five Union regiments in danger of being flanked. The five regiments of Lucas' cavalry, also fighting on foot, were in danger of being turned. If these units folded, the entire Union line was in jeopardy of being enveloped. Mouton's right was anchored by Randal's Texas brigade, holding the center of the Confederate line. As this brigade marched out in echelon, they found that they were squeezed between Polignac's charge and the road. Randal's men were forced to march slower.

Taylor watched the Texans and Louisianans engage the enemy from horseback. He was smoking a cigar and had one leg crossed over the saddle.[28] As soon as he saw the Union forces occupied with the first wave, he ordered General Walker to unleash his Texans on the federal forces. The Texans, who had been watching the action on the other side of the field were anxious to attack and did so in rapidly advancing solid lines, not echelon formations.[29]

R. B. Scott of the Sixty-Seventh Indiana Infantry Regiment was at the vertex of Lee's *L*. His regiment was to the right of Nims' battery on the

John G. Walker

Born Missouri 1822, Walker received his early education at the Jesuit College in St. Louis. Commissioned directly into the US Army in 1846, he served during the Mexica War and had attained the rank of captain by the time he resigned in 1861 to enter Confederate service. He was commissioned major of cavalry in the regular Confederate Army and was made brigadier general early in 1862. Walker distinguished himself with the Army of Northern Virginia through the Maryland Campaign and was promoted major general in November 1862; his division of two brigades took possession of Loudon Heights in the operations against Harper's Ferry in September 1862 and subsequently rendered gallant service during the Battle of Sharpsburg. At this juncture, he was transferred to the Trans-Mississippi Department, where he assumed command of the Texas Infantry Division. After participating in the Red River Campaign, he relieved General Richard Taylor in the District of West Louisiana, and at the close of the war, he was in command of a division in the District of Texas, New Mexico, and Arizona; his troops being composed at the time of Steele's, Bee's, and Bagby's cavalry divisions, Cooper's Indians, and Slaughter's Brigade. Walker went to Mexico without waiting for his personal parole at the end of hostilities. He later he served as US consul general at Bogota, Columbia, and as special commissioner to the South American republics on behalf of the Pan-American Convention. Walker died in Washington, D.C., in 1893 and is buried in Winchester, Virginia.

stagecoach road. Scott saw the Texans coming at his position and wrote they ran toward the Union line "like a cyclone. Yelling like infuriated demons."[30] The Texans ripped through Dudley's Third Massachusetts Cavalry Regiment and began to push the Union line in on itself. Nims' battery kept a deadly fire until three of its guns were captured and then turned around and used on the former friends.[31] The Twenty-Third Wisconsin and Sixty-Seventh Indiana regiments were crushed. Ransom ordered the Eighty-Third Ohio, the last infantry regiment on his right flank to move in support of the left.[32] They were already being flanked by Green's Texans. When they shifted to their new position, they found that

Camille A. J. M., Prince de Polignac

Polignac was a French prince and military officer and one of the best Confederate general officers during the Civil War. He was born into nobility in Millemont, Seine-et-Oise, France, on February 16, 1832. His family was closely related and allied to the royal family before the French Revolution. His father was a senior advisor and minister to the royal family. Polignac was related to the Grimaldi family that still ruled in Monaco. The young prince studied mathematics at St. Stanislaus College while in his late teens and then joined the French army in 1853. He served with gallantry during the Crimean War in 1854 and 1855, receiving a commission as a second lieutenant. He resigned from military service in 1859 and traveled to Central America and to the United States in 1861.

Polignac volunteered to service in Richmond. He served as a staff officer for P. G. T. Beauregard and Braxton Bragg with the rank of lieutenant colonel. He served at the Battle of Shiloh and the Siege of Corinth. In January 1863, he attained the rank of brigadier general. He transferred to the Trans-Mississippi Department in March. There, he commanded a Texas infantry brigade. His Texan troops had problems with his accent, his attention to personal grooming habits, and the fact that he oiled his hair; however, they quickly found the new commander was a dynamic leader and tough fighter. They had trouble pronouncing the name Polignac, but could easily refer to him as "General Polecat." It stuck.

Working under Major General Richard Taylor, with whom he enjoyed a great friendship, Polignac commanded his troops in northeastern Louisiana. In the spring of 1864, during the Red River Campaign, Polignac led his men during the Battle of Mansfield and then, on the death Brigadier Alfred Mouton, he received a battlefield promotion to division commander. He led the small Louisiana Division through the remainder of the Red River Campaign. Polignac was formally promoted to major general on June 14, 1864. The Confederacy sent him to Paris in March 1865 to try to convince Napoleon III to join the cause of the Confederacy. The war ended while he was en route.

After the war, Polignac based out of his estate in France and traveled to Central America. He rejoined the French Army as a brigadier general and commanded a division during the Franco-Prussian War. He married twice and had three daughters and a son, whom he named Victor Mansfield. He died on November 15, 1913, in Paris. He is buried with his wife's family at Frankfurt-am-Main.

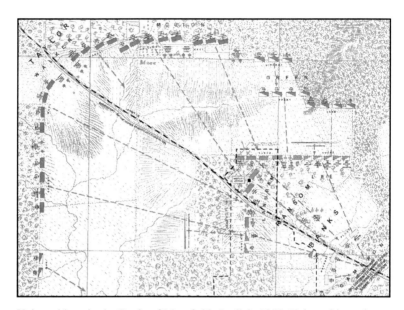

Unit positions in the Battle of Mansfield, April 8, 1864. Unit positions shown over Confederate engineer's base map drawn shortly after the battle. North is to the left of the map. Base map by Major Richard Venable. Additional cartography by Gary D. Joiner.

the left flank did not exist.[33] Ransom then ordered them back to support the Chicago Mercantile Battery.[34]

Ransom ordered his adjutant, Captain William H. Dickey, to instruct Landram to retreat on the same line as the 83rd Ohio. Dickey left and was shot in the head. The order was not carried out and most of the right-wing regiments were forced to surrender when surrounded. Two regiments, the 48th Ohio and the 130th Illinois simply ceased to exist. There were not enough survivors to rally or formally surrender.[35] Ransom described his 13th Corps as being caught in a nutcracker. Shortly after Dickey's death, the entire Union line collapsed.[36] Ransom rallied his men through the woods and around the Chicago Mercantile Battery, which was pouring accurate fire into the Confederate ranks. Ransom was mounted on his horse so his men could see him in swirling fight. As he ordered the remnants of his 13th Corps into their new positions, Ransom fell from his horse, hit in the knee by shrapnel.[37] Some of his men lifted Ransom on their shoulders and took him to the rear. Brigadier General Robert Cameron's Third Division finally made their way around the cavalry train and set up between the battery and the copse of trees standing in front of the crossroads.[38] The head of the wagon train was at the crossroads. In thirty minutes of fighting, the Union advance had been crushed. Ransom was wounded, and both of Landram's brigade commanders, Emerson and Vance, had been wounded and captured.[39]

Franklin came to the front with Cameron. As they formed their line behind the artillery battery, the remnants of Dudley's cavalry tried to rally to the new line. Lieutenant Colonel Lorenzo Thomas of the Third Massachusetts cavalry yelled to his men to rally on the new line to, "try to think that you are dead and buried, and you will have no fear."[40] Franklin made an accurate assessment of the situation to his front and ordered Brigadier General William Emory to form his First Division of the Nineteenth Corps in line of battle behind him on the first good position he could find.[41] Emory, coming forward from Ten Mile Bayou, picked a point about three miles behind the initial line on a stream called Chapman's Bayou with a ridgeline lying behind it.[42] There he waited.

As Cameron's men solidified their line, they were met with a crashing charge, not from the Confederates, but from the Union survivors of the opening phase of the battle. A northern reporter described the scene. "We found ourselves swallowed up, as it were, in a hissing, seething, bubbling whirlpool of agitated men."[43] The rout was endangering both the men running and the men of the Cameron's division. Soldiers were shedding guns, knapsacks, and any gear that slowed them down.[44] The Confederates behind them were still giving the Rebel Yell and the cacophony at the crossroads was maddening.[45] Franklin, unhorsed by the mob, fell and broke his left arm.[46] Banks tried to rally his men. No one doubted his personal courage, but he was ineffective. He shouted to them to, "Form a line here. I know you will not desert me."[47] But desert him they did. The wagons could not be turned around so the teamsters cut the lines to ride the horses and mules away from the disaster. The Corps d'Afrique added their number to the tide of men in retreat. The wagons acted as a barrier to any organized retreat. No artillery limbers could pass the train so they were captured piece by piece. Franklin was taken away to safety as Cameron tried to hold the line, but after only about twenty minutes his position collapsed as well.[48] He had only five regiments and they were flanked on both left and right. Cameron's men also joined the exodus of blue trying to reach safety somewhere behind them. It was now about 5:30, and the sun was low in the western sky.

Emory's men were coming forward from Ten Mile Bayou when he began to encounter trickles then masses of men, union soldiers, running or riding toward him, and then past him.[49] This slowed his division's progress tremendously. He stopped at a house on a ridge overlooking the small creek called Chapman's Bayou. Next to the house was an orchard and, although there are no local records to state why, Emory called it Pleasant Grove.[50] He positioned his men in front of the creek, correctly assuming that this was the only water for miles around, and certainly the only water between him and Ten Mile Bayou, little more than a small creek, seven miles behind him. His fresh troops stood their ground better than their predecessors.

The Confederates had lost unit cohesion in the wild assaults leading to the third Union position of the day, and the final attack was made as a mad rush. Confederate troops hit Emory's entire line in a massive assault, but they were exhausted from continuous fighting. As darkness fell, the Rebels managed to push the Union troops behind the creek and claimed the water for themselves.[51]

Emory redeployed his men on the low ridge above the bayou.[52] The Rebels made a last push up the ridge in the waning light but failed to dislodge the Union infantry. Fighting ended with the darkness. Emerson held the ridge against the Confederate mob. The Union soldiers could hear their wagons being moved to the north, cavalry units rallying to bugle ca'ls, and companies being mustered for formation in the darkness.[53] As the fighting was winding down, General Taylor received the reply to his letter to Kirby Smith from the previous night. General Kirby Smith told Taylor to avoid a general engagement. Taylor sent the courier back to

Shreveport with a message for the commanding general: "Too late, sir, the battle is won."[54]

The losses that day were high for both sides. Landram's Fourth Division of the Thirteenth Corps, the first line of Union infantry in the battle, lost almost half of their 2,400 men with 25 killed, 95 wounded, and 1,015 reported missing. Many of these missing were killed in the opening minutes of the battle, and hundreds were captured within the first half-hour of fighting.[55] Cameron's Third Division lost 317 of its 1,200 man roster. Lee's cavalry division lost 39 killed, 250 wounded, and 144 missing. Emory's division lost 347 killed of his 5,000 men. The total Union losses were 113 killed, 581 wounded, and 1,541 missing or 2,235 official casualties of a force of 12,000 participating in all three phases.[56] Taylor reported taking 2,500 prisoners.[57] The numbers of dead were certainly higher than Union estimates. They left their dead and wounded on the field to be cared for by Confederate doctors. Some Union doctors remained to help with the medical care.[58] An examination of individual regimental records increases the total casualties. The regimental casualty figures reveal 240 killed, 671 wounded, and 1,508 missing or 2,419 casualties.[59]

Confederate losses were listed as approximately 1,000 killed and wounded of 8,800 combat soldiers. Although a few Confederates were taken prisoner, the number of missing was insignificant. Two-thirds of these were from Mouton's division and were captured because of the echelon attack. This is easily proven when comparing General Walker's casualties.[60]

Taylor had lost many of his favorite commanders that day, but he had stopped the Union advance on Shreveport and was confident that early the next morning he would crush Bank's Nineteenth Corps. At 1:30 A.M. April 9, Taylor penned a letter to Walker telling him what they would do the next day. This plan was simple. At dawn that day his force would sweep over the ridge, led by Missouri and Arkansas troops to give the Texans and Louisianans a much-needed rest. Taylor ordered Green to take his cavalry to the Blair's Landing road to cut off the Union retreat and to try to keep reinforcements from joining Banks. In the plan, Brigadier General Mosby M. Parsons' division of Missouri infantry was to form the left wing and Brigadier General Thomas Churchill's division of Arkansas infantry was to form the right wing. Because the road was so narrow, Churchill's men were to wheel around in the woods and attack the Union on their left flank. Taylor told Walker that the only troops they faced were the Nineteenth Corps consisting of about seven thousand men, many of whom were raw recruits "who will make no fight. Yankees whom we have always whipped."[61] Taylor also thought that Banks might pull back during the night. In that event, the Confederates would pursue them and push them behind Pleasant Hill, forcing them to return to Natchitoches. Taylor also mentioned that it was impossible for reinforcements to reach Banks before late in the day and cautioned that they must fight him quickly. Taylor's intelligence reported troop transports coming up the river. This was Rear Admiral David Dixon Porter's force of six warships and twenty troop and supply transports coming to meet Banks at Springfield Landing. With the letter completed, Taylor slept a few hours on the battlefield. He would be ready for Banks in the morning.

Through the night the Confederates could here the clanking and rustling sounds of troops being repositioned. What they did not know, but Taylor suspected, was that Banks was withdrawing to Pleasant Hill. Taylor did not know that General Smith's 7,500 men forming the rear of the Union column had encamped at Pleasant Hill that night. Taylor's battle plan for the next day was set, but the location was to be fourteen miles down the road rather than over the ridge to his front.

6

THE BATTLE OF PLEASANT HILL

Major General Nathaniel P. Banks was pleased with Brigadier General William Emory's stand as night fell on April 8. He considered the ridge a wonderful place to defend and sent an aide back to Pleasant Hill to order Brigadier General Andrew Jackson Smith to bring his Sixteenth Corps forward.[1] Major General William B. Franklin, nursing his broken arm, pointed out that Smith would have just reached Pleasant Hill and he doubted Smith's ability to reach the ridge before the next morning. If they did arrive, would they be in any shape to fight after covering twenty-two miles in one day and immediately march fourteen miles overnight? Franklin pointed out the lack of water. Banks asked the opinion of his friend, General William Dwight, a brigade commander in Emory's division. Dwight advised Banks to retreat to safer ground and to do so promptly. Banks agreed and at 10:00 P.M. the army began its retreat.

Banks allowed the Thirteenth Corps to lead, followed by the cavalry, then the Nineteenth Corps. Dwight's brigade brought up the rear, guarding against Rebel attacks. The column moved slowly, picking its way through stragglers and hampered by the infantry's trains. The head of the column reached Pleasant Hill at 8:30 on the morning of April 9.[2]

After daylight, some Confederate cavalry began harassing the rear of the column, mostly worrying stragglers and disrupting the 153rd New York Infantry. General Smith began hearing rumors that the Thirteenth Corps had been cut to pieces early that morning. As small groups of weary men walked, mounted riders trotted, and teamsters bullied their teams into the village, Smith knew the rumors were true.[3] He ordered the Second Brigade, Third Division of his Sixteenth Corps, commanded by Colonel William Shaw, to take up a position on the road west of the village. They were hampered by the bulk of the column, which was now streaming into the village. Shaw's men were forced to abandon the road and made their way through the dense woods.[4] Shaw reported to Emory, who told him to relieve Brigadier General James McMillan's brigade. McMillan had picked a good location south of the road and formed his men perpendicular to it. On the north side of the road was a small hill that overlooked the position.

Shaw relieved the brigade and set up in line of battle three regiments of Iowans on the south side and one regiment of Missourians on the north side of the road.[5] He also had a four-gun battery to the north of the road. This position was detached from the nearest friendly troops by a quarter-mile. These were New Yorkers led by Colonel Lewis Benedict. Dwight's Brigade was positioned parallel to Benedict and on the north side of the road with his units facing north. This left both of Shaw's flanks exposed and Dwight with his left wing facing ninety degrees to the expected angle of attack. Benedict was positioned astride the Logansport road.[6] The bulk of General Smith's men were located in and around the village of about fifteen buildings on the tallest of the gently rolling ridges. Banks set up his headquarters on the east side of the village in the largest residence, the Childers House. The house stood near the intersection of the road that led to Blair's Landing.[7] Shaw's brigade was in line of battle more than a mile to the west from the bulk of the Sixteenth Corps, which was in and near the village.

The village of Pleasant Hill, established in the 1850s, contained a store, a recently built Methodist church, the Pearce Payne College, with two unfinished brick buildings designed to be wings of a larger structure, and about a dozen houses.[8] Pleasant Hill was situated on the east side of a large cleared field that ran along the stagecoach road. To the west of the village was a stand of dense pine trees and beyond this was a large open field.

Before dawn Taylor ordered his men to probe the ridge at the previous day's fighting, and they soon found that Banks had pulled out. In his message to General John G. Walker earlier that morning, General Richard Taylor told the Texan, "Arkansas and Missouri will lead the fight this morning. They must do what Texas and Louisiana did today [yesterday]."[9] During the remainder of the day, the plan he created the night before was followed.

Taylor and Major General Tom Green led the Texas cavalry down the road with orders for the infantry to follow. Six miles northwest of Pleasant Hill they found a large number of prisoners being herded back to the Confederate lines by Texas cavalrymen. These men were part of the 165th New York, a Zouave unit from Dwight's brigade. Viewing the Zouaves still dressed in their bright blue and red uniforms, one of Green's men said the war must be almost over because, "Lincoln was now reduced to sending his women to fight."[10] About 9:00 A.M. Green's cavalry came into contact with McMillan and Shaw's troops just as the former were to be relieved by Shaw. Taylor thought they were a rearguard protecting the trains. He had no way of knowing that Banks had pulled out the night before.[11] Taylor ordered the cavalry to reconnoiter the Union position.[12]

About 1:00 P.M., Churchill's men arrived some two miles west of Pleasant Hill.[13] Taylor talked to Churchill and found that the Arkansans had marched forty-five miles in the last thirty-six hours and were exhausted. Taylor told them to rest for a short time and that they would lead the attack.[14] Taylor then decided that all of his infantry units required rest to perform at optimal ability. He delayed his attack for three hours with orders for all the units to rest for two hours[15]. He knew he was wasting valuable daylight, but he also knew his men were in no condition to fight. The cavalry scouts reported the basic layout of the Union forces.

Brigadier General Thomas J. Churchill. From Francis Trevelyan Miller et al., eds., *The Photographic History of the Civil War in Ten Volumes* (New York: Review of Reviews Co., 1912), 10:257.

Taylor used the concept for battle he had created the night before making a slight variation. Churchill would sweep to the Confederate right over a mile into the woods. On his right were three regiments of cavalry to cut off the Union retreat. Churchill would then extend past the Union left, wheel around to his left, and reinforce the main line of attack from behind the Union line. This would effectively cut communications between Churchill and other Confederate units. Walker would form in line of battle south of the road and begin his advance when he heard Churchill's assault. Walker was charged with linking his right flank with Churchill's left. When it appeared the Union forces were drawn south of the road from the combined infantry attack, cavalry under Brigadier General Hamilton P. Bee and Colonel Augustus Buchel were to charge down the road and through the village. Two more cavalry units under Brigadier General James P. Major and Colonel Arthur P. Bagby were to seal off the Blair's Landing road. Brigadier General Alfred Mouton's division, now under the command of the Brigadier General Camille Armand Jules Marie de Polignac, was held in reserve. Taylor told his men to rely on the bayonet, "as we had neither time nor ammunition to waste."[16]

At 3:00 P.M., Churchill and his men headed down the road for two miles and then began their trek though the dense woods. They formed up line of battle with Brigadier General Mosby M. Parsons' division on the right and his own division composed of Brigadier General James C. Tappan's brigade and Colonel Lucien Gause's brigade on the left. The forest immediately posed problems to the two divisions. The woods were dense and did not allow a view of not more than a few feet ahead of the men. The terrain was hilly with steep slopes and ravines that broke the line of approach, making it difficult for the men to walk abreast. As they swept to their right, Parsons' left flank came in contact with federal units, so the entire force moved even farther to the right. With all of these movements, forward progress became more difficult to determine.[17]

After the Missouri and Arkansas troops disappeared into the woods, Taylor began a countdown to begin the battle. He gave Churchill an hour and a half to get into position. At 4:30 P.M., a twelve-gun battery opened up on the Union four-gun battery with Shaw's men to the north of road. The distance between the two batteries was about eight hundred yards. Within thirty minutes the counter battery fire had become so intense, the Union battery was withdrawn for their own safety.[18] As the Union battery withdrew, Churchill's men were heard yelling, signaling the beginning of their attack. Walker's Texans recognized this as the signal for their advance, and at 5:00 P.M. began their charge.[19]

General Green saw the Union battery limbering up. Believing that the forward Union units were collapsing under the weight of the Confederate artillery barrage, he ordered Bee to charge.[20] Bee charged his men across an old track and was met with a furious volley from Shaw's brigade. One third of Colonel Xavier Debray's regiment died in the assault. Colonel Buchel forced the now advancing Union infantry back to their original line and then fell mortally wounded. Debray's horse was hit and fell on him. He survived by losing his boot and slightly injuring his ankle. He limped back to his line using his sword for a cane.[21]

Walker's men marched against Shaw's Brigade, exchanging volleys as they approached. Shaw's men were in a band of trees and behind a rail fence. This position was exposed and he had no flank support. Walker's men drove through the Thirty-Second Iowa just as Major's cavalry, fighting dismounted, attacked the Union brigade's right flank.[22]

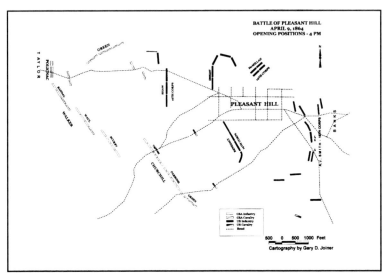

Opening positions of the Union and Confederate armies at the Battle of Pleasant Hill, 4:00 P.M., April 9, 1864. Cartography by Gary D. Joiner.

Churchill's divisions believed they were abreast of the Union line. They could hear the cannonade to their left rear. They saw a Union line ahead of them in a field, in the center of which lay a tree-filled, dry streambed. This was Colonel Lewis Benedict's Third Brigade of the First Division of the Nineteenth Corps. Most of the enemy was in the thicket and Churchill charged them. The Confederates had no use for their muskets in the thick stream bed undergrowth, so they used their weapons as clubs. The four regiments collapsed as a line and each routed. The three New York regiments broke first and the Thirtieth Maine retreated only after it was almost enveloped. Benedict was killed shortly after he told the Maine troops to pull back.[23] Flushed with this victory, Churchill's men captured an artillery battery and aimed for the village. They did not notice General Smith's men ahead and to their right. Churchill had wheeled too soon and had come into the Union lines almost in front of the Union left flank. It was a terrible mistake.[24]

When Benedict's brigade collapsed, there was no support on any side for Shaw. The Thirty-Second Iowa at the center of the line stubbornly

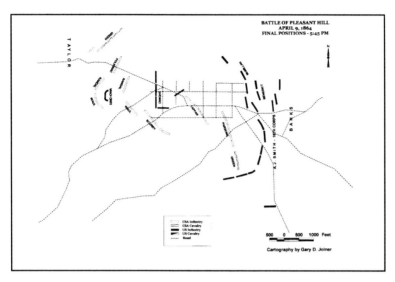

Final positions of the Union and Confederate armies at the Battle of Pleasant
Hill, 5:45 P.M., April 9, 1864. Cartography by Gary D. Joiner.

refused to leave and bent itself into a semi-circle. Brigadier General
Walker, wounded, was carried to the rear. Taylor called in Polignac's
weary reserves as Major's dismounted cavalrymen swept the regiment's
right. Shaw urged Dwight to move in to help, but Dwight refused to
move, saying he had no orders to do so. Smith ordered Shaw's Brigade
to withdraw, and three regiments did so. The steadfast Thirty-Second
Iowa was surrounded and cut off.[25] Dwight decided that if he did not
act, orders or not, he would suffer the same fate as Shaw. He ordered
two of his regiments to cross the road and set up on the south side.
General Emory then ordered McMillan's brigade, to fill the void created
by Dwight. This brigade had been relieved by Shaw and was held in
reserve. They marched into a hailstorm of shells from both sides.[26] A
soldier of the Thirtieth Maine wrote that the "air seemed all alive with
the sounds of various projectiles."[27]

    At that point in the battle, both sides thought the Confederates were
winning handily. The Union right and center had all but collapsed. The
left seemed to have evaporated. The one large contingent of the command

thus far not engaged was the bulk of the Sixteenth Corps and they were waiting for their chance. The Fifty-Eighth Illinois, which had been concealed in a copse of trees, began pouring accurate fire into Churchill's men. Other regiments of Lucas' Brigade joined in, and General Smith then ordered his entire line to charge the Confederates. Churchill's men still had forward momentum and reached the eastern side of the village.[28] The Confederates fell back to the stream bottom where Benedict's men had been found. The fighting was especially brutal here, and just as before, muskets were used as clubs due to the dense undergrowth.[29] As Parsons was driven back, Tappan was forced to retreat or his flank would be exposed and Smith's "gorillas" would drive a wedge between the two formations. As they withdrew, they ran into Scurry's Brigade of Walker's Division of Texans and were thrown a tight position. Taylor had to send both Horace Randal and Thomas Waul's brigades to Scurry's aid before he was enveloped.[30] The two armies had mutually separated at the end of the battle, which ended in a tactical tie.

During the battle the Confederates had forced the Union lines to bend back on the left and then had blown threw the Union center only to have their own right wing compromised at great loss. Darkness finally separated the armies. Taylor's plan worked as it was designed to, except for the unknown quantity of the Union Sixteenth Corps. Banks rode up to General Smith and shook his hand, thankfully saying, "God bless you general. You have saved the army."[31] Smith had little to say to Banks and went back to his troops to see to their welfare and to make them ready in the event of another Confederate attack. He did not attend a conference of Union commanders who met with Banks to decide their next course of action. The dead of both armies lay on the battlefield that night, and the wounded of both armies were heard pleading for help and water. They were in the no-man's land. Neither side could afford to offer assistance.[32] It was in the midst of this chorus of misery, which Banks decided on his next course of action.

Banks wanted to try again to take Shreveport and had told Smith of this intention.[33] In preparation, the commanding general ordered

Brigadier General Albert L. Lee to bring what was left of his trains back to Pleasant Hill. He met with Franklin, Dwight, and Emory to seek their counsel. Both Franklin and Emory suggested that the most prudent option was to take the road to Blair's Landing and link with Porter and the fleet. The supply transports held all the equipment and food the army needed. Dwight suggested that the army retrograde to Grand Ecore, telling Banks that no one had heard from Porter and that they did not know if Taylor's forces had captured or destroyed the fleet.[34] Banks listened to his friend and confidant over the objections of the two more seasoned generals. He decided to follow the same route by which they had come. At Grand Ecore he would determine what to do. The night was filled with the sound of the army packing and preparing to leave the way it had come. Lee was ordered to turn his train around again. The dead and wounded were to be left on the field where they lay for the second time in two days.[35]

General Smith was furious after midnight when he found out about Banks' plan. He stormed up to Banks to protest the action, stating the reasons for not retreating. First, he was angry at the thought of not burying his dead and leaving his wounded for the Confederates to tend to if they could or would do so. It was a matter of honor not to leave his men on the battlefield. Second, it would leave his 2,500 men with Porter at risk without the benefit of support. Banks said no on both counts. Smith then pleaded with Banks to let him stay behind with his men to tend to the dead and dying. Banks refused this as well saying that there was no water for the troops and they must return to Grand Ecore. The lack of water was certainly true, but Banks was to use this as the primary excuse for the upcoming retreat too often.[36]

Smith left Banks and made a visit to Franklin. Still seething at Banks' evident incompetence on the battlefield, and his eagerness to leave the dead and wounded, Smith asked Franklin to place Banks under arrest and take over the command of the army. He assured Franklin that he would have the full support of the Thirteenth, Sixteenth, and Seventeenth Corps. Franklin, still disgusted with Banks, considered this and then replied, "Smith, don't you know this is mutiny?"[37] Because mutiny was an offense that resulted in hanging on conviction of the crime, the generals dropped the conversation. Union losses by regimental tally were 289 killed and 773 wounded for a total of 1,605.[38] Confederate losses at Pleasant Hill were 1,200 killed and wounded and another 426 taken prisoner.[39]

The twin battles fought over two consecutive days left dead and wounded over a twenty-mile line, with the vast bulk of these on the two battlefields. Homes, schools, and all other available buildings were used as hospitals. Confederates and federal soldiers were treated side by side for several days afterward.[40] The Union trains provided much needed supplies, but the Confederates physicians were quickly overwhelmed with the numbers of wounded to be cared for. Food was unavailable for three days.[41]

The Confederates buried their dead first, with the Mansfield dead buried in the town's cemetery. The Confederate officers were placed in adjacent graves on the crest of the hill on which the cemetery was located.[42] Other Confederate dead were buried in makeshift graves near where they fell for reburial later. Some of the Union dead at Mansfield were buried near the town's cemetery. These were men who died while under medical care. Two mass grave trenches were dug near the second phase of the Mansfield battlefield and hundreds of Union soldiers were buried there.[43] Of the four hundred Union wounded left at Pleasant Hill, more than half died.[44] At Pleasant Hill, it took more than a day to bury Confederate dead near the village's cemetery.[45] Union dead at Pleasant Hill were buried in a makeshift graveyard in the rear of the Pearce Payne College. Some were buried in individual graves and others in common trenches.[46] Captured Union officers and soldiers were taken first to Shreveport and then to Camp Ford prison in Tyler, Texas.[47]

One of the Confederate prisoners held at Grand Ecore was David French Boyd, one of Taylor's engineers and Sherman's best friend when he was superintendent of the Louisiana Seminary at Pineville. He was kept aboard the *Polar Star*. On April 14, Boyd tried to smuggle out a letter to General Taylor, telling what he had observed at Grand Ecore.

The letter, written in the margins of a newspaper, was placed in Taylor's mailbox in Shreveport. He did not see it until the 1870s. Boyd had no way of knowing for sure that the dam had been blown at Tone's Bayou. The obstruction was apparently blown on or soon after March 18, 1864, and the river did not return to its main channel course until 1873. In the summer of 1864, a Texas cavalry unit (the W. P. Lane Rangers) came to the site and crossed Bayou Pierre in short order, but it took them half a day to cross Tone's Bayou.[48]

The Union Army had halted Confederate attacks on them for three straight days, including the short battle at Wilson's Farm, now moved back on the road to Natchitoches and then to Grand Ecore. It had sustained heavy casualties but was still very much a viable fighting force. The average soldier was disgusted with Banks and had little confidence in his ability as a commander. This was never more certain than with the western troops. The easterners had seen Lewis Benedict, one of their favorite commanders, killed. They had also seen Thomas E .G. Ransom, now almost a legend among Illinois troops, wounded, and carried off the field. The Nineteenth Corps commander had a broken arm from being knocked off his horse by his own men during the rout and was seen in a sling by all the troops whom he passed. What had they gained for their hard marching and fighting a determined, almost maniacal foe? Nothing.

Although the Battle of Pleasant Hill was a tactical tie, Banks' decision to retreat to Grand Ecore effectively turned the engagement, and eventually the entire campaign, into a strategic defeat for the Union. His army had not been shattered and his senior commanders had a desire to press ahead to avenge the two days of retreat. The forward elements of the navy were left without support and had to fend for themselves. Banks' excuse of lack of water was real in the army's immediate location, but the retreat to Grand Ecore was more for a sense of security than to slake the thirst of the column.

7
THE CAMDEN CAMPAIGN

The northern prong of Major General Nathaniel P. Banks' plan, the attack on Shreveport by Union forces based in Arkansas, was underway, although deep in the wilderness of pine barrens and river bottoms. The timing and planning of the campaign allowed the Union commander in Arkansas, Major General Frederick Steele, to select his route and to a great degree, the extent of his participation in the campaign. This wide leeway created immediate concerns. Was Steele to capture Shreveport or simply support Banks? Was there to be a siege or an assault on the town? What was he to do if he faced the bulk of Confederate forces that could be brought against him?

Steele's orders were to take a force down to Shreveport and work in concert with Banks and the fleet under Rear Admiral David Dixon Porter. How this would be accomplished was left up to Steele and his staff. The Arkansas commander at first planned to move southwest from Little Rock and approach the Ouachita River somewhere between Hot Springs and El Dorado. From there he would descend to Monroe, Louisiana, which was also located on the Ouachita River. This route offered several advantages. It was a straightforward line of travel that was devoid of major Confederate units until he reached Louisiana. If he did not cross the Ouachita River earlier, he would do so at Monroe and

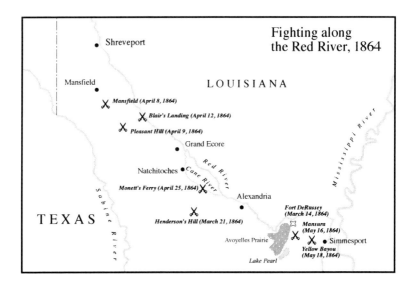

Fighting along
the Red River, 1864

Shreveport

Mansfield

LOUISIANA

Mansfield (April 8, 1864)

Blair's Landing (April 12, 1864)

Pleasant Hill (April 9, 1864)

Grand Ecore

Natchitoches

Monett's Ferry (April 25, 1864)

Alexandria

Fort DeRussey
(March 14, 1864)

Mansura
(May 16, 1864)

Simmesport

Yellow Bayou
(May 18, 1864)

Henderson's Hill (March 21, 1864)

Avoyelles Prairie

Lake Pearl

TEXAS

follow the uncompleted bed of the Southern Pacific Railroad west in an almost straight line to the Red River. This alternative afforded Steele the support role he requested without requiring a large troop commitment in a final battle. Although the route would take the Union force almost due south then almost due west to the Red River, it was the safest path.

For some reason, perhaps to solve potential political problems, Steele changed his mind. He decided to veer more to the southwest, to Arkadelphia and then to Washington, the capital of Confederate Arkansas, about seventy miles north of Shreveport.[1]

On March 17, Steele ordered Brigadier General John Thayer, the Frontier Division commander at Fort Smith, to march his troops to Arkadelphia, where he would join Steele's column coming from Little Rock. Steele gave Thayer until April 1 to march the 170 miles.[2] He then ordered the commander of the small garrison at Pine Bluff to send scouts to watch for any movement by Confederate forces to the south. Steele took the Third Division, Seventh Corps, and two brigades of cavalry from Little Rock on March 23. Steele's force consisted of 6,800 men and Thayer added another 3,600, making a force of 10,400.[3] Each man was loaded down with full equipment for a campaign and forty rounds of ammunition.[4]

Steele's men had not been campaigning but performing garrison duty. To ease them into the march, he set a leisurely pace. The column left Little Rock to the cadence of "Yankee Doodle."[5] The first day they traveled nine miles.[6] Early the next morning, A. F. Sperry, a soldier in the Thirty-Third Iowa Infantry and perhaps the best chronicler of the campaign, noted that the predawn darkness was broken as "Bugles rang as we had never heard them before."[7] The column formed up before the sun rose and marched the entire day. That night Steele ordered half rations for his men, except coffee, for the duration of the march.[8] The next day, March 26, the column reached the Ouachita River at the hamlet of Rockport, which they found deserted.[9] They easily crossed the shallow river, although they stopped to throw up a bridge in case rains made the stream rise. This activity slowed them and for the next three days, the column marched at a still leisurely pace to a point a few miles outside Arkadelphia. The advance elements entered the town on March 29.[10] Steele expected to find Thayer's column from Fort Smith either waiting for them or arriving shortly thereafter. Neither happened. Arkadelphia was a small town and the forage opportunities for a force of 6,800 men were limited. Steele opened his commissary wagons to the men and waited for Thayer. Many of the troops, hungry from the trek on half rations, ate ravenously from the limited local fare and their own supplies.[11]

Confederate forces in Arkansas were scattered but highly mobile, consisting primarily of seasoned cavalry units. Their division and brigade commanders were typically excellent field officers. However, the Rebels had a disadvantage in the district commander, Major General Sterling Price, who was only marginally competent.

Major General Richard Taylor, at that time before the Battle of Mansfield, planned the destruction or capture of the Union forces, but to accomplish this he needed all four of the available infantry divisions. Lieutenant General Edmund Kirby Smith vacillated between using his forces to destroy the larger enemy to his south or to assist in thwarting Steele as he descended from central Arkansas.[12] Taylor cajoled and pleaded with his superior to make up his mind. Taylor wrote angrily

Frederick Steele

Born New York 1819, Steele graduated from the US Military Academy in 1843, thirtieth in his class of thirty-nine that included Ulysses S. Grant. He was commissioned second lieutenant and posted to infantry. After performing routine frontier and garrison duty, he served with distinction in the Mexican War, winning brevets to first lieutenant and captain and promotion to first lieutenant, captain 1855, and major of the Eleventh Infantry 1861. In the opening stages of the Civil War, he commanded US regulars at the Battle of Wilson's Creek, Missouri; moving to the volunteer organization, he was named colonel of the Eighth Iowa Infantry in September 1861; brigadier general US Volunteers in January 1862; commanded the District of Southeast Missouri; led a division in the capture of Helena, Arkansas, and in General William T. Sherman's repulse at Chickasaw Bluffs; and major general US Volunteers March 1863. Steele commanded a division in the Army of the Tennessee during the Vicksburg Campaign of 1863 and was placed in command of the Department of Arkansas. He directed the Arkansas portion of the Red River Campaign in the spring of 1864, and after taking Camden, Steele was driven back to Little Rock with heavy losses. In 1865, he led a division in General E. R. S. Canby's campaign against Mobile. Brevetted through major general US Army, he was finally mustered out of volunteer service in 1867. He continued in the regular army as colonel of the Twentieth Infantry. In 1868, while on leave in California, Steele suffered an attack of apoplexy and fell from a carriage. He died shortly thereafter.

"Action, prompt, vigorous action, is required. While we are deliberating the enemy is marching. King James lost three kingdoms for a mass. We may lose three States without a battle."[13]

Before the Battle of Mansfield, Kirby Smith and Taylor met to discuss plans. Taylor offered to take the bulk of his forces and march to Arkansas, eliminate the threat posed by Steele, and return to Louisiana to stop Banks. Kirby Smith refused and gave Taylor a vague response.[14]

Taylor defeated Banks and his Union column at Mansfield on April 8 and fought the federals to a bloody tie the next day at Pleasant Hill. Kirby

Smith was not on the scene and withheld two divisions from action in an attempt to save the day if Taylor ran into trouble at Mansfield. These two divisions fought at Pleasant Hill on April 9.

Price commanded just five brigades of cavalry. They were concentrated in the southwest portion of the state and were mostly tough veterans.[15] His brigades were scattered when Steele began his expedition. Two were east of the Saline River, one near Monticello and the other near Mt. Elba—both east of the Ouachita River approximately halfway between the towns Pine Bluff and Camden. Brigadier General John S. Marmaduke led the other three.[16] Two of the three were with Marmaduke at Camden, one of these under Brigadier General Joseph Shelby, the other under Colonel Colton Greene. The third brigade was operating west of the Confederate capital of Washington on the Red River.[17] Marmaduke's brigades totaled 3,600 men. Price's forces were adequate to thwart a Union drive, but not destroy federal columns sent against them in mass.

Marmaduke's intelligence gathering was suffering from a time lag. On March 25, the brigades were dispatched to specific points, only to discover that Steele's column was already approaching Arkadelphia. Marmaduke decided to make a dash for the Little Missouri River and contest the crossing with all of his brigades.[18] As the Confederate and Union columns moved and counter-moved, this hostile environment left them asking more questions than the answers than they received.

Steele arrived at Arkadelphia for his expected link-up with Thayer, but Thayer was missing. Steele waited for three days. As his men rested and ate voraciously from the commissary wagons and local fare, Steele became anxious and finally felt he could wait no longer. On April 1, Steele moved the column toward Washington.[19] Confederate Brigadier General William L. Cabell's brigade of Brigadier General James F. Fagan's Cavalry Division began skirmishing with the Union column almost immediately. That night Marmaduke ordered Colonel Greene's Brigade to take up a position on the Washington Road near the Little Missouri River.[20] The next morning Cabell was ordered to join Greene. Marmaduke's plan to hold at the Little Missouri crossing seemed to be working. As the two brigades

Sterling Price

Born in Virginia in 1809, Price attended Hampden-Sydney College and studied law. He moved with his family to Missouri in 1830 and served in the state legislature. In 1844, he was elected to the US House of Representatives; Price resigned from Congress to lead a regiment of Missouri troops in the Mexican

War. He was promoted to brigadier general of volunteers in 1848 and served governor of Missouri from 1853 to 1857. He was president of the Missouri convention that voted against secession, but a dispute with radicals prompted his break from the Unionist ranks. He offered his services to secessionist Governor Claiborne Fox Jackson and accepted command of the Missouri state militia. Price worked to maintain peace in Missouri, but after negotiations with Union leaders broke down in June 1861, he prepared his troops to oppose federal forces. He combined with General Ben McCulloch's Confederate troops to defeat the federals at Wilson's Creek, Missouri, in August 1861. Price captured Lexington, Missouri, in September before retreating into Arkansas and led Missouri troops in General Earl Van Dorn's Confederate force at Elkhorn Tavern, Arkansas, in March 1862. Following that defeat, the Missouri troops were mustered into Confederate service and Price was commissioned major general. He was transferred to Mississippi despite his fervent protest and suffered defeats at Iuka and Corinth before returning to Arkansas. He was defeated at Helena in 1863 and supported General Edmund Kirby Smith in repulsing General Frederick Steele's Arkansas portion of the Red River Campaign in the spring of 1864. That fall he led an ambitious cavalry raid into Missouri, but after initial success, was turned back in eastern Kansas. Retreating through Indian Territory and northern Texas, Price's remnant returned to Arkansas in December. At the close of the war, Price refused to surrender and escaped to Mexico. After the collapse of Maximilian's empire in 1866, Price returned to Missouri, where he died the following year. Called "Old Pap" by his men, Price was a devoted soldier. While his 1864 raid and subsequent exodus to Mexico have been highly romanticized, his overall military performance was largely unimpressive.

prepared to hold their position, word came that the Union column had turned toward Elkin's Ferry, bypassing them.[21] There is no evidence that Steele knew of the trap prepared for him.

The Union troops seized and then began fortifying the ferry landing, mounting artillery on all the approach roads. Brigadier General Shelby's brigade attacked the rearguard with spirited cavalry charges but failed to dislodge the federals.[22] On April 3 and 4 Steele's column crossed the Little Missouri while Shelby continued to attack. Marmaduke then attacked the column while it was most vulnerable, crossing the river. He charged with 1,200 men and drove several regiments back. The Union soldiers stopped running when they joined the main concentration of federal troops, in

Brigadier General John M. Thayer. From Francis Trevelyan Miller et al., eds., *The Photographic History of the Civil War in Ten Volumes* (New York: Review of Reviews Co., 1912), 10:221.

part because they could run no farther. The strengthened column then offered greater resistance and took the initiative. Shortly thereafter Marmaduke was forced to withdraw.[23] Shelby then joined the other two brigades that night and the Confederates withdrew to Prairie d'Ane, where they hastily built earthworks. Marmaduke received reinforcements from the Indian Territory on April 6 in the form of Brigadier General Richard Gano's brigade. These hard-riding cavalrymen traveled from Laynesport near the southeastern corner of the Indian Territory. They were stationed there to prevent Steele or Thayer from raiding the Confederate works in Jefferson or Marshall, Texas.[24] When the threat axis was determined, they were assigned to assist Marmaduke.

Steele finally received news from Thayer's column. They were trying to find him as they marched from Hot Springs. Steele halted his column to give Thayer time to catch up, still uncertain of the distance between the two groups. A spring rainstorm deluged the camp area, destroyed the corduroy plank roads, and threatened to float the pontoon bridges away.[25] Steele's men repaired the damage on April 8 and 9 while the twin battles of Mansfield and Pleasant Hill were being fought in northwest Louisiana. Steele, of course, knew nothing about Banks' fortunes or Porter's problems with falling river levels, harassment by Confederate artillery, cavalry, and infantry sharpshooters north of Grand Ecore.[26] Thayer finally arrived and Steele's men were unimpressed by their reinforcements.[27] Thayer had apparently expected Steele to resupply him, but Steele issued no orders to that effect. Steele's men had been consuming supplies at a fast pace while waiting for Thayer and Thayer's commissary stores were almost depleted as well. Steele was forced to request supplies from Little Rock, dispatching an empty supply train. His quartermasters were told to resupply the column with thirty days of half-rations for fifteen thousand men.[28] This order would reduce the number of wagons needed in this resupply effort and hopefully reduce the waiting time. Most of Steele's actions henceforth would be cast in the light of this severe lack of rations for his men and forage for his cavalry horses and supply wagon mules.

On April 10, Steele moved across Prairie d'Ane, pushing two of Marmaduke's brigades before him. Shelby and Brigadier General Thomas P. Dockery's brigades joined and stiffened their positions by late afternoon and a larger engagement occurred. Both sides brought up artillery, and the battle escalated until nightfall. The next afternoon Steele tried to force the Confederates out of their lines by making a grand show of his line of battle. The Confederates would not accept the challenge to fight and Steele returned to his camp of the previous night.[29] Under cover of darkness, Price, who had arrived at the battlefield, withdrew his men about eight miles toward Washington, abandoning the earthworks his men had held without a fight.[30]

Steele's men occupied the trench works on the morning of April 12. Shortly afterward, the column reversed its direction and marched for Camden.[31] Price had no way of knowing how short of supplies Steele was.

John S. Marmaduke

Born in Missouri in 1833, Marmaduke attended both Yale and Harvard before entering the US Military Academy, where he graduated from in 1857, thirtieth in his class of thirty-eight. Commissioned second lieutenant and posted to infantry, he participated in the Mormon Expedition, He was still on frontier duty at the outbreak of the Civil War and resigned his commission to become colonel in the Missouri state militia. Marmaduke fought at Boonville in 1861, but he resigned his state commission to enter Confederate Service. He was commissioned first lieutenant and named lieutenant colonel of the First Arkansas Infantry Battalion. He was promoted to colonel, Third Confederate Infantry and was wounded in an outstanding performance at Shiloh in April 1862. He was then transferred to the Trans-Mississippi and commanded the cavalry in General T. C. Hindman's Corps, Army of the West. Promoted to brigadier general November 1862, Marmaduke led a cavalry division that raided twice into Missouri and fought at Helena and Little Rock; he dueled with and killed fellow Confederate General Lucius Walker at Little Rock in September 1863, for which he was arrested but soon released. During the Red River Campaign in the  spring of 1864 Marmaduke's cavalry, with General Samuel Bell Maxey's Texans and Indians, opposed General Frederick Steele's Arkansas operations at Poison Springs and Jenkins' Ferry. That fall, he commanded a cavalry division in General Sterling Price's Missouri invasion, and in November he was captured while directing a rearguard action in Kansas. Although Marmaduke was imprisoned at Fort Warren, Massachusetts, for the remainder of the war, he was nonetheless promoted to major general in March 1865, becoming the last Confederate officer to be elevated to that rank. Released from prison in July 1865, he worked in the insurance business after the war and edited an agricultural journal in Missouri. He was elected governor of that state in 1884 and died in office in 1887. He was a gifted cavalry commander whose efforts largely escaped recognition outside the isolated Trans-Mississippi.

Steele's men marched toward Camden on April 12 and 13. On the 13th, the rearguard was repeatedly attacked by fresh reinforcements that Price had received. These men were the remainders of the division of troops from the Indian Territory, including Colonel Tandy Walker's Second Indian Brigade of Choctaws.[32] The pro-Confederate Indians

had a decided distaste for blue-coated soldiers who had enforced the
reservation policies of the US government. The Confederates made a
combined attack on Thayer's rearguard. The Rebels were finally repulsed
after most of the Union column turned back to help the beleaguered
Frontier Division. The Rebels broke off the engagement and the march
resumed. The spring rains once again began to pour, slowing the column.

Marmaduke marched his entire division sixty miles from near
Washington around Steele's flank and took up a position across the road
fourteen miles from Camden. Steele had sufficient manpower to push
the Confederates aside. His intent was not to deal a deathblow, but to get
past the Confederates and enter Camden where he could dig in until his
supplies arrived.[33]

In Shreveport four days previously, Kirby Smith had decided to go
after Steele. There were adequate cavalry units in Arkansas to deny the
Union foraging capability, disrupt lines of communication, and block
access to northern Louisiana, but not sufficient numbers to eliminate
the threat to his Louisiana headquarters. Kirby Smith decided to play a
safe hand of poker and perhaps grab some of the glory that heretofore
had been General Taylor's alone after Banks was thwarted at the battles
of Mansfield on April 8 and Pleasant Hill on April 9. Kirby Smith's
plans did not include Taylor, who was kept out of the plans for action
in Arkansas.[34]

Kirby Smith prepared to support Price with three divisions and Taylor
found this disconcerting. The divisions that Kirby Smith intended for use
in Arkansas were the Texas, Missouri, and Arkansas units, leaving the
Louisiana Division under Taylor's command. This small division had
been badly mauled at Mansfield. All four were desperately needed if
Taylor had an opportunity to trap Banks.

Taylor offered to lead his infantry against Steele until that Union
column was either destroyed or forced to retreat to Little Rock. He would
then return to Louisiana to fight Banks with both his and Price's forces.[35]
Kirby Smith agreed to this arrangement, and on April 14 Taylor sent three
divisions to Shreveport. These were the Texas Division of Major General

John G. Walker, the First (Arkansas) Division commanded by Brigadier General Thomas J. Churchill (tactical command by Brigadier General James C. Tappan), and the Second (Missouri) Division commanded by Brigadier General Mosby M. Parsons. Prince de Polignac's small and hard-fought Louisiana Division was sent south down Red River to track Banks and make him think that Taylor was still in pursuit. Taylor was told to return south and keep an eye on Banks.

Kirby Smith was normally a cautious man, almost to the point of distraction, but in his new-found desire for quick action to destroy Steele's force, Kirby Smith missed a crucial detail. His army would need pontoon boats borne by wagons to cross rivers in the event they were swollen because of rains common in the spring. Steele included adequate pontoons and engineering troops as part of his train. Kirby Smith brought only a few, although they were available. The Fourth Confederate Engineer Battalion, Company H, was based in Shreveport. This company operated the bridging portable bridging pontoons for the Army of Western Louisiana. They were left in Shreveport and rather than following the army into Arkansas, they operated on the Red River between Shreveport and Natchitoches from April 29 to May 25.[36] This lack of bridging equipment would cost the Confederates dearly.

Kirby Smith marched his men out of Shreveport on April 15 and 16.[37] The three divisions used three different roads to facilitate faster travel and greater ease of forage. Walker was sent to Minden, thirty miles to the east, and then north on the Ft. Towson Road to guard against a possible action by Steele to join Banks. Walker's Division then encamped north of Minden until it was determined that Banks was not going to cross the Red River at Grand Ecore and move to Harrisonburg on the Ouachita or attempt a march up the Red or Ouachita rivers to reach Steele. Walker marched his men northeasterly toward Camden.[38] Parsons took the center road, crossing the Red River at Shreveport, then traveling north to Benton then northeasterly to Rocky Mount and Shongaloo before heading north to Camden. Churchill took the western road which followed the Benton Road north to Plain Dealing, at which point it paralleled Parsons' route and converged with it at Magnolia. Kirby Smith's force then marched north to Calhoun, Arkansas, only a few miles from Price's position.

The federals were forced to lay corduroy road before the wagons and artillery could pass through the rain-soaked bottomlands.[39] On April 14, after an exhausting march through the stream valleys through which the Camden road passed, the Union commander received word from scouts that a large Confederate force was assembling between him and his future supply base.[40]

Steele was desperate for supplies. Camden was well fortified, but if he could not feed fifteen thousand men, the earthworks were useless to him.[41] He sent a supply train of 198 wagons to forage for corn and food that could be acquired by any means. He sent two cannon and 668 men of the First Kansas Volunteer Infantry (Colored) and detachments from several white Kansas cavalry regiments. Union forces in the west often used black troops for garrison duty and to guard supply trains.[42] The train moved west about eighteen miles and then scattered on various roads to forage. Most were successful in retrieving corn. On the morning of April 18 the train reassembled for the return to Camden. They had moved about four miles when they were met by reinforcements including 375 infantry and ninety cavalry with two small mountain howitzers.[43] A guard force of a thousand men and four field guns were now with the train.

Marmaduke decided to attack the supply column and set out with two thousand men.[44] His plan was to hit the Union wagon train simultaneously from the front and the right flank. He received word of the reinforcements and halted, asking Price for permission to bring his entire force to interdict the supply train. Permission was granted and, after another flanking march, he set up a trap at a community called Poison Spring. Price sent reinforcements and before the supply train arrived, Marmaduke had 3,100 men waiting for the federal column.[45]

When the supply column came in contact with Confederate troops, Colonel James Williams of the First Kansas Infantry ordered the wagons

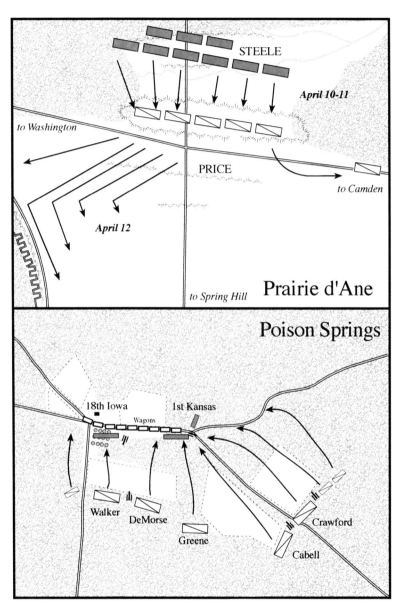

as close together as possible to protect them. He then moved his regiment to the front and along the flanks of the train facing outward, and the remaining men to the rear, also facing outward.[46]

The Confederates attacked the right flank first and the Union troops were so spread out protecting the 198 wagons that reinforcements could not reposition to counter new threats. Marmaduke then hit the train from the front and the black cavalrymen broke and ran into the woods. The Confederates gave chase and cut them down.[47]

Williams believed Steele's men in Camden, only four miles distant, would hear the commotion and rush to their assistance. This did not happen and the Confederates captured the train as the Union infantry and the remnants of the cavalry were routed. The Confederate Choctaws chased the survivors through the woods.[48]

The Rebels captured 170 wagons and burned 28 others. They also captured the four cannon with ammunition and powder plus one hundred prisoners.[49] Marmaduke suffered 115 killed, wounded, and missing. Union losses were 301 killed, wounded, and missing with 182 of them from the First Kansas Infantry.[50] The Confederates seemed to relish killing the Negro troops, at least according to their commander.[51] The survivors straggled back into Camden, without any wagons or field pieces, and with 300 fewer men. The loss of forage was devastating.

Steele hunkered down in Camden waiting for supplies from Little Rock. He could do little else. On April 18 a messenger arrived with word that Banks wanted Steele to join him. In the message Banks said he had won at Mansfield and Pleasant Hill but had withdrawn to Grand Ecore for supplies.[52] On April 22, Steele wrote Major General William T. Sherman that he could not defeat everything that Kirby Smith could send against him if Banks were defeated.[53] Steele then sent a courier to Banks saying that he probably could not link up with the southern column because he had received word that eight thousand Confederate infantry had just reinforced Price. Steele's letter rambled about possible lines of approach, each of which he dismissed.[54]

Kirby Smith arrived at Calhoun, Arkansas, near Magnolia, with the three divisions of infantry on April 17 and immediately took command of field operations.[55] From Calhoun, Kirby Smith had telegraph access to Shreveport.[56] He ordered Fagan's division with Shelby's brigade attached, to place themselves between Steele and Little Rock, and while doing so, to attack Steele's supply bases on his main line of retreat.[57]

Kirby Smith then ordered Parsons and Churchill to Camden from their western Arkansas positions. By the next day (April 20) they had moved to Magnolia, about half the distance to Little Rock from Shreveport. The movements of Parsons and Churchill were designed to make Steele believe that the main attack was on his fortified position at Camden.[58] Four days later Fagan arrived at El Dorado on the Ouachita and learned that Steele's supply train was returning to Camden with a heavy guard. Fagan then headed northwest to intercept it. Forty-five miles of fast marching placed Fagan on the Saline River at Mt. Elba. He allowed his exhausted men to bivouac at midnight. At dawn the next morning, Fagan moved to Marks' Mills, located on a road intersection on the Camden to Pine Bluff road. Finding no trace of the supply train at the intersection, he prepared to attack.[59]

Steele's supply train, commanded by Lieutenant Colonel Francis Drake, was heading southwest from Pine Bluff. At the core were 240 wagons, filled with the required half-day's rations for fifteen thousand men, plus other supplies for the column. Guarding this train were three regiments of Union infantry with a total of 1,200 men and 240 cavalry troopers.[60] Oddly, for a column heading potentially into harm's way, there were large numbers of hangers-on, including local citizens, cotton speculators, and three hundred Negroes, who were referred to as contrabands.[61] The column encamped near Marks' Mills on the evening of April 24 without knowing that Fagan was just down the road.[62] Drake apparently did not feel the need to post pickets.

At dawn Fagan hit the supply column with two brigades of cavalry before it could reach the Saline River.[63] A third brigade formed in the woods parallel to the road and hit the column in the flank. Cabell's brigade, attacking the Union left flank, chased Drake's men from the train and into the woods on the opposite side. Cabell then realized that Union infantry were massing to attack one of his flanking regiments. At this point he ordered an about-face and fell on the Union troops, thus

James F. Fagan

Born in Clark County, Kentucky, on March 1, 1828, Fagan's family moved to Little Rock, Arkansas, in 1838. His father died in 1840 and his mother married a prominent Arkansas politician, Samuel Adams. During the Mexican War, Fagan served with the Arkansas Mounted Volunteers and achieved the rank of lieutenant. After the war, he returned to his home in Saline County. He served in the Arkansas House of Representatives and then in the Arkansas Senate in the 1850s and early 1860s. When the Civil War broke out, he raised a company of soldiers that became part of the First Arkansas Infantry Regiment. Fagan was elected colonel of the regiment. They fought at First Manassas, or Bull Run, on July 21, 1861. They were transferred to the Army of the Mississippi and fought at the Battle of Shiloh. At "Bloody Shiloh," the First Arkansas suffered 45 percent casualties. Fagan was promoted to Brigadier General in September 1862. He was transferred to Arkansas, where he commanded a brigade under Lieutenant General Theophilus Holmes. The Arkansans made a failed assault on Helena on July 4, 1863. Fagan and the other commanders retreated to Little Rock before the Union forces took it. They then moved to southwestern Arkansas. Fagan and his cavalry were particularly useful during the Camden Campaign, the northern portion of the Red River Campaign in the spring of 1864. He led his men against a Union supply train at Marks Mills. They then participated in the pursuit of the Union Army back to Little Rock following the Battle of Jenkins' Ferry. Fagan was promoted to the rank of major general on April 25, 1864. His last operations were in Missouri during Sterling Price's ill-fated raid. After the war, Fagan received an appointment from President Ulysses S. Grant as a US Marshal from 1875 to 1877. He held the post of receiver in the Land Office in Little Rock. Fagan died in Little Rock on September 1, 1893. He is buried in Mount Holly Cemetery in Little Rock.

avoiding a trap. Cabell's troops fought hand-to-hand for an hour-and-a-half until Confederate reinforcements arrived to crush the Union line. As the Union troops were pushed back to fighting among the wagons, Shelby's brigade arrived after a ten-mile march. At this point two Union regiments surrendered when Drake was wounded.[64] The Confederates then directed attention to the third regiment that was still holding out and soon defeated them. Because of the way the column approached on one road, and the disposition of their forces, the Confederates were allowed to attack the federals piecemeal, one or two units at a time, thereby granting the Southerners superiority in numbers at each surge of fighting. The Confederates then attacked the cavalry that had been conducting rearguard duty several miles behind the train. The Union cavalrymen were driven off and Fagan owned the day and the supply train.[65] The battle lasted five hours, in which the Union suffered more than 1,300 military casualties. This did not include civilians, particularly the escaped slaves who had been killed.[66] Confederate casualty lists were incomplete. The numbers of killed, wounded, and missing were apparently about five hundred.[67] The battle at Marks' Mills was a twin to that of Poison Spring in tactics and results.

Steele heard about the battle at Marks' Mills and its disastrous results and was immediately forced to halt his waiting game. The supply problem was critical and there was no chance to replenish his force. He had sent thousand men and nine thousand horses in a land of pine barrens and swampy river bottoms, that is, a countryside that was devoid of forage. The next day he evacuated Camden and began a retreat to Little Rock.[68]

At this point the Confederates achieved a strategic victory. The enemy was forced to retreat to its home base. The Union column was in an untenable position. They might fight their way to Shreveport and hope to secure supplies, but their animals, and perhaps their men, might starve. If the Confederates did nothing, victory was theirs. Kirby Smith wanted more—to secure Little Rock and perhaps the entire state of Arkansas and perhaps Missouri. Glory was his if he could only stop the fleeing Union column and force a battle leading to the annihilation of the enemy. This desire was his undoing.

The Union retreat took on the look of a rout, though more organized. Steele ordered that everything that could not be taken by the troops should be destroyed. This strangely included a large amount of hardtack and bacon that could not be distributed.[69] The column set out after dark on April 26 after fooling the Confederates into believing they were bedding down for the night. By midnight, the column had crossed the

Ouachita, where they pulled up their pontoon bridge and slept along the road where they stopped.[70]

Kirby Smith had no idea that Steele had left. At 9:00 A.M. on April 27, the Confederates entered the abandoned works at Camden. The three infantry divisions that Kirby Smith brought with him from Louisiana all arrived late that afternoon. They could not quickly pursue because of the lack of pontoon bridges. Kirby Smith then sent Brigadier General Samuel B. Maxey's Cavalry Division back to the Indian Territory because he believed they would not be needed.[71] Kirby Smith's reasoning was flawed. Maxey's division would have provided extra man and fire power to either slow down or flank the retreating Union column. Tactically and strategically, the order made little sense. Marmaduke's cavalry crossed the Ouachita by swimming, but not until darkness fell. The next morning, Smith ordered his troops to begin bridging the river.[72]

Steele pushed his men as hard as he could along the road to Jenkins' Ferry rather than the Pine Bluff road. This allowed him to avoid the mud flats of the Moro Swamp.[73] Men threw away things they previously thought were important to lighten their loads. Rumors were rampant that the Confederates had overtaken them and were waiting somewhere ahead.[74] The Confederates, however, were having trouble of their own.

Fagan could not find a place to cross the Saline River. The water had risen as a result of the almost constant rains, and he was forced to cross farther north. He finally gave up and led his men to Arkadelphia on April 29 to find supplies.[75] Southern Arkansas was equally inhospitable to both sides. With Fagan now in Arkadelphia and Maxey ordered to retire to the west, Kirby Smith was short two veteran divisions. To Fagan's south, Marmaduke was pressing closer to Steele's column.

Steele reached Jenkins' Ferry that afternoon and found the Saline River equally unyielding as it had been for Fagan. He brought up the pontoon bridges, loaded on wagons, and bridged the torrent after 4:00 P.M.[76] Steele then began moving the wagons and artillery across the bridge leaving tactical command to Brigadier General Frederick Salomon. The infantry

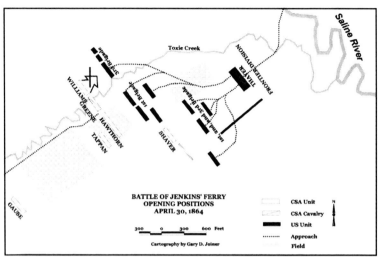

Opening positions of the Union and Confederate armies at the Battle of Jenkins'
Ferry April 30, 1864. Cartography by Gary D. Joiner.

and cavalry would cross last. As the train moved over the pontoon
bridges, Marmaduke was closing in on the federal column.

Marmaduke began to skirmish with the Union rearguard the next
morning, trying to pin them down until reinforcements arrived. He was
unable to identify which units or their type that remained on the south
side of the river. This lack of intelligence proved crucial. The Rebels
incorrectly believed they were facing the rearguard of Steele's column
and that pursuit would begin the next morning after they bridged the
Saline. Churchill's division, the first to arrive, caught the federal infantry
on the west side of the Saline River.[77] The road leading to the ferry
descended from a line of hills and bluffs into a narrow slit bordered on
the north by a line of bluffs, a small bayou, and a canebrake. To the south
were fields separated by and ringed with timber. There was little area
for either side to maneuver. In the fields close to the river, the Union
infantry felled trees into an abatis, an obstruction made of trees with the
trunks facing the defenders and the leafy growth facing the enemy. They
also began to form some of the trees into hastily contrived breastworks.
The field of fire was less than a quarter mile deep and wide.[78] The fields

Colonel Horace Randal and his wife. Ambrotype in the collection of the Henry E. Huntington Library.

were flooded with almost two feet of water. Across this swamp and into the abatis and breastworks, was the only approach the Confederates could use. The Rebel line of attack and the Union defensive positions eerily resembled the battlefield at Gettysburg on July 3, 1863, although with a few elevation differences. General George Pickett's charge at the Battle of Gettysburg would be replayed in the Saline bottoms of Arkansas with one major exception. There would be no grand push with all units marching forward. With Steele in retreat and such an inhospitable avenue of approach, the Rebels should have dug in and waited. They did not.

General Price ordered Marmaduke and Churchill to attack. This was done piecemeal, committing individual regiments because of the tight quarters.[79] Kirby Smith again made a tremendous error using unsound military practice. There was no thought to smashing a single point in the Union line by a massive surge of men. The small bayou, Toxie Creek (today known as Cox Creek), proved a problem for the advancing Confederates. Some of Steele's regiments, set as skirmishers across the stream, poured enfilade fire on the advancing Rebels.[80] Kirby Smith decided there were not enough forces engaged so he added all of Churchill's division and then Parsons' division, but incrementally. Marmaduke's inability to identify the number and nature of the enemy units to his front then became critical in the battle. The Confederates did not realize that Steele had been unable to cross his infantry en masse over the Saline and that

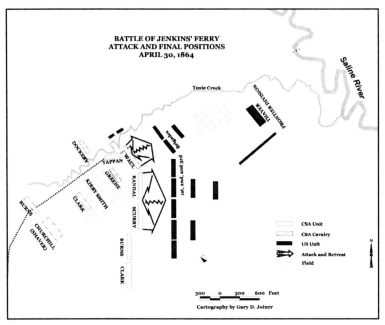

Final positions of the Union and Confederate armies at the Battle of Jenkins'
Ferry April 30, 1864. Cartography by Gary D. Joiner.

they were fighting the main force, not the rearguard. Both divisions were
forced to retreat in the withering fire coming from their front and their
left flank.[81] Visibility was almost nil as a result of fog and the smoke from
muskets and artillery. Both Price and Kirby Smith told the two divisions to
pull back. At about the same time, General John G. Walker's division arrived
and Kirby Smith committed them to attack on the Union left. Kirby Smith
wanted all three of Walker's brigades to advance and overpower the federal
position. He finally realized that he must pour men into the area near the
ferry landing, but by this time the Union line reconfigured for the onslaught.
This was a senseless attack and all three of the brigade commanders
suffered wounds, with Horace Randal and William R. Scurry mortally
wounded.[82] Kirby Smith's orders caused senseless carnage. As the
Confederates fell back, Steele brought the remainder of his forces over
the river in three hours. The Union troops then pulled the bridges to
their side and destroyed them.[83] Steele had no choice. His men were not

Brigadier William R. Scurry. Carte de Visite. Library of Congress, LC B812-8841.

physically able to fight a battle in a running pursuit. The river was the ally of the Union. The federals had no way to know that the Rebels had inadequate bridging equipment. They still believed a major force was to their front, waiting to pounce. Their memories of Poison Spring and Mark's Mills were still fresh.

The track behind Steele's retreat was littered with wagons that broke down and by pack animals that were freed because they were too weak to pull wagons or artillery limbers. As units at the front of the column discarded their equipment, those following were forced to move through these obstacles throughout May 1. They did not stop that night and marched until 4:00 A.M. without a break. Their meager food supplies gave out, and the column was finally given a short break before dawn.[84] After an all-too-brief respite, Steele began the march again, and by the afternoon, the men reached Benton where a supply train from Little Rock met them. Steele halted for the remainder of the day and evening.[85] The next morning the lead elements of the column moved into Little Rock.[86] The hard march brought the Union troops to safety. The campaign ended with the federals in Little Rock and the Confederates still south of the Saline River.

Confederate casualties at Jenkins' Ferry were listed as eight hundred to one thousand killed, wounded, or missing out of six thousand committed.[87] Union casualties were approximately seven hundred killed, wounded, and missing.[88]

In the campaign in Arkansas, the Confederate losses were reported as 2,300 to the Union's 2,750.[89] Steele suffered a huge loss in matériel

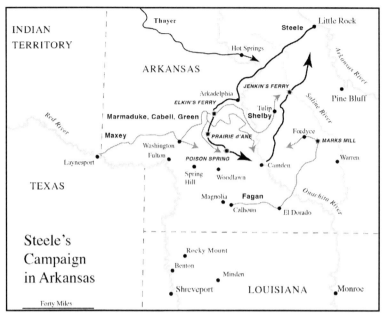

Steele's campaign in Arkansas. Cartography by Gary D. Joiner.

including 635 wagons, 2,500 mules, and nine artillery pieces.[90] The
Confederates, who did not travel with large trains, lost 35 wagons and
three field pieces.[91]

Kirby Smith moved his army back to the little village of Tulip,
located near the battlefield. On the night of April 30, both Scurry and
Randal died of their wounds and were buried in the village graveyard.[92]
For the next three days the army encamped while Kirby Smith pondered
what to do. On May 3, he ordered his three divisions to return to Taylor.[93]
They would not reach their Louisiana and Texas comrades in time to
assist them in pursuit of Banks.

8
THE NAVY

Rear Admiral David Dixon Porter left Grand Ecore on the morning of April 7 with a much smaller but still powerful fleet. The slowly dropping river level forced him to leave the *Eastport* behind. He chose his vessels for the final sprint to Shreveport for their firepower and their ability to navigate the tight meanders of the unpredictable river.[1]

The admiral selected one ironclad and two monitors to lead this portion of the mission. The monitors were the *Osage* and *Neosho*. Each was equipped with two 11-inch naval smoothbore guns in a single turret mounted at the bow. They needed only four-and-a-half feet of water beneath their decks to float. The ironclad was the *Chillicothe*. It required almost seven feet of water below the waterline to get under way.[2] The *Lexington* was one of the oldest warships in the inland fleet. As a timberclad sidewheeler, the *Lexington* used thick layers of wood to protect it from enemy guns. The timberclad required six feet of water to keep it afloat.[3] Porter also selected two tinclads. These were the *Fort Hindman* and the *Cricket*. The *Fort Hindman* required only two feet four inches of water to float.[4] The *Cricket* was a stern-wheeler and had a draft of four feet.[5] Porter picked the *Cricket* as his flagship. The remainder of the US Navy's contingent consisted of the tugs *Dahlia* and *William H. Brown* and the supply transport *Benefit*. Of the three, the *William H. Brown*

David Dixon Porter

Born in Pennsylvania in 1813, Porter was the son of Commodore David Porter and the cousin of Major General Fitz-John Porter. He accompanied his father's pirate suppression expeditions in the Gulf of Mexico. Having spent much of his early life at sea, he received little formal education, Porter joined the Mexican Navy as a midshipman in 1827, and joined US Navy as midshipman in 1829. He was promoted to lieutenant in 1841 and saw considerable service during the Mexican War. He served various merchant enterprises but returned to active duty in 1855. With the outbreak of Civil War, he served in blockade squadrons and was promoted to commander in 1861 after twenty years as a lieutenant. Porter capably led the mortar flotilla in the capture of New Orleans was then given command of the Mississippi River Squadron in October 1862. For his excellent service during the Vicksburg Campaign, he was elevated to rear admiral, bypassing the ranks of captain and commodore. Porter took a large fleet up the Red River to support Major General Nathaniel P. Banks' ill-fated campaign; the fleet was harassed by Confederate land forces and slowed by low-water levels during its difficult retreat. Sent East, Porter directed the North Atlantic Squadron for the balance of the war, participating in the capture of Fort Fisher, North Carolina. He served as superintendent of the US Naval Academy from 1865 to 1869 and was made vice admiral in 1866 and admiral in 1870. He was the author of numerous books including *Incidents of the Civil War* (1886) and *History of the Navy During the War of the Rebellion* (1890). Porter died 1891. The failure of the Red River Expedition notwithstanding, he played a significant role in the federal success in the West.

was the only one armed. It was large for a tug and was often used as a dispatch boat.[6]

These vessels guarded and herded the army's transports of at least twenty vessels. The quartermaster's boats held supplies for the main column and 1,600 of Brigadier General Andrew Jackson Smith's men of the Seventeenth Corps under Brigadier General Thomas Kilby Smith. Kilby Smith had armed most, if not all of these boats with army field cannon mounted on the decks. He had also placed bales of cotton and sacks of oats on the decks from which his men could fire in relative safety.[7] Among the transports was Major General Nathaniel P. Banks' headquarters boat *Black Hawk*, which Porter detested as an insult to his own favorite command vessel *Black Hawk*.[8]

The fleet headed north and reached Campti at 5:00 that afternoon.[9] The next morning as the force got underway, the transport *Iberville* ran aground almost immediately and was wedged so tightly against a sand bar that it took several hours to get the packet afloat. The water level dropped at a steady rate. As Porter passed north of the Grand Ecore hill complex and the mouth of Bayou Pierre, he had no way of knowing that the river was starved for water because of the Confederate destruction of the Tone's Bayou dam on March 18.

The *Iberville* was pulled off the bar, and the fleet slowly ascended the river as the crews called out the locations of snags in the channel bottom. Travel was slowed to just above steerageway in the now gentle current. The fleet reached the town of Coushatta and the mouth of Coushatta Chute at 6 P.M. At 9:00 the next morning, April 8, the fleet headed north again, moving in single file because of the narrow, winding river. Porter saw the river road that Banks could have used. He also saw the fields of corn and herds of cattle on which the army could have subsisted.[10] Other than the small band of Confederates seen at Coushatta, there was no opposition. The day passed uneventfully, as did April 9. At 2 P.M. on April 10, the fleet reached the mouth of Loggy Bayou, or what Porter believed to be Loggy Bayou.[11] This body of water was not the same stream shown on his map.[12]

While anchored opposite the stream, Kilby Smith sent a landing party to scatter some Confederates who were watching them. Then, after traveling another mile, Porter and Kilby Smith saw a sight that halted any further progress. They found a large steamboat blocking their path.

Porter began working on the problem of moving the *New Falls City* and Kilby Smith landed troops to secure the position. Shortly after this Captain William Andres of the Fourteenth New York Cavalry rode up with fifty of his troopers and told them of Banks' defeat on the April 8. He carried with him several dispatches and specific verbal orders for Kilby Smith to return to Grand Ecore.[13] No mention was made of Porter's fleet.

Kilby Smith and Porter decided that they must return to Grand Ecore before the Confederates could bring their artillery to the banks of the river and effectively blockade them. Porter and Kilby Smith ordered additional artillery placed on the upper decks of the transports, and barricades of any materials available were made for firing positions for the infantrymen.[14] The fleet then began the arduous downstream passage from the deepest penetration into the Red River Valley by federal forces.

Almost immediately the *Chillicothe* impaled itself on a submerged tree. The hull was pierced and needed patching. This halted the fleet for more than two hours. The *Chillicothe* was not able to move until the *Black Hawk*, using the *Chillicothe*'s hawser, was able to free the stricken boat.[15] Other vessels suffered damage as rudders became unshipped and paddles splintered, a common occurrence. As these boats were dealing with their own problems, the *Emerald* ran hard aground.[16] The Confederates began to fire at the fleet, and the sound of minie balls careening off hulls, casemates, and superstructure of the *Benefit*, *Black Hawk*, and *Osage* was ear shattering.[17] These vessels responded to the ineffective long-arm fire with the *Osage*'s 11-inch naval guns and this "must have been like hunting partridges with a howitzer."[18] When the fleet reached Coushatta Chute on the morning of April 12, the *Lexington* collided with the transport *Rob Roy*, spearing the latter's wheelhouse and launch and damaging the packet's smokestacks.[19]

On April 12, the fleet approached Blair's Landing, which was due west of Pleasant Hill and approximately forty-five miles north of Grand Ecore. Tom Green's cavalry had moved there to harass and, if possible, halt the progress of the fleet. Porter's fleet, transports, and armed vessels alike, passed the landing under cannon and small arms fire.[20] Some naval personnel were wounded and the vessels received damage from the Confederate artillery, which was well placed and concealed. Bringing up the rear of the flotilla were the timberclad *Lexington* and the monitor *Osage*. Strapped to the *Osage* was the transport *Black Hawk*. In making

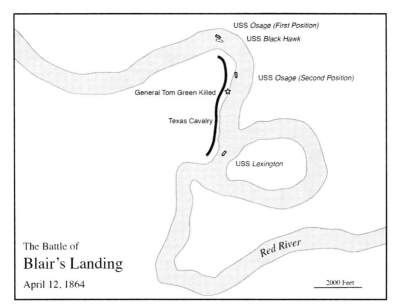

Battle of Blair's Landing. Cartography by Gary D. Joiner.

the tight turn above the landing, the *Osage* slewed and ran aground. Green and his 2,500 men were near the bank at this time. They dismounted, tied their horses, formed into three ranks and began pouring fire into the three boats. Banks' *Black Hawk* took such devastating fire that forty soldiers on its decks had to be evacuated into the safe confines of the cramped metal hull of the *Osage*. All hands aboard followed. Later Porter stated on examination of the *Black Hawk* "that there was not a place six inches square not perforated by a bullet."[21]

Porter was fortunate that the unprotected wooden transports had passed the landing earlier. If Green and his 2,500 men had possessed more artillery, the scene would have been much worse. Thomas O. Selfridge, Jr., commanding the *Osage*, wrote to Admiral Porter some sixteen years later, recounting it as "one of the most curious fights of the war, 2,500 infantry against a gunboat aground."[22]

The *Osage* and the *Black Hawk* strapped together were still aground with the wooden surfaces of the *Black Hawk* riddled like Swiss cheese

Thomas O. Selfridge, Jr.

Born in Massachusetts in 1836, Selfridge graduated from the US Naval Academy first in his class of 1854. He passed the midshipman exam in 1856, the master in 1858, and was made lieutenant 1860. He was present at the destruction of the Norfolk Navy Yard in 1861 and commanded the forward battery on the US frigate  *Cumberland* in its battle with the *Merrimack (Virginia)* in March 1862. Promoted to lieutenant commander 1862, Selfridge joined the Mississippi River Squadron for the Vicksburg Campaign. During the Red River Expedition of 1864, he was instrumental in the dam-building operations that allowed the federal fleet to continue. With Admiral David Dixon Porter, he joined the North Atlantic Squadron. He was conspicuously involved in the capture of Fort Fisher, North Carolina, in 1865. Selfridge continued in the US Navy following the war was promoted to commander in 1869. He participated in numerous surveys in Central and South America, including that of the Darien Isthmus (Panama) for which he received the Legion of Honor of France. He was promoted to captain in 1881, commodore in 1894, rear admiral in 1896, and retired in 1898. Selfridge died in 1924; his memoirs were published the same year. He had a knack for being where the action was and was involved in an amazing number of the Navy's most important events.

from musket and artillery fire. The vessels were forced to work the monitor off the bar and allow the *Lexington* to carry on the fight. After an intense engagement of more than an hour with no hint of the Confederates' lessening the strength of their attack, the *Lexington* finally silenced Green's four-gun artillery battery with its 8-inch guns.[23] Shortly before this duel, the *Osage* managed to move from the bar on which it was grounded. The *Osage* cut the lines to the *Black Hawk* and Selfridge let the current move the boat close to the Confederates without the engines running. Selfridge brought one of his 11-inch guns to bear on the troops and, at a distance of only twenty yards, fired a load of grape shot and canister directly at the officer on horseback who had been urging his men on with fiery passion. This blast decapitated the unfortunate man,

USS *Osage*. Library of Congress LC 816-3126.

General Green himself. The aiming of the naval accomplished by the first use of a periscope in battle.[24] The Confederates broke ranks and moved away from the riverbank.[25] There had been few casualties, but Green's loss was catastrophic for General Richard Taylor. Although Union estimates of Confederate casualties estimated two to five hundred killed and wounded, Confederate losses were quite low, perhaps less than ten. Union losses were also negligible.[26]

Porter kept the vessels moving past sunset and into the night. With only torches and perhaps moonlight to light the way, this was a perilous journey. The flotilla finally anchored at 1 A.M. on the morning of April 13. Several transports had run aground during the night. After dawn the next morning, the quartermaster's boat *John Warner* went aground and delayed the progress of the fleet. Porter made several attempts to extricate the *John Warner* throughout the day. The Confederates, who had placed field pieces on a high bank, began to fire at the vessels before *Osage* drove them off. The *Rob Roy* then lost its rudder and had to be placed undertow by the transport *Clara Bell*.[27]

Seth Ledyard Phelps

Born on June 13, 1824, in Parkman, Ohio, Phelps enlisted in the US Navy in October 1841. He served as a midshipman and junior officer in his early career, sailing in various squadrons to Africa, the Mediterranean, the Caribbean, and South America. While aboard the USS *Susquehanna* in 1858 sailing off the coast of Chile, Phelps contracted yellow fever and reported on his case before the US Senate. Rising to the rank of lieutenant commander, Phelps played a key role in the procurement and manning of the vessels in the Western Gunboat Flotilla and its successor, the Mississippi Squadron. Phelps was charged with creating the first timberclad warships for the inland fleet. In this capacity, working under Commander John Rodgers, Phelps helped in the design, construction, and conversion of the gunboats *Tyler, Lexington,* and *Conestoga.* Beginning in August 1861, Phelps commanded the *Conestoga.* In early January 1862, Phelps undertook a secret mission up the Tennessee River and discovered the Confederates were building Fort Henry. On another excursion, he was able to capture the unfinished Confederate ironclad *Eastport,* which was moved to Union shipyards at and near Cairo, Illinois, and converted the massive boat into one of the largest ironclads in existence. In June 1862, Phelps assumed command of the *Benton* and participated in the actions against Memphis, Tennessee. Phelps then took command of the *Eastport* and led Squadron Six based in Helena, Arkansas. Rear Admiral David Dixon Porter took command of the new Mississippi Squadron in late October. Porter moved Phelps to Cairo to examine improprieties in vessel conversions. Early in 1864, Phelps again commanded the *Eastport* and was part of the Red River Campaign. The vessel was too large for the river and proved more of a hindrance than help. It was struck by a torpedo south of Grand Ecore, Louisiana, and had to be scuttled near the mouth of the Cane River. Porter blamed Phelps for the loss and he resigned from the Navy in October 1864. Phelps later served as Commissioner of the District of Columbia and as US Minister to Peru. He died in Lima, Peru, on June 24, 1885.

The *John Warner* resisted all attempts to remove it from the sandy river bottom to which it was firmly affixed. Fearing that the Confederates were preparing a trap, at daylight on the morning of April 14, Kilby Smith ordered his transports and their protecting gunboats ahead to

Campti. He left the tinclad *Fort Hindman* to stay with the *John Warner* for protection. The next day the *Fort Hindman* managed to pull the vessel off the bar and they returned to the fleet at Grand Ecore on April 15, where the naval forces were safely under the army's guns.[28] The navy was now finally in contact with the army, largely as a result of the skills and composure of Porter and Kilby Smith.[29]

Finally arriving at Grand Ecore, Porter visited Banks in his headquarters tent. Banks made it plain that he considered he had won the Battle of Mansfield and that the subsequent battle of Pleasant Hill was simply a withdrawing action. Banks gave Porter the same excuse he had used with General Smith, that he only withdrew for lack of water. Totally disgusted with Banks and his excuses for retreat, Porter told Banks that under no circumstance would the navy go back upstream.[30]

With the river falling rapidly at Grand Ecore, the fleet and the army were forced to withdraw from this region that had held so much promise for them. The army began marching along the river road to Alexandria. On April 16, with some navigation problems and further mechanical failures, the fleet proceeded downstream three miles with *Eastport* in the lead. In mid-March, the Confederates, knowing that the fleet could only return on the same route it took north, had placed six torpedoes (or mines) below the ferry at Grand Ecore.[31] The *Eastport* struck one of these Confederate torpedoes, but only a few people aboard felt the shock. It took on water rapidly and came to rest on the bottom. Fortunately, the bottom was only a few feet at most below the keel and settled in the soft sand.[32]

The *Eastport* became a potential obstacle as threatening as the *New Falls City*, but perhaps more deadly. The great ironclad was wedged at the forefront of the flotilla and blocked its passage. The pump boat *Champion No. 5* was used to bilge out the water. The *Eastport*'s guns were removed and placed on flat rafts towed by the *Cricket*. The ironclad's captain, Lieutenant Commander Seth Ledyard Phelps, and his crew worked day and night to save the vessel.[33] It was finally refloated on April 21 and with some groundings because of still taking on water, the behemoth proceeded downstream another forty miles. Near the town of

USS *Cricket*. Naval Historical Center Photo NH 55524.

Montgomery the ironclad ran into submerged snags and became firmly stuck on April 26. The *Champion No. 3* and the *Fort Hindman* joined the pump boat *Champion No. 5* in attempts to wrest the vessel free. As the boats tried to move the behemoth back and forth, the efforts to save it only worsened the situation. The captain of the *Fort Hindman*, Acting Volunteer Lieutenant John Pearce and Phelps of the *Eastport* made several attempts to rock the *Eastport* free, but they were doomed to failure. Porter received news that the water level downstream was falling. Knowing that the fleet was in danger of being bottled up behind the great ironclad, Porter ordered a ton of powder placed throughout the vessel. Combustible materials available at the time were packed into the boat and at 1:45 P.M. on April 26 it was destroyed.[34]

The vessels that had been aiding and guarding the *Eastport*—the *Fort Hindman, Cricket, Juliet, Champion No. 3*, and *Champion No. 5*—

made their way downstream and approached the mouth of the Cane River. The Confederates had assembled four artillery pieces of Captain Florian O. Cornay's First (Louisiana) Battery, with two hundred riflemen from Camille Armand Jules Marie, Prince de Polignac's Division assisting.[35] They heaped fire on the vessels, and the *Champion No. 3* was sunk. Below decks, more than one hundred slaves being carried to freedom were scalded to death. The *Champion No. 5* was heavily damaged, grounded, and abandoned by the crew. The *Fort Hindman*, now commanded by Phelps, *Cricket*, with Porter aboard, and the *Juliet* were severely damaged but passed through the gauntlet.[36] A tribute to the ferocity of this attack is that in five minutes, the *Cricket* was hit some thirty-eight times, and suffered twenty-five dead and wounded. This constituted fully half of the crew. The *Juliet* also lost half its crew, suffering fifteen killed and wounded. The *Fort Hindman* suffered three killed and four or five wounded.[37]

Porter, aboard the *Cricket*, displayed great personal bravery in keeping the tinclad in the fight. A shell hit the aft gun and killed the entire gun crew. Another eliminated the forward gun and its crew. Cornay's Confederates were pouring accurate fire on the gunboats. A third shell hit the fire-room where the stokers kept steam pressure up in the boilers. All were killed but one man. Porter gathered some refugee slaves that the *Cricket* had taken aboard, showed them how to fire a gun and turned them into a gun crew to try to keep the Confederates' heads down long enough for the vessel to escape. He then went to the engine room and, finding the chief engineer dead, he put the assistant engineer in charge and told him to get the steam pressure up. Porter then went to the pilothouse and discovered that another shell had wounded one of the pilots and that the remaining crew on the bridge were hiding. With his customary aplomb, Porter took charge of the *Cricket* and moved the tinclad past the battery that had nearly sent it to the bottom.[38]

Porter's fleet limped into the northern approaches to Alexandria with the Red River falling rapidly. He had lost the most powerful ironclad in the fleet. Two of his pump boats had also been sunk, and three of his tinclads had been severely damaged. Most of the army transport vessels had received either mechanical or battle damage. To make matters worse, the river had fallen a full six feet and most of his fleet was now trapped above "the Falls."[39]

In places, the river appeared to be a string of ponds connected by rivulets. The fleet barely floated in the shallows, stranded upstream from "the Falls," the lowest water that the boats would have to cross before reaching safety in the deep water beyond. The Confederates had adequate artillery and cavalry to keep the enemy in sight and occupied, but inadequate infantry to lay siege to the town.

Taylor was in a peculiar position. He had surrounded an army of thirty-one thousand men with eighty cannon and a huge fleet of warships, with only six thousand men.[40] Taylor had cavalry patrols operating at Fort DeRussy and on Bayou Teche.[41] He positioned artillery batteries at various points on the river below Alexandria, including an important crossing at David's Ferry.[42]

Captain John A. West's Grosse Tete (Louisiana) Flying Artillery Battery, under Lieutenant W. H. Lyne, was sent to David's Ferry, located on the Red River about thirty miles below Alexandria. They almost immediately engaged and burned the transport *Emma* on May 1.[43] On May 4, they attacked and captured the *City Belle* on its way to Alexandria with reinforcements. On board were seven hundred men of the 120th Ohio Infantry. About half of these men were captured and the remainder were killed or wounded.[44]

The same day the *John Warner* and the *Covington* left Alexandria. They were joined by the *Signal*. The *John Warner* carried the men of the Fifty-Sixth Ohio Infantry who were leaving on veterans' furloughs.[45] The vessels had received small arms fire throughout the day. At night the small convoy tied up on the river bank about twenty miles south of Alexandria. Confederates fired at them as they ate the evening meal.[46] The next morning the gunboats got underway and at 4:45 A.M.; as they reached Dunn's Bayou, the *Warner* was fired on by artillery and musketry. The *Covington* and *Signal* fired back on the attackers. The Confederate artillery disabled

USS *Signal*. Naval Historical Center Photo NH 49978.

the *Warner*'s rudders and it drifted to the bank below the attack. The Rebel
artillery continued to fire at the boat and they were joined by Confederate
cavalry. The vessel was pounded into a floating pile of debris.[47] The Fifty-
Sixth Ohio, still aboard, was torn to shreds. The *Covington* tried to torch
the boat rather than allow it to be captured after the captain of the *Warner*
raised the white flag. The colonel of the Fifty-Sixth Ohio pleaded with the
party from the *Covington* not to burn it because the boat still held 125 of
his men who lay dead or dying on its decks.[48]

The artillery from Dunn's Bayou then arrived to pour more fire on
the warships. The *Covington* and *Signal* tried to retire upstream, but the
Signal lost its steering assembly and port engine. The *Covington* threw a
towline to the *Signal* and began pulling it against the current. An artillery
shell then hit one of the *Signal*'s steam pipes and the crew believed the

USS *Neosho*. From Francis Trevelyan Miller et al., eds., *The Photographic History of the Civil War in Ten Volumes* (New York: Review of Reviews Co., 1912), 6:228.

boilers were going to explode. The *Covington* cut its companion loose. The *Covington* tried to escape, but its rudder had been hit as well. The captain tied up to the opposite bank and his crew returned fire for a short time, until they ran out of ammunition. The captain ordered the guns spiked and set fire to the tinclad. The *Signal* was forced to surrender under the combined battery fire after the *Covington* began to burn. The Confederates reported that they drove off another gunboat that tried to offer assistance.[49] The navy suffered more losses in vessels and men than it had on April 22 below Grand Ecore.[50] But they were not alone in their adversity. Inside the defensive perimeter at Alexandria, Porter was dealing with other problems.

Porter's resolve was shaken as he considered the destruction of his fleet to keep it from falling into enemy hands. There seemed no way out of the dilemma. Near the time that a decision must be made to destroy or abandon the fleet, Lieutenant Colonel Joseph Bailey suggested a solution that was to make him famous during the war and give him the highest awards his country bestowed.

The navy was in desperate straits. The water level had fallen until the sand and rocks of the Falls were showing as only damp indications of their usual underwater treachery. The river level at the chute or navigable channel was only three feet four inches deep.[51] The *Louisville* and its sisters needed seven feet to float. The transports and gunboats that had been left behind as the remainder of the fleet ascended the river had been ordered below the falls as the river began to fall. The transports that accompanied Porter upstream were ordered across as well. But the potential disaster lay ahead in the fact that the majority of the most powerful vessels were trapped above the rocks. These included the *Lexington, Osage, Neosho, Mound City, Louisville, Pittsburg, Carondelet, Chillicothe, Ozark,* and *Fort Hindman.*[52] If the navy retreated, these vessels would have to be destroyed. It was unthinkable to lose these expensive, powerful boats, and their loss would seriously harm or destroy Porter's career. Porter's report to Gideon Welles resulted in General-in-Chief Ulysses S. Grant's decision to keep General Smith's men with Porter to protect the fleet, and this was fortunate for the Navy.

The number of possible actions was limited if the fleet was to be saved. A huge number of men would be tied down at Alexandria waiting for the autumn rains to raise the river level and that appealed to no one, particularly with General Taylor and his army nearby. The only other possibility was to force the water level to rise at Alexandria. Lieutenant Colonel Bailey of Wisconsin, one of Major General William B. Franklin's engineers, advanced this option.

Bailey had worked in the logging industry in Wisconsin and was familiar with the practice of building temporary dams to increase water levels to float logs downstream to saw mills in dry weather. He told Franklin about his idea and although Franklin was favorably impressed, he became distracted by command issues and nothing was done. After the *Eastport* sank, Franklin gave Bailey a letter of introduction to Porter, who gave little credence to an idea from an army officer offering a means to save his fleet.[53]

Franklin was also an engineer and appreciated Bailey's approach. Once again Franklin attempted to convince Porter, now at Alexandria.[54]

Joseph Bailey

Born May 6, 1825, in Morgan County, Ohio, Bailey earned an engineering degree at the University of Illinois and then moved to Wisconsin where he became a successful businessman, civil engineer, and lumberman. At the beginning of the Civil War, Bailey entered Union Army service as a captain of Company D of the Fourth Wisconsin

Infantry Regiment. The regiment served under Major General Benjamin Butler during the occupation of New Orleans in April 1862. He was promoted to major in May 1863 for his engineering efforts during the siege of Port Hudson. Bailey was promoted to lieutenant colonel in August 1863 when his regiment was realigned as a cavalry unit.

He became famous during the Red River Campaign of 1864 when General Nathaniel P. Banks and his Army of the Gulf attempted to invade Texas by ascending the Red River in Louisiana with the intent of crossing into Texas after taking the Confederate state capital at Shreveport. The effort ended in disaster and Bailey was credited with saving the Union Navy's Mississippi Squadron under Rear Admiral David Dixon Porter. Banks brought approximately 32,500 men to take Shreveport and another 10,000 men from Arkansas to descend on the Confederate city. Both columns were thwarted by Confederate forces.

As the Union forces fell back to Alexandria, Louisiana, the water in the Red River fell precipitously as a result of Confederate engineering efforts up river. It seemed as if the bulk of the Mississippi Squadron must be scuttled or burned to prevent capture. Bailey used his logging knowledge to propose a dam and a series of wing dams to increase the water level to float the vessels to safety. Both General Banks and Admiral Porter were reluctant. Bailey finally was given permission to use volunteers and he created his dams. Without the Navy's big guns, the Union Army would not be able to retreat from the valley. The project took ten days and troops worked from both banks of the river. The river began to rise on May 10, 1864, and fleet passed safely downstream.

Bailey received the "Thanks of Congress" and was awarded the Congressional Medal of Honor. He became the chief engineer of the Nineteenth Army Corps and then held various commands through the end of the war. President Abraham Lincoln appointed him a brigadier general. He achieved the rank of brevet major general after the war.

Immediately following the war, Bailey and his wife moved to Vernon County, Missouri, and he was elected sheriff. He was assassinated on March 21, 1867, while attempted to arrest hog thieves. He and his wife are buried in Evergreen Cemetery at Fort Scott, Kansas.

Mississippi Squadron vessels trapped above the Falls. USS *Chillicothe,* USS *Ozark,* USS *Fort Hindman,* and tug *Dahlia.* Louisiana and Lower Mississippi Valley Collection, LSU Libraries, Louisiana State University, Baton Rouge.

By this time Porter's options were even more limited and the water level was lowering with each passing hour. On April 29, Bailey attended a meeting with Banks and General David Hunter, who had been in Alexandria for two days with a message from Grant. Banks was interested because Hunter's message made it imperative that the army should withdraw from central Louisiana as quickly as possible. Banks also could not afford to leave Porter with Hunter there watching him. Sherman's belief that Banks would leave the fleet stranded if the army was forced to leave might have become a reality had Hunter not been sent with the message from Grant. Hunter, though skeptical, agreed to Bailey's proposal because Franklin promoted it.[55] The same day construction began; Franklin sought a leave of absence because of his wound and left Alexandria for convalescence.[56] Brigadier General William Emory was elevated to the command of the Nineteenth Corps and Brigadier General James W. McMillan replaced Emory as division commander.[57]

Bailey's task of dam building was more difficult than he expected. First, he had trouble securing work gangs. Some regimental commanders thought it was a waste of time.[58] Second, the site he chose for the main dam was large, 758 feet wide. The water level varied from four to six feet and as the dam was formed, the level rose and the current increased to ten miles per hour.[59] Third, building materials for the dam were not uniform. He began to disassemble buildings in Alexandria and across the river in Pineville. Bricks, stones, wall segments, even pieces of furniture were used. Ironically, some of the dam's structure included portions of Sherman's beloved Louisiana Seminary for Learning and Military Institute from across the river in Pineville.[60] Soldiers from Maine, most of whom had been lumbermen, felled trees and chopped them to appropriate lengths. Bricks and stones were gathered into barges to make cribs to meet the tree dam.[61] The structure was formed from both sides of the river, meeting in the center. Construction of the dam became quite a spectacle attracting the interest of bored soldiers. Primarily the Maine soldiers and US Colored Troops of the Corps d'Afrique built the dam.[62]

After a week of work, the tree dam extended three hundred feet from the western bank. Four coal barges loaded with brick and stone were lashed together and sunk to extend it farther. From the other side, the crib dam was extended to meet the barges on May 8.[63] The lightest draft vessels, the *Osage*, *Neosho*, and *Fort Hindman* floated to the area above the dam. The others did not follow, although the water was deep enough for them to do so. The ironclads were still filled with cotton and removing it would have lightened them sufficiently to pass through the dam on May 8, but they were not willing to lose the white gold. The water level was rising significantly and exerting pressure on the cribs and barges. Finally, at 5 A.M. on May 9 the river pushed the center barges aside. Porter ordered the *Lexington* through the gap before the water level fell and the timberclad managed to pull through with a full head of steam. The *Osage*, *Neosho*, and *Fort Hindman* followed with only the *Neosho* suffering minor hull damage from the rocks.[64]

Bailey's dam under construction at Alexandria. From Francis Trevelyan Miller et al., eds., *The Photographic History of the Civil War in Ten Volumes* (New York: Review of Reviews Co., 1912), 1:78–79.

The other vessels had not been moved up to the pool above the dam so when the water level decreased, they were unable to get through.[65] Bailey immediately began repairs on the dam and decided that other structures called wing dams must be built to channel the water above the main dam. This delay affected Banks' plan for evacuation. By May 9, Major General John McClernand had arrived from Texas and Banks now had more troops to deal with.[66] Although Banks had anticipated moving from Alexandria on May 9, he did not do so. By May 11 Banks sent word to Porter that the navy must be ready to move its boats as soon as the wing dams were built.[67]

Porter began removing guns and iron plating from the ironclads to lighten their weight. The guns, ammunition, and needed supplies were placed on wagons and carried below the falls. Iron plating was removed from some of the ironclads and dumped in the river. Tar was then smeared on the exposed wood to fool anyone who saw the vessels without their armor.[68] Porter chose not to carry eleven 32-pounder smoothbore cannon and had them spiked and dumped into the river.[69] By May 11, the wing dams were complete, but water was not rising sufficiently to float the vessels over the dam. A bracket dam was hastily built. Two days later the water was high enough for the ironclads to shoot through the gap.[70]

Bailey's complex series of dams were designed to use every aspect of the Red River near Alexandria. The river made a gentle curve just above the town, and at both ends of the arc were the boulders that formed the Falls. The wing dams were located at the northern end, supported by the bracket dams. The tree dam, supported by the cribs, was placed near the wharves on the town's riverfront.[71]

The dam system was a daring, innovative undertaking.[72] For his efforts and ingenuity, Bailey was awarded the Medal of Honor and the "Thanks of Congress." By May 15, Porter pushed his fleet out of the Red River and into the wide waters of the Mississippi. He wrote to his mother, "I am clear of my troubles and my fleet is safe out in the broad Mississippi. I have had a hard and anxious time of it."[73]

9
THE UNION RETREAT

During the retreat from Pleasant Hill, Major General Nathaniel P. Banks made a series of poor decisions. He tried to deflect the criticism he knew would come from his superiors. He fired veteran commanders who would offer opposing views, he marched his army onto an elongated island that led to potential entrapment, he chose a route on that island that kept the army away from the naval guns, and barely escaped a Confederate trap.

Banks' column was full of griping, angry men who believed that they were betrayed by incompetent commanders. The words of improvised songs floated up and down the line. One ditty sung by Massachusetts troops to the tune of "When Johnny Comes Marching Home," had a chorus of "We all skedaddled to Grand Ecore." The troops sometimes ended the bitter song with a yell of "Napoleon P. Banks."[1] The soldiers began referring to the commanding general as "Mister Banks," referring to his lack of military training and his accession to the lofty rank of major general without ever wearing so much as a private's stripes.[2]

The column covered the distance from Pleasant Hill to Grand Ecore in three days. Banks ordered the men to expand the outer perimeter of the Confederates' former defenses with the army's thirty thousand men packed into a fortification of about six square miles.[3] He believed General Richard Taylor had twenty-five thousand men to contest him.[4] Banks, apparently panicked, ordered the remaining division at Alexandria under Brigadier General Cuvier Grover to come to Grand Ecore immediately.[5] He then sent a message to Pass Cavallo, Texas, instructing Major General John McClernand to strip his command of all but two thousand soldiers and bring the bulk of his force to Grand Ecore. McClernand was to take over command of the Thirteenth Corps, replacing the wounded Brigadier General Thomas E. G. Ransom.[6]

Banks then reported to General-in-Chief Ulysses S. Grant the details of the campaign thus far. His major points were: (1) Shreveport was the prime focus of the Confederates defenses, (2) the Confederates were on the defensive, (3) the Rebels had been planning an invasion of Missouri, (4) Steele's advance on the line he was using rendered Banks no assistance at all, and (5) gunboats were useless to the army, considering the shallow depth of the river. He concluded, saying that he intended to advance on Shreveport using a different route.[7] Just as this missive was complete, word came from Major General William T. Sherman demanding the return of Brigadier General Andrew Jackson Smith and his men.[8] Banks countermanded Sherman's order because he was senior to Smith's commander.[9]

Banks made an apparent effort to shift blame and bolster his own support, lagging among the troops and within his staff, and fired his chief of staff, Brigadier General Charles P. Stone.[10] He relieved Brigadier General Albert L. Lee from command of the cavalry division and sent him to New Orleans.[11] With Lee was Colonel Nathan A. M. "Gold Lace" Dudley, who was also relieved of command. Scathing letters were attached to the men's files.[12] Banks replaced Stone with William Dwight.[13]

While the navy bumped and scraped its way along the sandy, rock-scattered river bottom, Banks led his men south toward Alexandria. The high bluffs of Grand Ecore did not directly connect to the river road. Four miles south of Grand Ecore lay Natchitoches. From there the road, which ran along the Red River, crossed the Cane River. The channel of the Cane River had once been the main course of the Red River.

These two channels ran roughly parallel for thirty miles before joining at Monett's Ferry. He chose the Cane River Road; however, it afforded him little assistance from the fleet until he reached the ferry. It followed a channel that was located west of the river and was not open to the naval vessels.[14] The river road followed the twisting channel of the Cane River, adding another fifteen miles to cross the island formed by the two streams. Had Banks taken an alternative route, traveling west and then turning south, he would have left the safety of the fleet and reentered the "howling wilderness."

Banks placed General Smith's division in Natchitoches as a safeguard between General Taylor and his own army. Smith's men would be the last to leave and on April 21 at 5 P.M., the column began to move.[15] The men torched the few buildings in Grand Ecore.[16] Three brigades of cavalry, now allowed to perform their duties properly, screened the column. As twilight led to darkness, the cavalrymen burned homesteads and barns to light the way for the infantry and to exact some revenge. Following the cavalry was the infantry led by Grover's division, just arrived from Alexandria. Banks positioned the combined trains behind these fresh troops. Next came the remainder of the Nineteenth Corps, and then the Thirteenth Corps. After the column passed through Natchitoches, General Smith's Seventeenth Corps and one brigade of cavalry brought up the rear.[17]

Banks received messages that Taylor was moving his forces south to cut the Union forces off at Monett's Ferry.[18] If the Confederates made a strong position at the ferry, the entire column would be cut off on this island and possibly, forced to surrender. Banks now drove his men to reach the ferry before the Confederates could arrive. Rebel advance troops cut trees to block the road ahead of the Union troops, slowing the column and raising tensions. There were no large streams on the island from which the men could fill their canteens. The banks of the Cane River were steep and not easily traversed. The men were pushed to the limit of their endurance with some staggering, some sleeping while marching and officers often asleep in their saddles.[19]

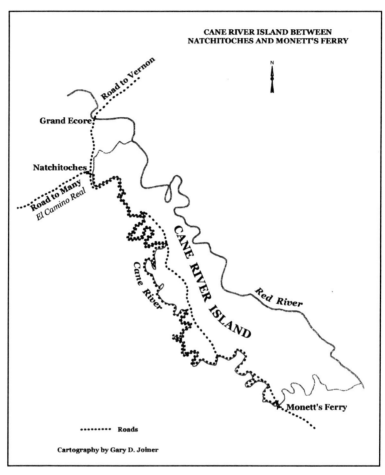

Map of Cane River Island. Cartography by Gary D. Joiner.

Taylor sent Major General Tom Green's cavalry, now under the command of Major General John Wharton, to harass the rearguard. The Confederate cavalry was adept at hit-and-run raiding tactics and this added to the charged atmosphere of the column. Wharton's timely arrival saved Natchitoches from being put to the torch by General Smith's men.[20]

The column pressed on through the night of April 21 and finally halted at 2:30 in the morning to allow the rear units to catch up. The lead elements had covered twenty miles in a little more than nine hours. At 11 A.M. on

April 22, the cavalry and infantry units took up the march again, just as the rearguard units were closing on the column. As the men began to bed down, Banks received word from scouts that the Confederates were on his side of the ferry.[21] At midnight, he ordered Brigadier General William Emory to take the entire army except the rear guard and secure the ferry landing. Banks then ordered General Smith to send a brigade to assist Emory. Smith refused, stating that he could not spare any men.[22] Emory pressed forward and by 4:30 A.M. drove the Confederate pickets across the river. As dawn broke, Emory and his men could finally see what awaited them. Across the river on a high and deeply wooded bluff, the Confederates had mounted numerous cannon. The position overlooked any line of approach the federal troops might mount on Taylor's troops, consisting of eight batteries of artillery and 1,600 cavalry were sent to seal off the ferry.[23] They commanded the best ground for miles around. Brigadier General Hamilton P. Bee was ordered by both Taylor and Wharton to hold the ferry crossing and not let Banks escape. What Emory and his men did not know was that Confederate infantry under Brigadier General Camille Armand Jules Marie de Polignac had secured the ford opposite Cloutierville and that other infantry under Brigadier General St. John R. Liddell was in position near the present-day site of Colfax on the other side of the Red River.[24] Wharton's cavalry was pressing General Smith so hard it was possible that he might not be able to hold the Confederates at bay.[25] If the column was to retreat to Grand Ecore, it would be forced to fight every inch of the way. All avenues of escape for the Army of the Gulf had been blocked. Emory sent his cavalry forward only to be driven out of range by the Rebel artillery. He then formed a line with his infantry to watch the Confederates and sent the cavalry to find another exit.[26] None was found. Taylor had achieved his goal.

Some of the Union troopers approached a Negro and asked him if there was a place to cross the river other than the ferry and were told of a point two miles behind them. The Negro led them to a ford that was not covered by the Confederates.[27] Grover's division led by Brigadier General Henry Birge, Benedict's Brigade now led by Colonel Francis Fessenden, and

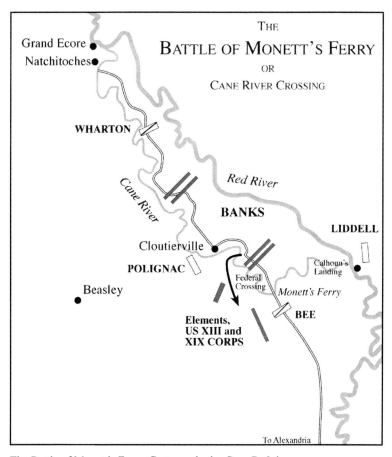

The Battle of Monett's Ferry. Cartography by Gary D. Joiner.

the remnants of the Thirteenth Corps, were selected to make the flank attack.[28]

The Union troops led by Birge made a long loop around both the Cane River and the Confederates blocking the ferry position. They approached in line of battle with skirmishers deployed to their front. This was a difficult maneuver because the terrain was wooded and sometimes marshy. They emerged unseen onto a broad cotton field. After crossing the field, the Union troops climbed a wooded ridge, where their skirmishers encountered Bee's pickets. From this ridge, Birge and his men could see the main Confederate position, a quarter of a mile ahead and across an open field. They could also look down at some of their own troops across the Cane River.[29]

Birge allowed Fessenden to prepare the attack. Benedict's old brigade held the right of the line and Birge's men held the left Cameron's division was held in reserve. Fessenden ordered the men to fix bayonets and to wait to fire in volley to increase effectiveness of the fire. The Union line moved forward and Fessenden was one of the first casualties, suffering a wound to his right leg, later amputated. The line wavered as it descended the ridge and crossed a slough. The field they now crossed was in the shape of a trapezoid and this forced the troops to crowd closer together. As the Union line reached the foot of the ridge where the Confederates were lodged, they charged.[30]

The Confederates were Colonel George Baylor and the Second Arizona Cavalry. Seeing the size of the force to their front, the Rebels fell back to a line behind an overgrown fence. Here Colonel Isham Chisum's Second Texas Partisan Rangers Cavalry Regiment joined them. Baylor asked Bee for two regiments to plug a hole in his flank, but none were sent.[31]

Birge halted his men and dressed their line. He then rode with some of his staff to examine what lay ahead of them. As the men went into a gully they were hit by murderous artillery and small arms fire, the location of which they could not determine. At this moment Birge and his party rode back through the line to save themselves, creating confusion. The Union regiments simply hit the ground or broke and ran. Two regiments crossed into a ravine for cover.[32]

Emory watched from across the Cane River and directed an artillery battery to provide fire support. He ordered his troops to make a feint as if forcing the ferry crossing to distract the Confederates. The ruse worked and the Rebels were forced to split their artillery fire between Birge and Emory. Bee then received word, incorrectly, that his right flank was being attacked.[33] There were no federal forces there, but Bee concluded that Banks had out maneuvered him and that the battle was lost. Bee ordered Baylor, who was expecting fire support, to retreat.[34]

Taylor was south of Cloutierville doing his best to pin down General Smith. The Confederates here were making great progress and Taylor believed his trap was working.[35] Bee retreated and left the ferry landing open. Emory crossed and ordered the cavalry division to chase Bee's men. Emory's troops took a wrong road and missed the fleeing Confederates.[36] The road to Alexandria lay open for the Union column. Smith's men were the last to cross the river at two in the afternoon the next day. Wharton had driven them to the ferry just as Polignac joined up his forces with Taylor.[37] The Confederates were now at the narrow end of the island and the Union forces were gone. In the running battles of April 22 and 23, Union losses were three hundred killed wounded and missing. Confederate losses were less than half that. Bee had suffered only fifty casualties.[38]

Taylor censured Bee and later fired him.[39] Lieutenant General Edmund Kirby Smith and Bee's peers defended him, but his premature actions in retreat place the tactical blame squarely on him for the battle's loss.[40] Ultimately, perhaps the loss is equally the fault of Kirby Smith, who removed three divisions of infantry to chase Major General Frederick Steele in Arkansas and thus left Taylor with inadequate resources to trap Banks. Taylor did not have enough men to keep the Union forces from creating a bridgehead at the ferry. Emory could have forced it by the next day, especially with Birge cooperating in a flanking maneuver.

The Union column force-marched into Alexandria with the lead elements entering the town on the afternoon of April 25.[41] At the rear of the column, General Smith's men scorched the earth around them and arrived the next day.[42] As they marched in, hordes of runaway slaves entered with them, freed from the torched plantations along the river. Major General William B. Franklin issued orders against looting, pillaging, and burning, but the evidence of destruction was seen in the charred ruins of the plantations and homesteads north of Alexandria.[43]

Banks only vaguely realized the political firestorm in which he was involved. The campaign had begun five weeks before his return to the central Louisiana town. In that short time, Grant had become general-in-chief, Major General Henry Halleck was chief of staff, and Sherman was making final preparations for his thrust into Georgia. Banks' carefully worded messages to his superiors, to President Abraham Lincoln and others, concerning tactical situations, had been mixed with exuberant exaggerations and expectations. He was not privy to conversations and letters exchanged among the people with whom he was communicating. Banks was also not aware of newspaper reports and letters from within his own command condemning his actions.[44]

Grant sent Banks orders on March 31 that were plainly stated. First, if Banks captured Shreveport, he was to hand over the city to Steele and let the navy handle the defense of the river. Second, with the sole exception of the Rio Grande River, Banks was to withdraw from every point he occupied on the Texas coast. Third, he was to reduce garrison posts and troop concentrations to compose a force of twenty-five thousand troops to take Mobile.[45] Banks received the orders on April 18, while the army was at Grand Ecore.[46] While Grant's orders were being delivered to Banks, Banks' message of April 2 was being forwarded to Grant. This letter told Grant of Banks' intention of chasing Kirby Smith into Texas.[47]

The letter infuriated Grant. On April 17, Grant sent Major General David Hunter to Banks with a copy of his orders. He was to make it plain to Banks that Mobile was more important than Shreveport. If he found Banks had taken Shreveport and was in East Texas, he was to order Banks to retrace his steps and prepare for the attack on Mobile.[48] Hunter arrived in Alexandria on April 27.

On April 18, other correspondence was generated between Secretary of War Edwin M. Stanton and the naval base at Cairo, Illinois, Rear Admiral David Dixon Porter's headquarters. Stanton was told that navy dispatches had been received from Porter explaining that Banks had been defeated at Mansfield, retreated to Pleasant Hill, and had fought another battle there, which he had won.[49] At that point no mention was made of the retreat to Grand Ecore. Stanton also received the first newspaper reports about the battles. Stanton immediately sent the naval dispatches and newspaper reports to Grant.[50] Shortly after this, Stanton received word from Cairo that Sherman's aide, Brigadier General John M. Corse, had arrived there with word from General Smith that Banks had lost four thousand men, sixteen guns, two hundred wagons, and had retreated to Grand Ecore with his force in poor condition.[51] These were forwarded to Grant as well.

Grant was furious. He telegraphed Halleck that he wanted Banks removed from command and replaced by Major General Joseph J. Reynolds, then in command of New Orleans.[52] Halleck took Grant's telegram to President Lincoln who told the chief of staff to delay action on Banks' removal. Lincoln needed New England in the upcoming November elections so firing Banks was politically out of the question.[53]

On April 25, Grant issued an order countermanding his demand that Smith and his men be sent to Sherman.[54] This was done purely to protect the fleet and was based on reports from Porter to Secretary of the Navy Gideon Welles.[55] On the same day Grant received an anonymous letter from (apparently) an officer in the Thirteenth Corps, railing against Banks' deplorable mismanagement.[56] This was too much. On April 27, Halleck ordered Banks to turn over command to the next ranking officer and return to New Orleans and carry out previous instructions [the attack on Mobile].[57] The order was not delivered because it was apparently aboard the *City Belle*, a transport packet, when it was attacked on May 4.[58] Grant abandoned the attack on Mobile, realizing that troops from west of the Mississippi could not feasibly be moved in time to coordinate attacks.[59] He then suggested that the Gulf region be reorganized. Grant even suggested to Halleck that he take over command of the Army of the Gulf. Halleck declined.[60] Grant and Halleck then informed Banks that no troops were to be withdrawn from the region at that time.[61]

Lincoln was silent on Banks' removal, certainly adding to the delay in action on reallocating forces for the spring campaigns. Although no formal written communication exists, Lincoln must have agreed to the wishes of Halleck and Grant.[62] On May 7, Major General E. R. S. Canby was given command of the newly reorganized

Military Division of West Mississippi, including the Departments of the Gulf and Arkansas.[63] A delicate balance was struck in this promotion. Canby was given broad discretionary powers in his command. Banks was to command the Department of the Gulf, but as a subordinate officer to Canby. Banks' position still carried the trappings of power, but it was only an illusion.[64] Banks, of course, knew nothing of this. He was in Alexandria with his army and the fleet was trapped above the Falls with Taylor and his Confederates at his heels.

Banks wanted to leave Alexandria as quickly and quietly as possible. Tired and disgruntled, he had no intention of offering battle to Taylor. The general staff and the president had castigated him for his failures and his presidential plans were in ruins. An ambitious but honest man, he observed the events crushing his career with detached bemusement. He never seemed to understand how the promising campaign turned into a major embarrassment. Remaining was the task of extricating his army from the valley. He continued to overestimate the number of Confederate troops that operated against him.

The demoralized army was a source of problems. Banks did not trust General Smith's men or officers, and he believed they would wreak havoc on the local citizens and their property, and this was a counterproductive to the president's plans for reconstruction. Smith's men had burned several buildings between Natchitoches and Alexandria. Banks believed that if Alexandria were put to the torch, Taylor might contest his passage all the way to Simmesport. He made preparations against the incendiary proclivities of the westerners, but he could not be sure that his favored eastern troops would decline to participate in such activities.

Taylor was still hoping for his three divisions to return from Arkansas. He watched helplessly as the Union fleet left. His only hope of defeating or capturing the Union force was to hold them inside Alexandria or to block their retreat at some point to the south. He had inadequate resources to lay siege to the town, but he could observe his opponents' movements. He prepared to meet Banks' column when they retreated, again at a place of his choosing. He watched anxiously, praying for his reinforcements to arrive.

After the dam broke on May 9, Banks had time to prepare for his departure in more detail. He was evidently worried that Smith's "gorillas" might cause problems and make Taylor aware of the army's impending departure. He ordered Brigadier General Richard Arnold, his new chief of cavalry, to place five hundred cavalrymen under "reliable" officers inside the town during the departure to prevent a conflagration.[65] Smith's men were not pleased, with Brigadier General Oliver Gooding overheard to say, "This is just like old Banks."[66]

The first troops left Alexandria at 7 A.M. on May 13. A little more than an hour later, with most of the column still in town, buildings began to burn. Some Union soldiers, and possibly pro-Union residents of the town, had buckets with a mixture of turpentine and camphene (a precursor to napalm) and mops. These men smeared the volatile mixture on buildings and one was reported as saying they were "preparing the place for Hell!"[67] The town turned into an inferno. One man reported that the cavalry officers who were assigned to protect them were actually directing the burning.[68] Even stout pro-Unionists, who had been under the protection of the army until then, saw their homes torched. People whose sons had just enlisted in the Union army were burned out, and they asked for refuge on the boats, knowing that their neighbors would seek retribution.[69] Several members of Banks' staff and the provost guards tried to stop the flames. Explosives were used to try to extinguish the fire, but the sources were too numerous and a wind fanned the conflagration. In three hours the entire center of town had ceased to exist.[70] Banks had not ordered the torching, but he certainly failed to halt it. His ultimate purpose for not burning the town had not been accomplished. The flames could be seen for miles, and Taylor certainly knew the Union forces were on the move.

Banks set his usual order of march, although he allowed the cavalry to screen forward and to the flanks. Next came the Nineteenth Corps, the combined supply train, the Thirteenth Corps, and then Smith's Sixteenth Corps units.[71] The men torched buildings all along the road, and nothing was left useable for the people of the region.[72] Taylor was doing his best

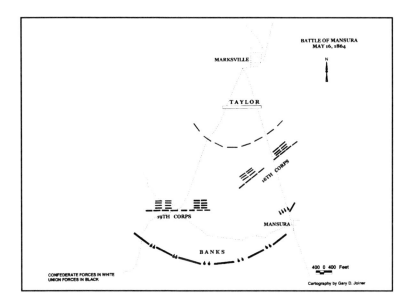

with the forces at his disposal. His cavalry was harassing the column from both front and rear. His men blocked the roads beginning twelve miles south of Alexandria, trying to buy time for reinforcements that never came.

The next day Banks' pioneers cleared the road and spanned Bayou Choctaw with a pontoon bridge. That evening they bivouacked beside the wrecks of the *John Warner*, *Signal*, and *Covington* and saw their mail strewn over the ground.[73] On May 15, the column slowly traversed the Bayou Choctaw Swamp and ascended to the tablelands of the Avoyelles Prairie. The lead elements were attacked several times by Wharton's cavalry. The Nineteenth Corps finally brought enough troops to the open country to push the Rebels back. The Confederates retreated to set up again farther down the road and the head of the column continued until at nightfall they entered the town of Marksville.[74]

On the morning of May 16, Banks found that Taylor had drawn all of his available forces to meet him six miles ahead at the village of Mansura. Taylor used the buildings of the village as his center and placed eight cavalry regiments on his right with nineteen cannon. Polignac and his infantry were on the left with thirteen guns.[75] Also on the left were two regiments of cavalry. About half of the field guns aimed at the federal troops had been taken from them at Mansfield. The Union troops formed line of battle, and an artillery duel ensued. Taylor later said that it was a beautiful sight with the lines of battle being three miles long on prairie land as "smooth as a billiard table."[76]

Both sides recorded the beauty of the scene as regiments marched into order. Cavalry skirted about seeking a place to charge and a myriad of silken flags fluttered in the late spring breezes. The air was filled with glittering accoutrements of war and many diaries and reports reflected the grandeur of the spectacle.[77] The Nineteenth Corps moved forward but Taylor's former-Union guns kept them at bay. A sporadic artillery duel lasted nearly four hours until. Smith's men were brought up from the rear and the entire line moved forward at the pace set by the westerners. Taylor, confronted with eighteen thousand men moving against his six thousand, retreated.[78] There were few casualties, which added to the vivid memories of the diarists.[79]

Banks pushed on to Bayou de Glaise. From there the road led to Moreauville, Yellow Bayou, Simmesport, Old River, and the Atchafalaya. The army was close to safety even though Confederate cavalry was vigorously skirmishing with the rearguard and slowing them down. The Confederates also tried to attack the wagon train, but with little success. When the lead elements arrived at Simmesport, or the charred ruins of where it had been located, they believed the campaign was over. The entire army drew up in and around the former town.[80]

General Smith was tired of Confederate cavalry harassing him while he guarded the tail of the column. He sent Brigadier General Joseph A. Mower back to Yellow Bayou with three brigades to push the Rebels back. Mower crossed the small bayou and pushed on another two miles where he found Wharton's cavalry and Polignac's infantry drawn up in line of battle.[81]

Polignac fired his artillery and then advanced his infantry into Mower. Mower's men pushed them back and then withdrew. He was

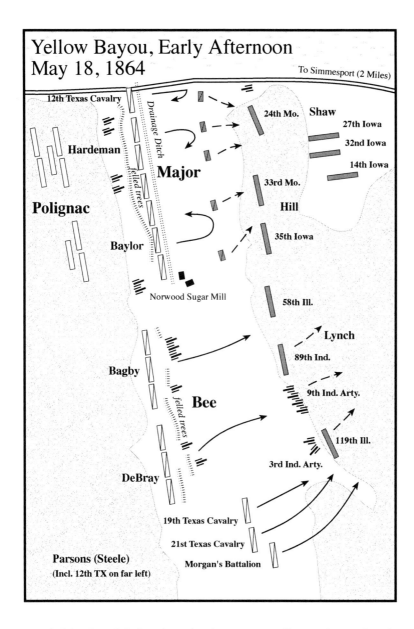

Yellow Bayou, Early Afternoon
May 18, 1864

To Simmesport (2 Miles)

12th Texas Cavalry

Drainage Ditch

24th Mo. Shaw

27th Iowa

32nd Iowa

Hardeman

14th Iowa

felled trees

Major

33rd Mo.

Polignac

Hill

Baylor

35th Iowa

Norwood Sugar Mill

58th Ill.

Lynch

89th Ind.

Bagby

9th Ind. Arty.

Bee

felled trees

119th Ill.

DeBray

3rd Ind. Arty.

19th Texas Cavalry

21st Texas Cavalry

Parsons (Steele)
(Incl. 12th TX on far left)

Morgan's Battalion

worried that he might be advancing into a trap. Polignac advanced again but was repulsed. The fighting moved into a thicket of dry trees, brush corn and cane stubble, which caught fire. The battlefield was blinded by

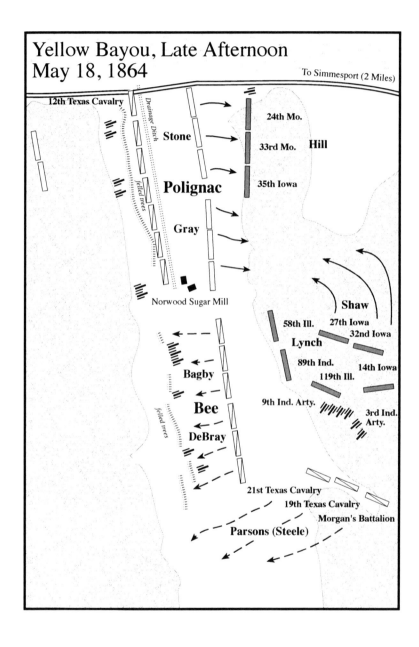

Yellow Bayou, Late Afternoon
May 18, 1864

To Simmesport (2 Miles)

12th Texas Cavalry

Drainage Ditch

felled trees

Stone

24th Mo.

33rd Mo.   Hill

35th Iowa

Polignac

Gray

Norwood Sugar Mill

Shaw

58th Ill.   27th Iowa
             32nd Iowa

Lynch

89th Ind.   14th Iowa

Bagby

119th Ill.

felled trees

9th Ind. Arty.   3rd Ind.
                              Arty.

Bee

DeBray

21st Texas Cavalry

19th Texas Cavalry

Morgan's Battalion

Parsons (Steele)

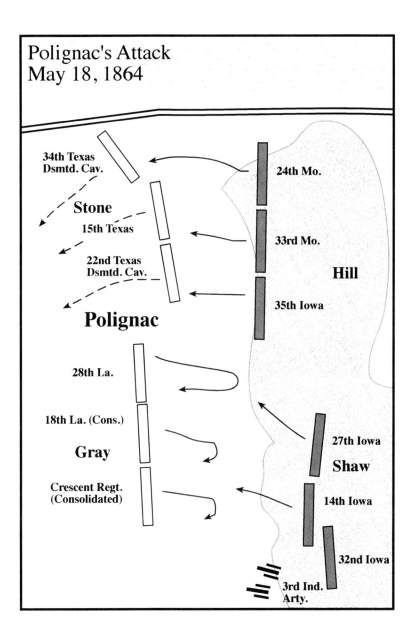

Polignac's Attack
May 18, 1864

34th Texas
Dsmtd. Cav.

Stone

15th Texas

22nd Texas
Dsmtd. Cav.

Polignac

28th La.

18th La. (Cons.)

Gray

Crescent Regt.
(Consolidated)

24th Mo.

33rd Mo.

Hill

35th Iowa

27th Iowa

Shaw

14th Iowa

32nd Iowa

3rd Ind.
Arty.

Colonel Bailey's bridge of boats across the Atchafalaya River. Photograph from an engraving. Image 48750101, John Langdon Ward Magic Lantern Slide Papers, Louisiana and Lower Mississippi Valley Collection, LSU Libraries, Louisiana State University, Baton Rouge.

the thick, acrid smoke. Neither side could successfully maneuver. Hand-to-hand fighting lasted for hours in small pockets.

The Confederate artillery prevented Mower from giving chase. Polignac had about 5,000 men on the field to Mower's 4,500. Polignac lost 608 men killed, wounded, and missing. Mower lost 350.[82] Taylor simply did not have enough men to trap Banks, and the Battle at Yellow Bayou proved it. The Confederate's successes in the campaign ended with another tactical tie and the lack of ability to chase the foe. Mower's men could boast that they were the first in and last out in the campaign and had certainly seen more than their share of the fighting.

As the men of Banks' column came to the landing to leave the Red River Country, they encountered high water, something they had missed during the entire campaign. Pontoon bridges were not useful in the fast-flowing current. The army again faced the possibility of being trapped. It seemed as if the earth itself was on the side of the Confederates. Lieutenant Colonel Joseph Bailey, undoubtedly one of the most resourceful engineering officers in the Union army, made a floating bridge by anchoring the transports to each shore and lashing them together side by side. Using the boats as a roadbed, he put a plank road across them for the supply trains and artillery to cross the deep-channeled Atchafalaya River.[83] The infantry was ferried over in transports making bank-to-bank journeys. The entire force was able to cross on May 19 and 20. After the last man crossed, the transports were unlashed, the anchors were hoisted and there was no way for Taylor to pursue any further.[84] An Iowa soldier wrote, "General Banks looked dejected and worn, and is hooted at by his men."[85]

Canby arrived at Simmesport on May 18 and was waiting for Banks. He informed Banks of the reorganization ordered by Washington. Banks returned to New Orleans and became primarily a political officer, writing reports, and doing nothing that Canby did not approve.[86] That fall he secured a leave of absence to go to Washington and tried to salvage his career.[87] By that time the presidential elections were over and Lincoln had no reason to help him. He was picked to lead the Reconstruction government in Louisiana for the president and that put him in disfavor with the Radical Republicans in Congress.[88]

In December 1864, Congress reconvened the Joint Committee on the Conduct of the War to investigate the Red River Expedition, chaired by Senator Ben Wade.[89] Testimony was given from December 14, 1864 through April 21, 1865. Banks was the first in a long list of witnesses. The Radicals were out for blood, and Banks was an easy target. Banks appears to have tried to answer everything with honesty and integrity. No one could make a case that he had personally gained from the campaign. The Wade Committee published its findings and walked away in disgust. When the committee finished, no direct action was taken against any of the officers. Lincoln sent Banks back to Louisiana to reorganize the government, but before Banks reached New Orleans, the president had been assassinated and Andrew Johnson became president. In June 1865, Banks resigned from the army and returned to Massachusetts.[90]

In Shreveport, Kirby Smith had returned from Arkansas believing that he had saved his department. Taylor could not stand the sight of the commanding general. On June 5, he wrote a letter that blamed Kirby Smith for his [Taylor's] inability to capture the fleet and Banks' army. He asked to be relieved of command.[91] Kirby Smith put Taylor under arrest five days later and sent a message to President Jefferson Davis regarding his actions.[92] The same day, June 10, the Confederate Congress passed a joint resolution praising Taylor.[93] Troops loyal to Taylor almost came to blows with troops loyal to Kirby Smith. Soon after, Taylor was promoted to lieutenant general and given command of the Department of Alabama, Mississippi, and East Louisiana. He surrendered that department at the end of the war.

The campaign that began with such promise ended with nothing substantive to show for the great effort by both the Union army and navy. The Confederates felt cheated as well. Taylor wrote, "I feel bitterly about this [the removal of the three divisions to Arkansas], because my army has been robbed of the just measure of its glory and the country of the most brilliant and complete success of the war."[94]

Union attitudes were almost uniform in their disgust. A reporter for the St. Louis *Daily Missouri Republican* summarized the campaign as "A fit sequel to a scheme, conceived in politics and brought forth in iniquity."[95]

Appendix 1

Orders of Battle for the Red River Campaign during March–May 1864: Operations in Louisiana

CONFEDERATE FORCES

Lieutenant General Edmund Kirby Smith commanding the Army of the Trans-Mississippi
Maj. Gen. Richard Taylor commanding the District of Western Louisiana
Unattached—Second Battalion Louisiana Reserves

First Infantry Division
Major Gen. John G. Walker

First Brigade—Brig. Gen. Thomas N. Waul
      Twelfth Texas Infantry—Col. Overton C. Young
      Eighteenth Texas Infantry—Col. Wilburn H. King
      Twenty-Second Texas Infantry—Col. Richard B. Hubbard
      Thirteenth Texas Cavalry, Dismounted—Col. Anderson F. Crawford

Second Brigade—Brig. Gen. Horace Randal
      Eleventh Texas Infantry—Col. Oran M. Roberts
      Fourteenth Texas Infantry—Col. Edward Clark
      Twenty-Eighth Texas Cavalry, Dismounted—Lt. Col. Eli H. Baxter, Jr.
      Sixth (Gould's) Texas Cavalry Battalion—Lt. Col. Robert S. Gould

Third Brigade—Brig. Gen. William R Scurry
      Third Texas Infantry—Col. Phillip N. Luckett
      Sixteenth Texas Infantry—Col. George Flournoy
      Seventeenth Texas Infantry—Col. Robert T. P. Allen
      Nineteenth Texas Infantry—Col. Richard Waterhouse, Jr.
      Sixteenth Texas Cavalry, Dismounted—Col. William Fitzhugh

First Division Artillery
      Haldeman's Texas Battery—Capt. Horace Haldeman
      Gibson's Battery
      Daniel's Texas Battery—Capt. James M. Daniel

Second Infantry Division
Brig. Gen. Jean Jacque Alfred Alexander Mouton, Brig. Gen. Camille Jules Armand Marie, The Prince de Polignac

First Brigade—Col. Henry Gray
      Eighteenth Louisiana Consolidated Infantry—Col. Leopold L. Armant
      Twenty-Eighth Louisiana Infantry—Maj. Thomas W. Pool
      Consolidated Crescent Regiment—Maj. Thomas W. Pool

Second Brigade—Lt. Col. Robert D. Stone

        Fifteenth Texas Infantry—Lt. Col. Robert D. Stone

        Seventeenth Texas Consolidated Cavalry, Dismounted—Col. James R Taylor

        Twenty-Second Texas Cavalry, Dismounted—Maj. George W. Merrick

        Thirty-First Texas Cavalry, Dismounted—Maj. Frederick J. Malone

        Thirty-Fourth Texas Cavalry, Dismounted—Lt. Col. John H. Caudle

Second Division Artillery

        Cornay's Battery—Captain Florian O. Cornay

        West's Battery—Grosse Tete Flying Artillery—Captain John A. West

Churchill's Division

Brig. Gen. Thomas James Churchill (divided into divisions)

First Division

Gen. James C. Tappan

Tappan's Brigade—Col. H. L. Grinstead

        Nineteenth (Dawson's) and Twenty-Fourth Arkansas Infantry—Col. R G. Shaver

        Thirty-Third/Twenty-Fourth Arkansas Infantry—Col. H. L. Grinstead

Gause's Brigade—Col. Lucien C. Gause

        Twenty-Sixth Arkansas Infantry—Lt. Col. Iverson L. Brooks

        Thirty-Second Arkansas Infantry—Lt. Col. William Hicks

        Thirty-Sixth Arkansas Infantry—Col. James M. Davie

Second Division

Brig. Gen. Mosby M. Parsons

First Brigade—Brig. Gen. John B. Clark, Jr.

        Eighth Missouri Infantry—Col. Charles S. Mitchell

        Ninth Missouri Infantry—Col. Richard H. Musser

Second Brigade—Col. Simon P. Burns

        Tenth Missouri Infantry—Col. William M. Moore

        Eleventh Missouri Infantry—Lt. Col. Thomas H. Murray

        Twelfth Missouri Infantry—Col. William M. Ponder

        Sixteenth Missouri Infantry—Lt. Col. Pleasant W. H. Cumming

        Ninth Missouri Battalion Sharpshooters—Maj. Lebbeus A. Pindall

Artillery—Etter's Arkansas Artillery Battery

Cavalry Corps
Brig Gen. Thomas Jefferson Green (divided into divisions)

Bee's Brigade—Brig. Gen. Hamilton P. Bee
       First Texas Cavalry—Col. Augustus C. Buchel
       Twenty-Sixth Texas Cavalry—Col. Xavier B. Debray
       Terrell's Texas Cavalry—Col. Alexander W. Terrell

Major's Division—Brig. Gen. James P. Major

Lane's Brigade—Col. Walter P. Lane
       First Texas Partisan Rangers—Lt. Col. R P. Crump
       Second Texas Partisan Rangers—Col. Isham Chisum
       Second Regt., Arizona Brigade—Col. George W. Baker
       Third Regt., Arizona Brigade—Lt. Col. George T. Madison

Bagby's Brigade—Col. Arthur P. Bagby
       Fourth Texas Cavalry—Col. William P. Hardeman
       Fifth Texas Cavalry—Maj. Hugh A. McPhaill
       Seventh Texas Cavalry—Lt. Col. Philemon T. Herbert, Jr.
       Thirteenth Texas Cavalry Battalion—Lt. Col. Edward Waller, Jr.
       Thirty-Fifth Texas Cavalry—Col. James B. Likens

Vincent's Brigade—Col. William G. Vincent
       Second Louisiana Cavalry—Maj. Winter O. Breazeale
       Fourth (Seventh) Louisiana Cavalry—Col. Louis Bush

Horse Artillery—Maj. Oliver J. Semmes
       Grosse Tete Flying Artillery Battery
       McMahan's Texas Artillery Battery
       Moseley's Texas Artillery Battery
       Valverde Artillery Battery

UNION FORCES
Major General Nathaniel Prentiss Banks, Commander Department of the Gulf

Thirteenth Army Corps (Detachment)
Brig. Gen. Thomas E. G. Ransom

Third Division—Brig. Gen. Robert A. Cameron

First Brigade—Lt. Col. Aaron M. Flory
       Forty-Sixth Indiana Infantry—Capt. William M. DeHart
       Twenty-Ninth Wisconsin Infantry—Major Bradford Hancock

Second Brigade—Col. William H. Raynor
        Twenty-Fourth Iowa Infantry—Major Edward Wright
        Twenty-Eighth Iowa Infantry—Col. John Connell
        Fifty-Sixth Ohio Infantry—Capt. Maschil Manring Artillery
        First Missouri Light Artillery, Battery A—Lt. Col. Elisha Cole
        Ohio Light Artillery, 2nd Battery—Lt. William H. Harper

Fourth Division—Col. William J. Landram

First Brigade—Col. Frank Emerson
        Seventy-Seventh Illinois Infantry—Lt. Col. Lysander R. Webb
        Sixty-Seventh Indiana Infantry—Major Francis A. Sears
        Nineteenth Kentucky Infantry—Lt. Col. John Cowan
        Twenty-Third Wisconsin Infantry—Major Joseph E. Greene

Second Brigade—Col. Joseph W. Vance.
        130th Illinois Infantry—Major John B. Reid
        48th Ohio Infantry—Lt. Col. Joseph W. Lindsey
        83rd Ohio Infantry—Lt. Col. William H. Baldwin
        96th Ohio Infantry—Lt. Col. Albert H. Brown Artillery
        Indiana Light Artillery, 1st Battery—Capt. Martin Klauss
        Chicago Mercantile Battery—Lt. Pinkney S. Cone

Nineteenth Army Corps
Maj. Gen. William B. Franklin

First Division—Brig. Gen. William H. Emory

First Brigade—Brig. Gen. William Dwight
        29th Maine Infantry—Col. George L. Beal
        114th New York Infantry—Lt. Col. Henry B. Morse
        116th New York Infantry—Col. George M. Love
        153rd New York Infantry—Col. Edwin P. Davis
        161st New York Infantry—Lt. Col. William B. Kinsey

Second Brigade—Brig. Gen. James W. McMillan
        15th Maine Infantry—Col. Isaac Dyer
        160th New York Infantry—Lt. Col. John B. Van Petten
        47th Pennsylvania Infantry—Col. Tilghman H. Good
        13th Maine Infantry—Col. Henry Rust, Jr.

Third Brigade—Col. Lewis Benedict
        30th Maine Infantry—Col. Francis Fessenden
        162nd New York Infantry—Lt. Col. Justus W. Blanchard
        173rd New York Infantry—Col. Lewis M. Peck
        165th New York Infantry—Lt. Col. Gouverneur Carr Artillery

First Delaware Battery—Capt. Benjamin Nields
Battery L, 1st US Artillery—Lt. Franck E. Taylor
First Vermont Battery—George T. Hebard

Cavalry Division
Brig. Gen. Albert L. Lee

First Brigade—Col. Thomas J. Lucas
        Fourteenth New York Cavalry—Major Abraham Bassford
        Sixteenth Indiana Mounted Infantry—Lt. Col. James H. Redfield
        Second Louisiana Mounted Infantry—Maj. Alfred Hodsdon

Third Brigade—Col. Harai Robinson
        First Louisiana Cavalry (US)—Major Algernon S. Badger
        Eighty-Seventh Illinois Mounted Infantry—Lt. Col. John M. Crebs

Fourth Brigade—Col. Nathan A. M. "Goldlace" Dudley
        Second Illinois Cavalry—Major Benjamin F. Marsh, Jr.
        Third Massachusetts Cavalry (Thirty-First Mass. Mounted Infantry)—
        Lt. Col. Lorenzo D. Sargent
        Second New Hampshire Cavalry (Eighth N.H. Mounted Infantry)—Lt. Col. George A. Flanders

Fifth Brigade—Col. Oliver R Gooding
        Eighteenth New York Cavalry, Cos. K & D—Capt. William Davis
        Third Rhode Island Cavalry (detachment)—Major George R Davis
        Second New York Veteran Cavalry (?)—Col. Morgan H. Chrysler

Artillery
        Rawles' Battery (Battery G, 5th US Light Artillery)—Lt. Jacob B. Rawles
        Sixth Missouri Cavalry, Howitzer Battery—Capt. H. H. Rottakan

Sixteenth Army Corps, Army of the Tennessee
Brig. Gen. Andrew Jackson Smith

Also under Smith's command was the Provisional Division of the Seventeenth Corps, and the Mississippi Marine Brigade.

First Division
Second Brigade—Col. Lucius F. Hubbard
        Forty-Seventh Illinois Infantry—Col. John D. McClure
        Fifth Minnesota Infantry—Major John C. Becht
        Eighth Wisconsin Infantry—Lt. Col. John W. Jefferson

Third Brigade—Col. Sylvester G. Hill
        Thirty-Fifth Iowa (non-veterans Eighth & Twelfth Iowa attached)—
        Lt. Col. William B. Keeler
        Thirty-Third Missouri (non-veterans, Eleventh Missouri attached)—Col. William H. Heath

Third Division
Brigadier General Joseph A. Mower

First Brigade—Col. William F. Lynch
        58th Illinois Infantry—Major Thomas Newlan
        119th Illinois Infantry—Col. Thomas J. Kinney
        89th Indiana (non-veterans, 52nd Indiana attached)—Col. C. D. Murray

Second Brigade—Col. William T. Shaw
        Fourteenth Iowa Infantry—Lt. Col. Newbold
        Twenty-Seventh Iowa Infantry—Col. James J. Gilbert
        Thirty-Second Iowa Infantry—Col. John Scott
        Twenty-Fourth Missouri (non-veterans, Twenty-First Missouri attached)
           —Major Robert W. Ryan

Third Brigade—Col. Risdon M. Moore
        49th Illinois Infantry—Thomas W. Morgan
        117th Illinois Infantry—Lt. Col. Jonathan Merriam
        178th New York—Col. Edward Wehler

Artillery
        Third Indiana Battery—Capt. James M. Cockefair
        Ninth Indiana Battery—Capt. George R. Brown

Seventeenth Corps
Detached to Brig. Gen. Andrew Jackson Smith (Sixteenth Corps)

Second (Provisional) Division
Brig. Gen. Thomas Kilby Smith

First Brigade—Col. Jonathan B. Moore
        Forty-First Illinois Infantry—Col. John M. Nale
        Third Iowa Infantry—Lt. Col. James Tullis
        Thirty-Third Wisconsin Infantry—Maj. Horatio H. Virgin

Second Brigade—Col. Lyman M. Ward
        Eighty-First Illinois Infantry—Lt. Col. Andrew W. Rogers
        Ninety-Fifth Illinois Infantry—Col. Thomas W. Humphrey
        Fourteenth Wisconsin Infantry—Capt. Carlos M. G. Mansfield

Artillery
        Fist Missouri Light Artillery, Battery M—Lt. John M. Tiemeyer

Mississippi Marine Brigade
Brig. Gen. A.W. Ellet

Infantry Regiment—Col. Charles R. Ellet
Cavalry Battalion—Maj. James M. Hubbard

Corps d'Afrique—U.S. Colored Troops
First Division

First Brigade—Col. William Dickey
        Seventy-Third Regiment U.S.C.T.—Col. Chauncey J. Bassett, Maj. Hiram E. Perkins
        Seventy-Fifth Regiment U.S.C.T.—Col. Henry W. Fuller
        Eighty-Fourth Regiment U.S.C.T.—Col. James H. Corrin
        Ninety-Second Regiment U.S.C.T.—Col. Henry N. Frisbie, Lt. Col. John C. Chadwick

Engineer Brigade—Col. George D. Robinson
        Ninety-Seventh Regiment U.S.C.T.—Lt. Col. George A. Harmount
        Ninety-Ninth Regiment U.S.C.T.—Lt. Col. Uri B. Pearsall

Garrison Troops holding Alexandria that did not actively participate in the campaign farther north but were sent to Grand Ecore as reserves after the Battles of Mansfield and Pleasant Hill:

19th Army Corps
Maj. Gen. William B. Franklin

Second Division—Brig. Gen. Cuvier Grover

Second Brigade—Col. Edward L. Molineaux
        13th Connecticut Infantry—Col. Charles D. Blinn
        1st Louisiana Infantry—Col. William O. Fiske
        90th New York Infantry (3 companies)— Maj. John C. Smart
        159th New York Infantry—Lt. Col. Edward L. Gaul

Third Brigade—Col. Jacob Sharpe
        38th Massachusetts Infantry—Lt. Col. James P. Richardson
        128th New York Infantry—Col. James Smith
        156th New York Infantry—Capt. James J. Hoyt
        175th New York Infantry—(three companies) Capt. Charles McCarthey

Artillery
        Seventh Massachusetts Battery—Capt. Newman W. Storer
        Twenty-Sixth New York Battery—Capt. George W. Fox
        Battery F, First US Artillery—Lt. Hardman P. Norris
        Battery C, Second US Artillery—Lt. John I. Rodgers

Cavalry
        Third Maryland Cavalry—Col. C. Carroll Tevis

Reinforcements ordered Alexandria from Texas following the battles of Mansfield and Pleasant Hill. They that did not actively participate in the campaign farther north and did not participate in the battles of Mansura or Yellow Bayou:

Thireenth Army Corps
Maj. Gen. John A. McClernand

First Division

Second Brigade—Brig. Gen. Michael K. Lawler
        49th Indiana—Col. James Keigwin
        69th Indiana—Lt. Col. Oran Perry
        34th Iowa—Col. George W. Clark
        22nd Kentucky—Col. George W. Monroe
        16th Ohio—Lt. Col. Philip Kershner
        114th Ohio—Lt. Col. John H. Kelly

Orders of Battle for the Red River Campaign during April–May, 1864 Operations in Arkansas

Confederate Forces

Lieutenant General (later General) Edmund Kirby Smith, Department Commander and Commander of the Army of Arkansas

District of Arkansas—Maj. Gen. Sterling Price

Escort—Fourteenth Missouri Cavalry Battalion—Maj. Robert C. Woods

Fagan's Cavalry Division—Brig. Gen. James F. Fagan

Cabell's Brigade—Brig. Gen. William L. Cabell
        First Arkansas Cavalry—Col James C. Monroe
        Second Arkansas Cavalry—Col. T. J. Morgan
        Fourth Arkansas Cavalry—Col. A. Gordon
        Seventh Arkansas Cavalry—Col John F. Hill
        Trader's Regiment of Arkansas State Troops—Col. W. H. Trader
        Gunter's Arkansas Cavalry Battalion—Lt. Col. T.M. Gunter
        Blocher's Arkansas Battery

Crawford's Brigade—Col. William A. Crawford
        Second Arkansas Cavalry—Capt. O. B. Tebbs
        Crawford's Arkansas Cavalry Regiment—Col. William A. Crawford
        Wright's Arkansas Cavalry Regiment—Col. J. C. Wright
        Poe's Arkansas Cavalry Battalion—Maj. J. T. Poe
        McMurtrey's Arkansas Cavalry Battalion—Maj. E. L. McMurtrey

Dockery's Brigade—Brig. Gen. Thomas P. Dockery
       Eighteenth Arkansas Mounted Infantry
       Nineteenth Arkansas (Dockery's) Mounted Infantry—Lt. Col. H. G. P. Williams
       Twentieth Arkansas Mounted Infantry
       Twelfthth Arkansas Mounted Infantry Battalion (Sharpshooters)

Artillery—
       Hughey's Arkansas Battery—Capt. W. M. Hughey

Marmaduke's Cavalry Division—Brig. Gen. John S. Marmaduke

Greene's Brigade—Col. Colton Greene
       Third Missouri Cavalry—Lt. Col. L. A. Campbell
       Fourth Missouri Cavalry—Lt. Col. William J. Preston
       Eighth Missouri Cavalry—Col. William L. Jeffers
       Tenth Missouri Cavalry—Col. Robert R. Lawther
       Harris' Missouri Battery—Capt. S. S. Harris

Shelby's Brigade—Brig. Gen. Joseph O. Shelby
       First Missouri Battalion Cavalry—Maj. Benjamin Elliot
       Fifth Missouri Cavalry—Col. B. Frank Gordon
       Eleventh Missouri Cavalry—Col. M. W (or V). Smith
       Twelfth Missouri Cavalry—Col. David Shanks
       Hunter's Missouri Regiment—Col. DeWitt C. Hunter
       Collins' Missouri Battery—Capt. Richard A. Collins

Maxey's Cavalry Division—Brig. Gen. Samuel B. Maxey

Gano's Brigade—Col. Charles DeMorse
       Twenty-Ninth Texas Cavalry—Maj. J. A. Carroll
       Thirtieth Texas Cavalry—Lt. Col. N. W. Battle
       Thirty-First Texas Cavalry—Maj. Michael Looscan
       Welch's Texas Company—Lt. Frank M. Gano
       Krumbhaar's Texas Battery—Capt. W. Butler Krumbhaar

Second Indian Brigade—Col. Tandy Walker
       First Choctaw Regiment—Lt. Col. James Riley
       Second Choctaw Regiment—Col. Simpson W. Folsom

First Infantry Division
Brig. Gen. Thomas James Churchill

Tappan's Brigade—Brig. Gen. James C. Tappan
Nineteenth (Dawson's) and Twenty-Fourth Arkansas Infantry—Lt. Col. William R. Hardy
Twenty-Seventh and Thirty-Eighth Arkansas Infantry—Col. R. G. Shaver
Thirty-Third Arkansas Infantry—Col. H. L. Grinstead
Etter's Arkansas Battery—Capt. Chambers B. Etter

Gause's Brigade—Col. Lucien C. Gause
Twenty-Sixth Arkansas Infantry—Lt. Col. Iverson L. Brooks
Thirty-Second Arkansas Infantry—Lt. Col. William Hicks
Thirty-Sixth Arkansas Infantry—Col. James M. Davie
Thirty-Ninth Arkansas Infantry—Col James W. Rogan
Marshall's Arkansas Battery—Capt. John G. Marshall

Hawthorne's Brigade—Brig. Gen. Alexander T. Hawthorne
Thirty-Fourth Arkansas Infantry—Col. William H. Brooks
Thirty-Fifth Arkansas Infantry—Col Henry J. McCord
Thirty-Seventh Arkansas Infantry—Col Samuel S. Bell
Cocke's Arkansas Battery—Col John B. Cocke

Second Division
Brig. Gen. Mosby M. Parsons

First Brigade—Brig. Gen. John B. Clark, Jr.
Eighth Missouri Infantry—Col. Charles S. Mitchell
Ninth Missouri Infantry—Col. Richard H. Musser
Ruffner's Missouri Battery—Capt. Samuel T. Ruffner

Second Brigade—Col. Simon P. Burns
Tenth Missouri Infantry—Col. William M. Moore
Eleventh Missouri Infantry—Lt. Col. Thomas H. Murray
Twelfth Missouri Infantry—Col. William M. Ponder
Sixteenth Missouri Infantry—Lt. Col. Pleasant W. H. Cumming
Ninth Missouri Battalion Sharpshooters—Maj. Lebbeus A. Pindall
Lesueur's Missouri Battery—Capt. A. A. Lesueur

Walker's Texas Division—Maj. Gen. John G. Walker

First Brigade—Brig. Gen. Thomas N. Waul
Twelfth Texas Infantry—Col. Overton C. Young
Eighteenth Texas Infantry—Col. Wilburn H. King
Twenty-Second Texas Infantry—Col. Richard B. Hubbard
Thirteenth Texas Cavalry, Dismounted—Col. Anderson F. Crawford
Haldeman's Texas Battery—Capt. Horace Haldeman

Second Brigade—Brig. Gen. Horace Randal
   Eleventh Texas Infantry—Col. Oran M. Roberts
   Fourteenth Texas Infantry—Col. Edward Clark
   Twenty-Eighth Texas Cavalry, Dismounted—Lt. Col. Eli H. Baxter, Jr.
   Sixth (Gould's) Texas Cavalry Battalion—Lt. Col. Robert S. Gould
   Daniel's Texas Battery—Capt. James M. Daniel

Third Brigade—Brig. Gen. William R Scurry
   Third Texas Infantry—Col. Phillip N. Luckett
   Sixteenth Texas Infantry—Col. George Flournoy
   Seventeenth Texas Infantry—Col. Robert T. P. Allen
   Nineteenth Texas Infantry—Col. Richard Waterhouse, Jr.
   Sixteenth Texas Cavalry, Dismounted—Col. William Fitzhugh

Union Forces

Major Gen. Frederick Steele, Commander, Department of Arkansas and the Army of Arkansas

Headquarters Escort—
   Co. D., Third Illinois Cavalry—Lt. Solomon M. Tabor
   Co. H., Fifteenth Illinois Cavalry—Capt. Thomas J. Beebe

Third Division
Brig. Gen. Frederick Salomon

First Brigade—Brig. Gen. Samuel A. Rice
   Fiftieth Illinois Infantry—Lt. Col. Thomas H. Benton, Jr.
   Twenty-Ninth Iowa Infantry—Col. Thomas H. Benton, Jr.
   Thirty-Third Iowa Infantry—Maj. Hiram D. Gibson
   Ninth Wisconsin Infantry—Col. C.E. Salomon

Second Brigade—Col. William E. McLean
   Forty-Third Indiana Infantry—Maj. Wesley M. Norris
   Thirty-Sixth Iowa Infantry—Col. Charles W. Kittredge
   Seventy-Seventh Ohio Infantry—Col. William B. Mason

Third Brigade—Col. Adolph Engelmann
   Forty-Third Illinois Infantry—Lt. Col. Adolph Dengler
   Fortieth Iowa Infantry—Col. John A. Garrett
   Twenty-Seventh Wisconsin Infantry—Col. Conrad Krez

Artillery—Capt. Gustave Strange
   Battery E, Second Missouri Light Artillery—Lt. Charles Peetz
   Springfield Illinois Light Artillery (Vaughn's Illinois Battery)—Lt. Charles W. Thomas

Company F, Ninth Wisconsin Infantry (Voegele's Wisconsin Battery)—Capt. Martin
Voegele

Frontier Division
Brig. Gen. John M. Thayer

First Brigade—Col. John M. Edwards
　　　　First Arkansas Infantry—Lt. Col. Elhanon H. Searle
　　　　Second Arkansas Infantry (8 cos.)—Maj. Marshall J. Stephenson
　　　　Eighteenth Iowa Infantry—Capt. William M. Duncan
　　　　Second Battery, Indiana Light Artillery—Lt. Hugh Espey

Second Brigade—Col. Charles W. Adams
　　　　First Kansas Colored Infantry—Col. James M. Williams
　　　　Second Kansas Colored Infantry—Col. Samuel J. Crawford
　　　　Twelfth Kansas Infantry—Lt. Col. Josiah E. Hayes
　　　　First Battery, Arkansas Light Artillery—Capt. Denton D. Stark

Third (Cavalry) Brigade—Lt. Col. Owen A. Bassett
　　　　Second Kansas Cavalry—Maj. Julius G. Fisk
　　　　Sixth Kansas Cavalry—Lt. Col. William T. Campbell
　　　　Fourteenth Kansas Cavalry—Lt. Col. John G. Brown

Cavalry Division
Brig. Gen. Eugene A. Carr

　　　　Co. B., Thirteenth Illinois Cavalry—Capt. Adolph Bechand
　　　　Third Iowa Cavalry (Detachment)—Lt. Franz W. Arnim
　　　　First Missouri Cavalry (8 cos.)—Capt. Miles Kehoe
　　　　Second Missouri Cavalry—Capt. William H. Higdon

Third Brigade—Col. Daniel Anderson
　　　　Tenth Illinois Cavalry—Lt. Col. James Stuart
　　　　First Iowa Cavalry—Lt. Col. Joseph W. Caldwell
　　　　Third Missouri Cavalry—Maj. John A. Lennon

Garrison Troops at Pine Bluff—Col. Powell Clayton
　　　　Eighteenth Illinois Infantry—Lt. Col. Samuel B. Marks
　　　　First Indiana Cavalry (8 cos.)—Maj. Julian D. Owens
　　　　Fifth Kansas Cavalry (10 cos.)—Lt. Col. Wilton A. Jenkins
　　　　Seventh Missouri Infantry—Maj. Henry P. Spellman
　　　　Twenty-Eighth Wisconsin Infantry—Lt. Col. Edmund B. Gray

Appendix 2

Mississippi Squadron Vessels Deployed in the Red River Campaign, March–May 1864

Union vessels that participated in the Red River Campaign. The list includes US naval vessels, US Army Quartermaster Corps vessels, and those of the Mississippi Marine Brigade.

Vessel Name	Type	Vessel Name	Type
Benton	Converted Ironclad	Dahlia	Tug
Choctaw	Converted Ironclad	Fern	Tug
Eastport*[1]	Converted Ironclad	Thistle	Tug
Essex	Converted Ironclad	Judge Torrence	Ordnance Boat
Lafayette	Converted Ironclad	Samson	Floating Machine Shop
Carondelet	Ironclad	Alf Cutting	Mississippi Marine Brigade/Tug
Louisville	Ironclad	Autocrat	Mississippi Marine Brigade/Transport
Mound City	Ironclad	Baltic	Mississippi Marine Brigade/Transport
Pittsburg	Ironclad	Cleveland	Mississippi Marine Brigade/Tug
Chillicothe	Ironclad	Diana	Mississippi Marine Brigade/Transport
Neosho	River Monitor	John Raine	Mississippi Marine Brigade/Transport
Osage	River Monitor	Lioness	Mississippi Marine Brigade/Ram
Ozark	River Monitor	Little Rebel	Mississippi Marine Brigade/Gunboat
Black Hawk	Large Tinclad	T. D. Horner	Mississippi Marine Brigade/Transport
Ouachita	Large Tinclad	Woodford*[6]	Mississippi Marine Brigade/Hospital Boat
Lexington	Timberclad	Bell Darlington	Mississippi Marine Brigade/Tug
Argosy	Tinclad/Sternwheeler	Adriatic	US Army QMC Transport Vessel
Avenger	Tinclad/Side-wheeler	Alice Vivian	US Army QMC Transport Vessel
Covington*[2]	Tinclad/Side-wheeler	Any One	US Army QMC Transport Vessel
Fort Hindman	Tinclad/Side-wheeler	Arizona	US Army QMC Transport Vessel
Gazelle	Tinclad/Side-wheeler	Bella Donna	US Army QMC Transport Vessel
Cricket	Tinclad/Stern-wheeler	Belle Creole	US Army QMC Transport Vessel
Forest Rose	Tinclad/Stern-wheeler	Black Hawk	US Army QMC Transport Vessel
Juliet	Tinclad/Stern-wheeler	City Belle*[7]	US Army QMC Transport Vessel
General Bragg	Tinclad-Side-Wheeler	Clara Bell	US Army QMC Transport Vessel
Naiad	Tinclad-Stern-wheeler	Colonel Cowles	US Army QMC Transport Vessel
Nymph	Tinclad-Stern-wheeler	Des Moines	US Army QMC Transport Vessel
Signal*[3]	Tinclad/Stern-wheeler	Diadem	US Army QMC Transport Vessel
Saint Clair	Tinclad/Stern-wheeler	Emerald	US Army QMC Transport Vessel
Tallahatchie	Tinclad/Stern-wheeler	Emma*[8]	US Army QMC Transport Vessel
General Sterling Price	Ram/Armed Supply Vessel	Gillum	US Army QMC Transport Vessel
New National	Mail/Supply/Receiving Vessel	Hamilton	US Army QMC Transport Vessel
General Lyon	Ordnance/Stores, Dispatch Vessel	Hastings*[9]	US Army QMC Transport Vessel
Benefit	River Service Vessel Side-wheeler	Henry Chouteau	US Army QMC Transport Vessel
William H. Brown	River Service Vessel Stern-wheeler	Iberville	US Army QMC Transport Vessel
Champion No. 3*[4]	Tug/Pump boat/Side-wheeler	Ike Davis	US Army QMC Transport Vessel
Champion No. 5*[5]	Tug/Pump boat/Side-wheeler	Illinois	US Army QMC Transport Vessel

Vessel Name	Type	Vessel Name	Type
J. C. Lacy	US Army QMC Transport Vessel	*Pauline*	US Army QMC Transport Vessel
James Battle	US Army QMC Transport Vessel	*Polar Star*	US Army QMC Transport Vessel
Jennie Rogers	US Army QMC Transport Vessel	*Red Chief No. 2*	US Army QMC Transport Vessel
John H. Groesbeck	US Army QMC Transport Vessel	*Rob Roy*	US Army QMC Transport Vessel
John Warner[*10]	US Army QMC Transport Vessel	*Sallie Robinson*	US Army QMC Transport Vessel
Kate Dale	US Army QMC Transport Vessel	*Shreveport*	US Army QMC Transport Vessel
La Crosse[*11]	US Army QMC Transport Vessel	*Shenango*	US Army QMC Transport Vessel
Laurel Hill	US Army QMC Transport Vessel	*Silver Lake No. 2*	US Army QMC Transport Vessel
Liberty	US Army QMC Transport Vessel	*Silver Wave*	US Army QMC Transport Vessel
Little Rebel	US Army QMC Transport Vessel	*Sioux City*	US Army QMC Transport Vessel
Louisiana Belle	US Army QMC Transport Vessel	*South Wester*	US Army QMC Transport Vessel
Luminary	US Army QMC Transport Vessel	*Starlight*	US Army QMC Transport Vessel
Madison	US Army QMC Transport Vessel	*Superior*	US Army QMC Transport Vessel
Mars	US Army QMC Transport Vessel	*Texas*	US Army QMC Transport Vessel
Meteor	US Army QMC Transport Vessel	*Thomas E. Tutt*	US Army QMC Transport Vessel
Mittie Stephens	US Army QMC Transport Vessel	*Universe*	US Army QMC Transport Vessel
Ohio Belle	US Army QMC Transport Vessel	*W. L. Ewing*	US Army QMC Transport Vessel

US Navy	42
Mississippi Marine Brigade	11
US Army QMC	55
Total Vessels	108

* indicates the vessel was lost during the expedition.

1. Sunk April 16, 1864 by Confederate torpedo.
2. Destroyed by Confederate artillery at Dunn's Bayou, twenty miles below Alexandria on May 5, 1864
3. Destroyed by Confederate artillery at Dunn's Bayou, twenty miles below Alexandria on May 5, 1864.
4. Destroyed by Confederate artillery and infantry at mouth of Cane River on April 26, 1864.
5. Destroyed by Confederate artillery and infantry at mouth of Cane River on April 26, 1864.
6. Ran aground and burned at Alexandria prior to March 27, 1864.
7. Captured by Confederate artillery at David's Ferry (Snaggy Point), thirty miles below Alexandria on May 5, 1864.
8. Destroyed by Confederate artillery at David's Ferry, on May 1, 1864.
9. Snagged and lost at Alexandria April 23, 1864.
10. Destroyed by Confederate artillery at Dunn's Bayou, twenty miles below Alexandria on May 4, 1864.
11. Destroyed by Confederate artillery at Egg Bend April 12, 1864.

Appendix 3

Confederate vessels operating on the Red River during the Red River Campaign

1. *Missouri*
2. *Mary T—Cotton II*
3. *Webb*
4. *Osceola*
5. *New Falls City*
6. *Louis D'Or*
7. *Beauregard*
8. *Indian No. 2*
9. *Pauline*
10. *Anna Perrette*
11. *T. D. Hine*
12. *Dixie*
13. *Colonel Terry* (from ORA 34/2, p. 1051)
14. *Countess*
15. *Frolic*
16. *General Quitman* (from ORA 48/2, p. 402)
17. *Lafourche*

Four unnamed submarines, sisters of the *Hunley*, based at Shreveport.

Appendix 4

Red River Campaign Timeline

March 7	• Lead elements of the US Thirteenth and Nineteenth Corps assemble in and near Brashear City (Morgan City); they are five days behind schedule; these troops are to meet the navy in Alexandria on March 17
March 8	• The advance of the column, led by the Cavalry Division of the Nineteenth Corps heads west from Brashear City toward Opelousas
March 10	• US Brigadier General Andrew Jackson Smith of William T. Sherman's command (Thirteenth, Sixteenth, and Seventeenth Corps) leaves Vicksburg aboard transports
March 11	• Evening: Army transports and Mississippi Squadron under Rear Admiral David Dixon Porter rendezvous at mouth of the Red River
March 12	• Combined fleet enters Red River • Simmesport secured as bridgehead
March 13	• Advance units of Mississippi Squadron move up river • Andrew Jackson Smith moves inland to Marksville after taking four unfinished Confederate forts at Yellow Bayou, two miles from Simmesport
March 14	• Admiral Porter clears piling dam and Smith's forces take Fort DeRussy with support from USS *Eastport* • CSA First (Texas) Division under Major General John G. Walker withdraws to Bayou de Glaize
March 15	• Admiral Porter orders USS *Osage* to demand surrender of Alexandria; the town surrenders without firing a shot
March 15–16	• Andrew Jackson Smith's men attempt to destroy Fort DeRussy and USS *Benton* and USS *Essex* pound the fort and fail to destroy it
March 16	• CSA Major General Richard Taylor orders forces to gather west of Alexandria and for all Confederate vessels and army units to evacuate the town • Third Division of Sixteenth Corps under Brigadier General Joseph Mower takes control of Alexandria

	• Admiral Porter enters Alexandria with the fleet minus the USS *Benton* and USS *Essex*
March 16–24	• The fleet and Sherman's men at Alexandria stealing more than three thousand bales of cotton from surrounding area
	• Porter monitors the river falling and does understand why it should not be rising following the spring rains
March 17	• Arkansas: Union Major General Frederick Steele orders Brigadier General John M. Thayer of the Frontier Division to lead a force from Fort Smith to Arkadelphia and link up with him for the drive on Shreveport; Steele, coming from Little Rock, is the senior Union commander in Arkansas; his two columns are to join and draw off Confederate forces against Major General Nathaniel P. Banks
March 18	• CSA Trans-Mississippi Department commander Lieutenant General Edmund Kirby Smith orders a huge transport, the *New Falls City*, to be removed from Coushatta Chute (Bayou Coushatta) and to be taken to the foot of Scopini's Cut Off (near the village of Robson in southern Caddo Parish) and to be wedged across the river to block it
	• A chain forged at a local plantation is being strung across the river upstream from the *New Falls City*
	• Smith also orders a dam (the Hotchkiss Dam) at Tone's Bayou (about two miles south of Louisiana State University–Shreveport on the Port of Shreveport–Bossier property) to be blown up and water diverted from Red River into Bayou Pierre, thus starving the river of water and hopefully trapping the Union fleet
March 21	• CSA Second Louisiana Cavalry Regiment under Col. William Vincent captured at Henderson's Hill near Boyce; the Confederates have no reconnaissance arm
	• Major General Banks, the senior Union army commander leaves Baton Rouge after installing the new governor in office; rather than march with his men, he ascends the river aboard a US Army Quartermaster Vessel, the *Black Hawk*; he has with him, several cotton speculators
March 23	• Arkansas: Steele leaves Little Rock with his column
March 25	• Lead elements of the Nineteenth Corps Cavalry Division encamp outside Alexandria, seven days late; the Union column extends behind the lead units for about twenty-five miles
	• Banks arrives at the wharf in Alexandria late in the day and is thwarted in cotton stealing by the navy
	• Arkansas: Confederate Brigadier General John S. Marmaduke sends out units to find the Union columns; Marmaduke is at Camden
March 26	• The last regiments in Banks' column march into Alexandria
	• About 2,500 African American troops of the *Corps d'Afrique* arrive by steamboat
	• Banks now has 32,500 combat troops in Alexandria
	• Banks orders the Cavalry Division to advance upstream to Grand Ecore, the port of Natchitoches; the column follows
	• Porter leaves about half the fleet at Alexandria because of low water;t he remainder accompanies the army up the river
	• Banks receives a letter from Lieutenant General Ulysses S. Grant informing him that Sherman's ten thousand veterans must be returned no later than April 15 and that Banks is not to enter Texas
	• Arkansas: Steele reaches Arkadelphia; Thayer is not there
March 28	• The last of the army's column leaves Alexandria that morning
	• Banks stays behind to organize elections
March 30	• Cavalry division arrives in Natchitoches; no Confederates are there

April 1
- Banks holds elections in Alexandria
- First US infantry units arrive in Natchitoches
- Banks sends a letter to army Chief of Staff Henry Halleck stating that he would be Shreveport by April 10 and would chase the Confederate army into Texas if needed, ignoring Grant
- Porter anchors his fleet at Grand Ecore, four miles from Natchitoches
- Taylor orders the brigades from the Louisiana and Texas Divisions to meet at Mansfield; he also requests that the Texas Cavalry Corps be released for action in Louisiana and that the Arkansas and Missouri Divisions in southern Arkansas be moved to Shreveport and then Mansfield
- Arkansas: Steele leaves Arkadelphia for Washington, Arkansas, the Confederate provisional capital

April 2
- Banks leaves for Grand Ecore aboard an army transport vessel

April 3
- Banks arrives at Grand Ecore

April 4
- Porter sends a raiding party up stream to Campti where two Confederates are captured
- Banks decides to hold an election in Grand Ecore
- Banks receives bad advice about roads and determines to move his army inland away from the protecting guns of the navy
- Porter and Banks have a conference in which they determine to meet at Springfield Landing (on Smithport Lake in northern DeSoto Parish) on April 10
- Porter pleads to wait until he can perform an armed reconnaissance along the river, but Banks refuses

April 5
- Banks holds elections at Grand Ecore
- The Confederate commander of the District of Texas, Major General John B. Magruder, releases the Texas Cavalry Corps under Brigadier General Tom Green, for operations in Louisiana; the cavalrymen leave camp in Hemphill, Texas, and ride toward Logansport

April 6
- The Union Cavalry Division takes the lead west out of Natchitoches along the old Spanish Royal Road (La Hwy 6); they turn northwest at White's Store (Robeline) and continue north at Crump's Corner (Bellmont) and then head north on the Natchitoches–Shreveport Stagecoach Road (La Hwy 175)
- Green's Texas cavalry reach Keachi where they bivouac for the night
- The Union Cavalry Division beds down at Pleasant Hill (then in southern DeSoto Parish)
- Arkansas: Marmaduke receives reinforcements from the Indian Territory (Oklahoma)

April 7
- Porter selects six gunboats to escort twenty transports upriver for the final push on Shreveport; the river level is too low for his largest vessels
- Green meets Taylor at Mansfield and is ordered to range forward to slow down the Union column
- Taylor picks a large field three miles south of Mansfield to lay his trap for the federal column
- Green blocks the road at Wilson's Farm, about three miles north of Pleasant Hill; a short fight ensues, delaying the Union column
- Green harasses the Union cavalry for another seven miles until the federals stop for the night at Carroll Jones' mill, about half way between Pleasant Hill and Mansfield

April 8
- Green slows the Union column down for about four hours until they reach Honeycutt Hill, three miles south of Mansfield

- Taylor positions his two divisions of infantry across the road in a giant *L* shape and waits for Banks to attack him
- The Union Cavalry Division supported by the small Union Thirteenth Corps prepares a smaller *L* line to respond to the Confederates about noon
- Banks is seven miles behind the forward units; he begins to move forward after reinforcements are requested
- A small division of infantry in the Union Nineteenth Corps is brought up behind the forward line and sets up at Sabine Crossroads (present-day intersection of DeSoto Parish Addison Road and La Hwy 175)
- Another division is brought forward to the ridge south of Chapman's Bayou
- Kirby Smith refuses to allow the Arkansas and Missouri divisions to come to the battlefield before the battle
- At 4 P.M. the Confederates attack
- The wagon train of the Cavalry Division blocks the road from Honeycutt Hill back more than three miles, keeping adequate reinforcements from coming forward and blocking the retreat of the Union forces
- Within an hour and a half the initial Union line is destroyed
- The second Union collapses about 5:30 P.M.
- The third Union line is pushed back across Chapman's Bayou and darkness ends the fighting about 7 P.M.
- Confederate casualties are about one thousand men including eleven field commanders
- Union casualties are about 2,500 including the commander of the Thirteenth Corps and two of the brigade leaders
- Banks leaves the field during the night and withdraws his army to Pleasant Hill
- Arkansas: Steele bridges the Little Missouri River during torrential spring rains

April 9
- At 1:30 A.M. Taylor lays out his plans for the next day's battle
- At dawn Taylor gives chase and catches Banks army at Pleasant Hill
- The battle began at 4 P.M. with the Confederates using Taylor's plan of the night before
- The Arkansas and Missouri divisions attack through the woods on the Confederate right but wheel too soon and enter the battlefield in front of Sherman's men; Taylor did not believe Sherman's men were there, but on the river guarding the fleet; they had always been at the back of the column
- The Louisiana and Texas divisions attack down the road and the battle ended with darkness as the day before, but this time in a tactical tie
- Arkansas: Steele and Thayer join; Thayer's column is low on supplies as is Steele's; Steele sends an empty supply train back for supplies

April 10
- Arkansas: Steele pushes the Confederates back at Prairie d'Ann
- Kirby Smith removes the Texas, Arkansas, and Missouri divisions from Taylor's command, sends them to Shreveport and prepares for operations in Arkansas
- Admiral Porter, with six gunboats and twenty transports reaches what he thinks is the mouth of Loggy Bayou; he is four to five miles north of it, one mile south of Tone's Bayou; his progress is stopped by the *New Falls City*
- A Union cavalry unit finds Porter and tells the army escort of the Seventeenth Corps to return to Grand Ecore, that Banks has met "with a reversal"
- The fleet begins the retreat

April 11
- Arkansas: Confederates abandon Camden and gather at Old Washington

April 12
- Green and 2,500 Texan cavalry attempt to trap the fleet at Blair's Landing (now in southern Red River Parish); Green fights a two-and-a-half-hour battle against the

USS *Osage*, the USS *Lexington*, and a transport; there are few casualties, except Green, who was decapitated by a canister round from the *Osage* in the first use of a periscope in battle
- Banks' column arrives at Grand Ecore after a three-day retreat; Banks begins to fortify the bluffs

April 12–13
- Arkansas: Steele's combined column enters Camden
- Kirby Smith sends the Texas, Arkansas, and Missouri divisions to Arkansas via separate routes; the units are to rendezvous at Calhoun, Arkansas

April 13
- Porter's fleet anchors at Grand Ecore at 1 A.M.

April 16
- The USS *Eastport* is sent down river from Grand Ecore before the fleet; two miles downstream it strikes a mine laid by the CSS *Missouri*, based in Shreveport, before the fleet reached Grand Ecore; efforts to refloat the vessel take several days

April 18
- Arkansas: Marmaduke destroys Steele's supply train at Poison Spring
- Arkansas: Steele receives a message from Banks to join him at Grand Ecore; Steele does not comply because he has no supplies and believes there is no way to get them to the South

April 19
- Arkansas: Kirby Smith arrives at Calhoun, Arkansas with the Arkansas, Texas, and Missouri divisions

April 21
- The Eastport is refloated and begins her trek downstream; efforts to raise the vessel from the shallow river are successful, but the gash in her full proves a problem; she will almost trap the fleet behind her on several occasions as she makes her way downstream and she will travel another forty miles and become wedged in a log jam near the village of Montgomery (in Grant Parish); all efforts to extricate the vessel are in vain
- Banks moves the column away from Grand Ecore and the river at 5 P.M. Andrew Jackson Smith's men torch the buildings of Grand Ecore
- Through the night the column covered twenty miles; they did not torch Natchitoches because Confederate cavalry harasses the rear units
- Banks makes another large tactical error; he moves the column onto Cane River Island, the land between the Cane and Red rivers; he hugs the western road away from the fleet and finds that there are no exits except far the south at Monett's Ferry (Bluff)
- Taylor dispatches cavalry under Brigadier General Hamilton P. Bee to block Monett's Ferry; the Louisiana Division, under the Prince de Polignac, is sent to south to cover any possible crossing north of the ferry; Taylor pleads for the Texas, Arkansas, and Missouri divisions to be returned

April 23
- Bee fails to stop the Union column from exiting Cane River Island; an African American runaway slave leads the Union troops to a ford behind the Confederates and Bee is outflanked; this is the last great chance to capture Banks' column

April 25
- The lead elements of Banks' column enter Alexandria
- Arkansas: A second Union supply train is ambushed at Marks' Mill ending hopes of reinforcements for Steele

April 26
- Arkansas: Steele abandons Camden heading for Little Rock
- Porter decides to destroy the *Eastport* by putting a ton of black powder aboard and detonating it; the fleet loses its most powerful warship

April 27
- Arkansas: Confederate enter the abandoned Camden
- Confederate cavalry and infantry attack the fleet near the mouth of Cane River; Porter loses the *Champion No. 3* and *Champion No. 5*; the *Cricket* and *Juliet* are heavily damaged

	• Porter's fleet limped into the area just above Alexandria in the evening; he finds the river so low that the rocks forming the "Falls" or rapids are clearly visible; his fleet is now trapped in two groups, those above the Falls and those below; his most heavily armed vessels are above the town
April 28	• Porter begins to remove guns from the armor plating from ironclads to lighten the vessels
April 29	• Porter and Banks accept a plan by Lieutenant Colonel Joseph Bailey to construct a dam to raise the water level in the Red River and allow the fleet to pass into the deeper water downstream; construction begins using African American engineering troops of the Corps d'Afrique and Maine troops who were lumbermen
	• Arkansas: Kirby Smith catches Steele's column trying to cross the Saline River at Jenkins' Ferry; most of the Union column had crossed; Smith makes an ill-fated frontal attack reminiscent of Pickett's Charge at Gettysburg in 1863 and wastes large portion of his three divisions; two of the three Texas Division brigade commanders are mortally wounded
	• Arkansas: Steele crosses the river and burns his bridges; Kirby Smith has no pontoon bridges and cannot follow; Steele returns to Little Rock
May 1	• Confederate artillery sinks the transport *Emma* at David's Ferry (near Echo)
May 2–9	• Bailey's dam is constructed; on May 9, the large dam gave way as a result of excess water pressure, the device worked too well; Bailey begins to reconstruct the dam and adds two wing dams a short distance upstream to ease the water pressure on the main dam
May 3	• Arkansas: Smith releases the three divisions for operations with Richard Taylor, but they will return too late to have any effect on fighting in Louisiana
May 4	• Confederate artillery sinks the transport *City Belle* at David's Ferry
May 5	• Confederate artillery sinks the *John Warner*, *Signal*, and *Covington* at Dunn's Bayou
May 10	• The *Lexington*, the monitors *Osage* and *Neosho*, and the ironclads *Mound City*, *Carondelet*, and *Pittsburg* cross the Falls
May 13	• The first troops of Banks' column leave Alexandria at 7 A.M.
	• The *Ozark*, *Louisville*, and Chillicothe cross the Falls
	• Union troops set fire to Alexandria and burn most of the business district and downtown residences
May 15	• The *St. Clair* engages Confederate artillery at Eunice's Bluff below Alexandria
May 16	• Richard Taylor attempts to block the Union column at Marksville; the two armies side step each other and the two forces fight an artillery duel at Mansura
	• Back flow water from the Mississippi River extends up the Red River to near Alexandria and increases the depth to the extent that the Mississippi Squadron steams downstream and out into the great river without difficulty
May 18	• The Confederates make a final attempt to halt the retreat of the Union army at Yellow Bayou, two miles west of Simmesport; they fail to stop the Union column
	• Union Major General E. R. S. Canby arrives at Simmesport and notifies Banks that he has been fired, the command has been reorganized, and that Banks is now working for him in an administrative capacity
May 19–20	• High water almost traps the army, but Bailey again rescues the troops by building a bridge by lashing the army's steamboats together and building a plank road across them; after the last units cross the Atchafalaya River, the steamboats are separated and the Confederates cannot follow; this ends the campaign

Notes

1 Origins of the Red River Campaign

1. Portions of this work have appeared in different forms in Gary D. Joiner, *One Damn Blunder From Beginning to End: The Red River Campaign of 1864* (Lanham, MD: Scholarly Resources, 2003), *Through the Howling Wilderness: The 1864 Red River Campaign and Union Failure in the West* (Knoxville: University of Tennessee Press, 2006), *Mr. Lincoln's Brown Water Navy: The Mississippi Squadron* (Lanham, MD: Scholarly Resources, 2007), and "Fred Steele's Dilemma and Kirby Smith's Quest For Glory," in Mark K. Christ, ed. *The Earth Reeled and Trees Trembled: Civil War Arkansas, 1863–1864* (Little Rock, AK: The Old State House Museum, 2007), 90–105.

2. Grady McWhiney, *Cracker Culture: Celtic Ways in the Old South* (Tuscaloosa: University of Alabama Press, 1988), 1–49.

3. U.S. Army Corps of Engineers, *Red River Index, ARK.-TEX. to Mississippi River, Index of 1990 Mosaics* (U.S. Army Engineer District, Vicksburg Corps of Engineers, 1990). River miles are given in post-Red River Navigation Project miles. In 1864, the Red River was almost twice as long as it became after straightening and channeling works. In Louisiana, counties are called *parishes*.

4. Personal communication with Clifton Cardin, official Bossier Parish historian, November 5, 2001.

5. Maude Hearn O'Pry, *Chronicles of Shreveport and Caddo Parish* (Shreveport, LA: N. P., 1928), 167.

6. John D. Winters, *The Civil War in Louisiana* (Baton Rouge: Louisiana State University Press, 1963), 211; Francis Fearn, ed., *Diary of a Refugee* (New York: N. P., 1910), 29–34.

7. Fearn, *Diary of a Refugee*, 29–34.

8. Perry Snyder, "Shreveport, Louisiana: 1861–1865: From Secession to Surrender," *Louisiana Studies*, 11, no.1, (Spring, 1972): 50–70; Jeffery Prushankin, *A Crisis in Confederate Command: Edmund Kirby Smith, Richard Taylor and the Army of the Trans-Mississippi* (Baton Rouge: Louisiana State University Press, 2005), *passim*.

9. U.S. Congress, *Report on the Joint Committee on the Conduct of the War, 1863–1866*, Vol. 2, *Red River Expedition* (Washington, D.C.: U.S. Government Printing Office [USGPO], 1865), 285.

10. Ibid.

11. A map of the inner defenses of Shreveport by Confederate Major Richard Venable from 1864 titled "Shreveport and Environs" in Jeremy Francis Gilmer papers, Southern Historical Collection, University of North Carolina, Chapel Hill, copy at Louisiana State University in Shreveport, Archives and Special Collections, Noel Memorial Library.

12. U.S. War Department, *War of the Rebellion: The Official Records of the Union and Confederate Armies* (Washington, D.C. 1890–1901) 128 vols. 32, pt. ii: 122. All references to the *O.R.* are to Series I and part i of the specific volume unless otherwise identified. The abbreviation *pt* indicates the part number.

13. Thomas L. Connelly, "Vicksburg: Strategic Point or Propaganda Device?" *Military Affairs* 34 (1970): 49–53.

14. Richard Lowe, *Walker's Texas Division C.S.A.: Greyhounds of the Trans-Mississippi* (Baton Rouge: Louisiana State University Press, 2004), 148–168.

15. *New York Times*, October 30, 1862.
16. Benjamin F. Butler, memorandum dated January 1862 in Edwin M. Stanton Papers, Division of Manuscripts, Library of Congress.
17. Ibid.
18. *De Bow's Review*, 2 (Revised Series, 1866), 419.
19. Frederick L. Olmsted, *A Journey Through Texas or, a Saddle-Trip on the Southwestern Frontier; with a Statistical Appendix.* (New York: Dix, Edwards, and Company, 1857), 140–141, 172–183, 358–360, 414–415, 428–441; Laura W. Roper, "Frederick Law Olmstead and the Western Texas Free-Soil Movement," *American Historical Review*, 56 (1950–1951), 58–64.
20. Butler memorandum dated January 19, 1862, Stanton Papers in the Library of Congress.
21. Ludwell Johnson, *Red River Campaign: Politics and Cotton in the Civil War* (Baltimore, MD: The Johns Hopkins Press, 1958), 20; James G. Hollandsworth, Jr., *Pretense of Glory: The Life of General Nathaniel P. Banks* (Baton Rouge: Louisiana State University Press, 1998), 84–85.
22. *O.R.* 15, 590.
23. *O.R.* Series III, 3: 522; Senate Executive Documents, No. 2, 38th Congress, 2nd session, No. II, 459–460, 470.
24. . *O.R.* Series III, 3: 522; Senate Executive Documents, No. 2, 38th Congress, 2nd session, No. II, 459–460, 470; *O.R.* 26, 673.
25. *O.R.* 26, 287–288.
26. Ibid., 288–297.
27. Nathaniel Banks to his wife, dated September 22, 1863, Banks Papers, Essex Institute, Salem, Massachusetts. Microfilm copy at University of Texas, Austin, Texas; Hollandsworth, *Pretense of Glory*, 138.
28. *O.R.* 26, 292; Richard Taylor, *Destruction and Reconstruction: Personal Experiences in the Civil War* (New York: D. Appleton and Company, 1879), 150; for an excellent examination of the Texas Overland Expedition, see Richard Lowe, *The Texas Overland Expedition of 1863* (Fort Worth: Ryan Place Publishers, 1996), and David C. Edmonds, *Yankee Autumn in Acadiana: A Narrative of the Great Texas Overland Expedition through Southwestern Louisiana October–December 1863* (Lafeyette, LA: Center for Louisiana Studies, 1979).
29. *O.R.* 26, 397.
30. Ibid., 20–21.
31. Fred Harvey Harrington, *Fighting Politician: Major General N. P. Banks* (Philadelphia: University of Pennsylvania Press, 1948), 133.
32. *O.R.* 26, 834–835.
33. Ibid., 683, 807; *O.R.* 34 pt. ii, 267.
34. William T. Sherman, *Memoirs of Gen. W. T. Sherman Written by Himself* (New York: Charles L. Webster & Co., 1892), I, 172–193.
35. *O.R.* 34 pt ii, 46; *JCCW*, 7.
36. Abraham Lincoln, *The Collected Works of Abraham Lincoln*, edited by Roy P. Basler (New Brunswick, NJ: The Abraham Lincoln Association, 1953), 7, 90.
37. C. A. Dana, *Recollections of the Civil War* (New York: D. Appleton and Co., 1898), 103.
38. Bruce Tap, *Over Lincoln's Shoulder: The Committee on the Conduct of the War* (Lawrence: University Press of Kansas, 1998), 214–215.
39. Lincoln, *Collected Works of Lincoln*, 6, 364–365; 7, 1–2, 90; Hollandsworth, *Pretense of Glory*, 205–206.

2 The Confederates Prepare

1. *O.R.* 26, pt. 2, 117, 293–294, 341–312; *O.R.* 34, pt. 2, 819.
2. Taylor, *Destruction and Reconstruction*, 153.
3. Prushankin, *Crisis in Command, passim*. This volume offers a superbly detailed analysis of the difference in command style of the two generals and their tenuous relationship.
4. Gary D. Joiner and Stephen R. James, "Phase I Cultural Resources Investigation: Harrah's Entertainment Project, City of Shreveport, Caddo Parish, Louisiana" unpublished technical report submitted to the Vicksburg District of U.S. Army Corps of Engineers, (1997), 27. Hereafter cited as "Harrah's.
5. *O.R.* 22, pt. 2, 1137–1139; Waldo Moore, "The Defense of Shreveport—The Confederacy's Last Redoubt" in *Military Analysis of the Civil War, An Anthology by the Editors of Military Affairs* (New York: American Military Institute, 1977), 396.
6. Venable Map.
7. Caddo Parish Records, Conveyance Book N, folio 295.
8. Lt. Jonathon Carter to the Directors of the Vicksburg, Shreveport and Texas Railroad, February 28, 1863.
9. Lawrence Estaville, *Confederate Neckties: Louisiana Railroads in the Civil War* (Ruston, LA: McGinty Publications, 1989), 62; U.S. War Department, *Official Records of the Union and Confederate Navies in the War of the Rebellion* (Washington, D.C., 1895–1929), 31 vols., 26, 438–439. Hereafter cited as *O.R.N.*; Mark K. Ragan, *Union and Confederate Submarine Warfare in the Civil War* (Mason City, IA: Savas Beattie, 1999), 288n.
10. *O.R.* 22, pt.2, 781–782.
11. William R. Boggs, *Military Reminiscences of Gen. Wm. R. Boggs, C.S.A.* edited by William K. Boyd (Durham, NC: Trinity College Historical Society, 1913), 57; Prushankin, *Crisis in Command*, 24–29.
12. Ibid.
13. *O.R.* 26, pt. 2, 216–218.
14. Ibid., 322.
15. *O.R.* 34, 574–576; Taylor, *Destruction and Reconstruction*, 148–149.
16. Ibid.; Prushankin, *Crisis in Command*, 29.
17. Johnson, *Red River Campaign*, 91.
18. Taylor, *Destruction and Reconstruction*, 155.
19. Gary D. Joiner and Charles E. Vetter, "Union Naval Expedition on the Red River," *Civil War Regiments*, 4, no. 2: 41.
20. Ibid.
21. David D. Porter, *Naval History of the Civil War* (New York: The Sherman Publishing Company, 1885), 496.
22. Ulysses S. Grant, *Personal Memoirs of U.S. Grant* (New York: Charles L. Webster & Company, 1885), 19.
23. *O.R.* 34, pt. 2, 126.
24. Lavender US Soil Survey map of 1906, the Louisiana State University in Shreveport archives. Hereafter cited as Lavender Map.
25. George W. Shannon, Jr., *Cultural Resources Survey of The Port of Shreveport-Bossier, Caddo and Bossier Parishes, Louisiana, unpublished report for the Caddo/Bossier Port Commission* (1996). Archives of the Division of Archaeology, State of Louisiana, Baton Rouge, Louisiana, 53. Hereafter cited as *Cultural Resources*.

26. W. W. Heartsill, *Fourteen Hundred and 91 Days in the Confederate Army: A Journal Kept by W. W. Heartsill for Four Years, One Month and One Day or Camp Life; Day by Day, of the W. P. Lane Rangers from April 19, 1861 to May 20th, 1865* edited by Bill Irvin Wiley (Wilmington, NC: Broadfoot Publishing Co., 1992), 211 Hereinafter cited as Heartsill, *Fourteen Hundred and 91 Days.*
27. Ibid. Today the Red River has changed course, and this fort sits on the east bank of the stream. The ravages of floods have almost completely destroyed it.
28. Frederick Way, Jr., *Way's Packet Directory, 1848–1994.* Rev. Ed. (Athens: Ohio University Press, 1994), 344.
29. *O.R.* 34, pt. 2, pp. 1056–1057. The *O.R.* transcription incorrectly names the place as "Scopern's."
30. Lavender Map.
31. Unpublished family diary in the collection of James Marston, Shreveport, Louisiana.
32. Venable Map
33. Eric J. Brock, "City Geared for Battle That Never Came" Presence of the Past column *Shreveport Journal Page* Nov. 25, 1995.
34. D. H. Mahan, *Treatise on Field Fortification, Containing Instructions on the Methods of Laying Out, Constructing, Defending and Attacking Entrenchments, With the General Outlines Also of The Arrangement, the Attack and Defense of Permanent Fortifications* (Richmond, VA: West & Johnson, 1863), Plate I. The first edition was printed in 1836.
35. For a full explanation of the locations of fortifications see Brock, "City Geared for Battle That Never Came," the Venable map, and O'Pry, *Chronicles of Shreveport and Caddo Parish.*
36. Gary D. Joiner, "40 Archaeological sites in the Red River Campaign." Unpublished report to the Louisiana State Department of Culture, Recreation and Tourism, Division of Archaeology. 1997.
37. Edwin Bearss and Willie Tunnard, *A Southern Record: The Story of the 3rd Louisiana Infantry, C.S.A.* (Dayton, OH: Morningside Bookshop, 1988), 326.
38. Venable Map.
39. Ibid.
40. *O.R.* 34, 489.
41. Ibid., 494.
42. Ibid., 479, 494; pt. 2, 1027.
43. Ibid., 479.
44. Taylor, *Destruction and Reconstruction,* 154–155.
45. *Atlas to Accompany the Official Records of the Union and Confederate Armies* (Washington, 1891–1895), Plate LII. Hereinafter cited as *O.R. Atlas; O.R.* 34, 599.

3 Union Plans to Take Louisiana

1. Richard B. Irwin, *History of the Nineteenth Army Corps* (New York: G. P. Putnam's Sons, 1892), 56. Hereafter cited as *Nineteenth Corps.*
2. Lawrence Lee Hewitt, *Port Hudson: Confederate Bastion on the Mississippi* (Baton Rouge: Louisiana State University Press, 1987), *passim.*
3. *O.R.* 26, 664, 672–673; Johnson, *Red River Campaign,* 35.
4. Lincoln, *The Collected Works of Abraham Lincoln,* 6: 364.
5. *O.R.* 26, 18–19, 285–312, 783.
6. Ibid., 341, 354, 779.

7. *O.R.* 34, pt. 2, 133.
8. Ibid., 15, 42, 46, 145, 267; *JCCW*, 227; Tap, *Over Lincoln's Shoulder*, 225, 230.
9. Banks Papers, various correspondence from August 20, 1863 through February 1864.
10. *O.R.* 34, pt. 2, 10.
11. *O.R.* 34, pt. 2, 224–225.
12. *O.R.N.* 26, 747–748.
13. Sherman, *Memoirs*, I, 425–426.
14. *O.R.* 32, pt. 3, 289.
15. M. A. DeWolfe Howe, ed., *Home Letters of General Sherman* (New York: Charles Scribner's Sons, 1909), 286–287.
16. *O.R.* 34, 68; pt.2, 545.
17. *O.R.* 34, pt. 2, 481, 494, 496.
18. Stephen E. Ambrose, *Halleck: Lincoln's Chief of Staff* (Baton Rouge: Louisiana State University Press, 1962), 161.
19. *O.R.* 32, pt. 2, 224–225.
20. John Scott, *Story of the Thirty Second Iowa Volunteers*, (Nevada: IA: John Scott, 1896), 136. Hereinafter cited as *32nd Iowa*; Wickham Hoffman, *Camp, Court and Siege, A Narrative of Personal Adventure and Observation during Two Wars 1861–1865, 1870–1871* (New York: Harper and Brothers, 1877), 93. Harrington, *Fighting Politician*, 152–153.
21. Jim Huffstodt, *Hard Dying Men: The Story of General W. H. L. Wallace, General T. E. G. Ransom, and their "Old Eleventh" Illinois Infantry in the American Civil War (1861–1865)* (Bowie, MD: Heritage Books, 1991), 1–23. Huffstodt describes the urban and rural complex nature of this regiment in detail.
22. William R. Brooksher, *War Along the Bayous: The 1864 Red River Campaign in Louisiana*, (Washington, DC: Brassey's, 1998), 50.
23. Harrington, *Fighting Politician*, 152–153.
24. *O.R.* 34, 179–180.
25. Sherman, *Memoirs*, 1, 425–426.
26. *O.R.* 34, pt. 2, 576.
27. Ibid., 616.
28. Ibid., 179, 266.
29. *O.R.* 34, pt. 2, 293.
30. *O.R.N.* 26, 747–748.
31. Robert U. Johnson and Clarence C. Buel, eds. *Battles and Leaders of the Civil War* (Secaucus, NJ: Castle Books, 1986), Vol. 4: 366; Porter, *Naval History*, 494–533, 548–553.
32. *O.R.* 34, 68, 203; Johnson and Buel, eds. *Battles and Leaders*, 4: 350–351.
33. Paul H. Silverstone, *Warships of the Civil War* (Annapolis, MD: Naval Institute Press, 1989), 156.
34. H. B. Sprague, *History of the Thirteenth Infantry Regiment of Connecticut Volunteers* (Hartford, CT: Case, Lockwood & Company, 1867, 186. Hereafter cited as *Thirteenth Connecticut*.
35. *O.R.* 34, 167–168; Johnson and Buel, eds. *Battles and Leaders*, 4, 366.
36. *O.R.* 34, pt. 3, 601.
37. *JCCW*, 154–157; Tap, *Over Lincoln's Shoulder*, 213.
38. Venable Map.
39. *O.R.* 34, pt.2, 638, 707.
40. Ibid., 704.

4 The Union Advances

1. Scott, *32nd Iowa*, 130; Edmund Newsome, *Experience in the War of the Rebellion* (Carbondale, IL: Author, 1880), 111; Walter G. Smith, ed., *Life and Letters of T. Kilby Smith* (New York: G. P. Putnam's Sons, 1898), 356. Hereafter cited as *T. Kilby Smith*.
2. *O.R.* 34, 304.
3. Ibid.
4. *O.R.N.* 25, 787–788.
5. *O.R.* 34, 312; Ezra Warner, *Generals in Blue: Lives of the Union Commanders* (Baton Rouge: Louisiana State University Press, 1992), 338–389.
6. For a thorough examination of Fort DeRussy, its associated defenses, and the actions at the fort, see, Steven M. Mayeux, *Earthen Walls, Iron Men: Fort DeRussy, Louisiana, and the Defense of Red River* (Knoxville: University of Tennessee Press, 2007).
7. *O.R.* 34, 599; Lowe, *Walker's Texas Division*, 170–177.
8. *O.R.* 34, 305.
9. Scott, *32nd Iowa*, 132.
10. Ibid.; *O.R.* 34, 305, 338–339.
11. *O.R.N.* 26, 25.
12. Porter, *Naval History*, 397.
13. *O.R.* 34, 305; Scott, *32nd Iowa*, 131.
14. Johnson and Buel, eds., *Battles and Leaders*, 4: 362.
15. Taylor, *Destruction and Reconstruction*, 156.
16. Ibid.
17. Gary B. Mills, *The Forgotten People: Cane River's Creoles of Color* (Baton Rouge: Louisiana State University Press, 199), 215n.
18. Johnson, *Red River Campaign*, 96; *O.R. Atlas*, Plate LII.
19. Taylor, *Destruction and Reconstruction*, 157.
20. Richard H. Zeitlin, *Old Abe the War Eagle: A True Story of the Civil War and Reconstruction* (Madison: State Historical Society of Wisconsin, 1986), 53.
21. Ibid.; *O.R.* 34, 315–316, 334–335, 463–464, 501; Taylor, *Destruction and Reconstruction*, 157; Joseph P. Blessington, *The Campaigns of Walker's Texas Division* (New York: Lange, Little & Co., 1875; Repr. Austin: State House Press, 1994), 178. Hereafter cited as *Walker's Division*; James K. Ewer, *The Third Massachusetts Cavalry in the War for the Union* (Maplewood, MA: Historical Committee of the Regimental Association, 1903), 137–139. Hereafter cited as *3rd Massachusetts Cavalry*.
22. *JCCW*, 28; Tap, *Over Lincoln's Shoulder*, 213–215.
23. *JCCW*, 28; Tap, *Over Lincoln's Shoulder*, 213–215.
24. Sprague, *Thirteenth Connecticut*, 186.
25. *O.R. Atlas*, Plate LII.
26. Scott Dearman, "Statistical Report of Union Troop Strength at the Battle of Mansfield, Louisiana April 8, 1864." Unpublished report at Mansfield State Historic Site, Mansfield, Louisiana.
27. *JCCW*, 28; Tap, *Over Lincoln's Shoulder*, 213–215.
28. *JCCW*, 28–29.
29. T. H. Bringhurst and Frank Swigart, *History of the Forty-Sixth Regiment Indiana Volunteer Infantry* (Logansport, IN: Wilson Humphreys & Co. Press, 1888), 85–86. Hereafter cited as *46th Indiana*.

30. *O.R. Atlas*, Plate LII.

31. *O.R.* 34, 426–427.

32. Johnson, *Red River Campaign*, 99; Joiner and Vetter, "Union Naval Expedition," 47. There are discrepancies in the spelling of Banks' vessel. Some sources list it as *Blackhawk*, whereas others name it the *Black Hawk*. Even Admiral Porter used them interchangeably.

33. Johnson and Buel, eds. *Battles and Leaders* 4: 366, Porter, *Naval History*, 494–533.

34. Johnson, *Red River Expedition*, 118.

35. *O.R.* 34, 426–427.

36. *JCCW*, 18, 71, 74, 224–225; Tap, *Over Lincoln's Shoulder,* 213–214.

37. *JCCW*, 281–283; Tap, *Over Lincoln's Shoulder,* 213–214.

38. Porter, *Naval History*, 500.

39. Ibid.

40. *O.R.* 34 pt. ii, 1056–1057.

41. Lavender Map.

42. *O.R.* 34 pt. iii, 172.

43. Scott, *32nd* Iowa, 135; Ewer, *3rd Massachusetts Cavalry*, 139; Richard B. Irwin, *Nineteenth Corps*, 294.

44. *O.R.* 34, 428, 445; Bringhurst and Swigart, *46th Indiana*, 86.

45. *JCCW*, 282, 286; Tap, *Over Lincoln's Shoulder,* 213–214.

46. Joiner, *Through the Howling Wilderness*, 73–76.

47. Ewer, *3rd Massachusetts*, 201, 276, 323.

48. *JCCW*, 201, 276, 323.

49. *O.R. Atlas*, Plate LII.

50. *O.R.* 34, 284; *JCCW*, 323; *O.R.N.* 26, 51.

51. Johnson and Buel, eds. *Battles and Leaders*, 4: 363.

52. *O.R.N.* 26, 51; *JCCW*, 201, 323; Newsome, *Experience in the War*, 124.

53. *JCCW*, 32; Tap, *Over Lincoln's Shoulder*, 213–215.

54. Hollandsworth, *Pretense of Glory*, 90–91.

55. *O.R.* 34, 284, 322, 331, 428, 446; *JCCW*, 32, 58.

56. *O.R.* 34, 284, 322, 331, 428, 446; *JCCW*, 32, 58.

57. Irwin, *Nineteenth Army Corps*, 296.

58. Ewer, *3rd* Massachusetts, 142.

59. Taylor, *Destruction and Reconstruction*, 178; Francis R. Lubbock, *Six Decades in Texas* (Austin, TX: Ben C. Jones & Co., 1900), 536.

60. *O.R. Atlas*, Plate LII.

61. *O.R.* 34, 520; Taylor, *Destruction and Reconstruction*, 158.

62. *O.R.* 34, 449; *JCCW*, 185.

63. *JCCW*, 185; Tap, *Over Lincoln's Shoulder*, 214, 225

64. *O.R.*34, 167, 290; pt. iii, 72; *JCCW*, 29, 59–60, 194–195.

65. Ibid.

66. *O.R.* 34, 290.

67. *JCCW*, 32, 61–62, 68; Huffstodt, *Hard Dying Men*, 175–176; Tap, *Over Lincoln's Shoulder*, 214.

68. The hill was named for the family that farmed the ridge and had a homestead on the west side of the road. Personal communication with Scott Dearman, Mansfield State Historic Site, 1 December 2001; John G. Belisle, *History of Sabine Parish Louisiana* (Many, LA: Sabine Banner Press, 1912), 159. Hereafter cited as *Sabine Parish*.

69. Irwin, *Nineteenth Corps*, 299; *O.R.* 34, 291, 456; Taylor, *Destruction and Reconstruction*, 160–161; JCCW, 60–62; Tap, *Over Lincoln's Shoulder*, 214.

5 The Battle of Mansfield

1. The hill was named for the family that farmed the ridge and had a homestead on the west side of the road. John G. Belisle, *Sabine Parish*, 159.
2. Irwin, *Nineteenth Corps*, 299; *O.R.* 34, 291, 456; Taylor, *Destruction and Reconstruction*, 160–61; *JCCW*, 60–62; Tap, *Over Lincoln's Shoulder*, 214.
3. *O.R.* 34, 512–513, 517, 519.
4. Ibid., 522.
5. Prushankin, *Crisis in Command*, 83.
6. Ibid., 528.
7. Johnson, *Red River Campaign*, 129; Prushankin, *Crisis in Command*, 84.
8. Taylor, *Destruction and Reconstruction*, 159.
9. Ibid., 161.
10. Ibid.
11. *O.R.* 34, 526.
12. Map of the Mansfield battlefield dated April 1864 by Major Richard Venable, Jerome Gilmer Papers, Southern Historical Collection, Wilson Library, University of North Carolina, Chapel Hill, North Carolina.
13. Prushankin, *Crisis in Command*, 87–88.
14. *O.R.* 34, 563–564; Taylor, *Destruction and Reconstruction*, 162; Blessington, *Walker's Division*, 185–186.
15. Taylor, *Destruction and Reconstruction*, 162.
16. Ibid.
17. Interview with Scott Dearman, Manager of Mansfield State Historic Site. Diaries and letters at the site indicate large numbers of parolees fought in the battle. October 10, 2009.
18. Taylor, *Destruction and Reconstruction*, 162; O.R. 34, 564.
19. *O.R.* 34, 167, 264, 266; Irwin, *Nineteenth Corps*, 303.
20. Richard Brady Williams, *Chicago's Battery Boys: The Chicago Mercantile Battery in the Civil War's Western Theater* (New York: Savas Beatie, 2005), 233.
21. *O.R.* 34, 464; *JCCW*, 61.
22. *JCCW*, 61; Johnson, *Red River Campaign*, 134.
23. *O.R.* 34, 564.
24. Ibid., 266–267, 295–296, 300–301; Irwin, *Nineteenth Corps*, 304.
25. *O.R.* 34, 564; Mary L. B. Bankston, *Camp-Fire Stories of the Mississippi Valley Campaign* (New Orleans: L. Graham Company, 1914), 152–153; John Dimitry, "Louisiana," in *Confederate Military History*, X (Atlanta: Confederate Publishing Company, 1899), 140–141; Napier Bartlett, "The Trans-Mississippi," *Military Record of Louisiana: Including Biographical and Historical Papers Relating to the Military Organization of the State* (New Orleans: L. Graham and Company, 1875), 13, 42.
26. *O.R.* 34, 266–267, 295–296, 300–301; Irwin, *Nineteenth Corps*, 304.
27. *O.R.* 34, 564.
28. Bartlett, "The Trans-Mississippi," 13.
29. *O.R.* 34, 564.
30. R. B. Scott, *The History of the 67th Regiment Indiana Infantry* (Bedford, IN: Author, 1892), 71–72. Hereafter cited as *67th Indiana*; O.R. 34, 462; Frank M. Flinn,

Campaigning with Banks in Louisiana, '63 and '64, and Sheridan in the Shenandoah Valley in '64 and '65 (Lynn, MA: Thos. P. Nichols, 1887), 108.

31. Scott, *67th Indiana*, 462; Flinn, *Campaigning with Banks*, 108.
32. *O.R.* 34, 266–267, 300–301; T. B. Marshall, *History of the Eighty-Third Ohio Volunteer Infantry, The Greyhound Regiment* (Cincinnati, OH: Eighty-third Ohio Voluntary Infantry Regiment Association, 1913), 134. Hereafter cited as *83rd Ohio.*
33. Marshall, *83rd Ohio*, 134.
34. Jim Huffstodt, *Hard Dying Men*, 177; Williams, *Chicago's Battery Boys*, 233.
35. John A. Bering and Thomas Montgomery, *History of the Forty-Eighth Ohio Veteran Volunteer Infantry* (Hillsboro, OH: Highland News Office, 1880), 132; Belisle, *Sabine Parish*, 161.
36. Huffstodt, *Hard Dying Men*, 177.
37. Ibid., 179; *O.R.* 34, 273–274, 292, 302; Irwin, *Nineteenth Corps*, 304.
38. *O.R.* 34, 274–275.
39. Ibid., 274–275, 292, 301; Irwin, *Nineteenth Corps*, 304.
40. Ewer, *3rd Massachusetts Cavalry*, 156; *O.R.* 34, 273–274.
41. *O.R.* 34, pp. 257, 273–274.
42. L. David Norris, James C. Milligan, and Odie B. Faulk, *William H. Emory: Soldier Scientist* (Tucson: University of Arizona Press, 1998), 228–229.
43. *Philadelphia Press*, April 25, 1864.
44. *O.R.* 34, 273–274; Ewer, *3rd Massachusetts Cavalry*, 149; Scott, *67th Indiana*, 72; Hoffman, *Camp, Court and Siege*, 89; John M. Stanyan, *A History of the Eighth Regiment of New Hampshire Volunteers* (Concord, NH: Ira C. Evans, Printer, 1892), 409.
45. *O.R.* 34, 273–274; Ewer, *3rd Massachusetts Cavalry*, 149. Norris et al., *William H. Emory*, 228.
46. *O.R.* 34, 273–274; medical certificate in the William B. Franklin Papers, Division of Manuscripts, Library of Congress.
47. *O.R.* 34, 273–274; Ewer, *3rd Massachusetts Cavalry*, 149; Scott, *67th Indiana*, 72; Henry M. Shorey, *The Story of the Maine Fifteenth Volunteer Infantry Regiment* (Brighton, ME: Press of the Bridgton News, 1890), 83–84. Hereafter cited as *15th Maine.*
48. *O.R.* 34, 257; Ewer, *3rd Massachusetts Cavalry*, 155; Flinn, *Campaigning with Banks*, 109.
49. *O.R.* 34, 391–392; Harris H. Beecher, *Record of the 114th, New York N.Y.S.V. Where It Went, What It Saw, and What It Did* (Norwich, NY: J. F. Hubbard, Jr., 1866), 311. Hereafter cited as *114th New York.*
50. Belisle, *Sabine Parish*, 163.
51. *O.R.* 34, 392, 421–442, 429, 606–607, 616–617; Taylor, *Destruction and Reconstruction*, 164; Orton S. Clark, *The One Hundred and Sixteenth Regiment of New York Volunteers . . .* (Buffalo: Printing House of Matthews and Warren, 1868), 155–157. Hereinafter cited as *116th New York*; Thomas J. Williams, *An Historical Sketch of the 56th Ohio Volunteer Infantry . . .* (Columbus, OH: The Lawrence Press, 1899), 66. Hereafter cited as *56th Ohio.*
52. Norris et al., *William H. Emory*, 228.
53. *JCCW*, 218; Hoffman, *Camp, Court and Siege*, 91; Pellet, *114th, New York*, 193–194, 202.
54. Sarah A. Dorsey, *Recollections of Henry Watkins Allen* (New York: M. Doolady, 1866), 263.
55. *O.R.* 34, 167, 263–264, 273.

56. Ibid., 263, 421.
57. Taylor, *Destruction and Reconstruction*, 164.
58. Dr. Benjamin A. Fordyce, *Echoes: From the Letters of A Civil War Surgeon*, Lydia P. Hecht, ed. (n.p., 1996), 248.
59. Unpublished casualty lists and reports at Mansfield State Historic Site, Mansfield, Louisiana; Interview with Steve Bounds, Site Manager at Mansfield State Historic Site, Mansfield, Louisiana, September, 15, 2001.
60. *O.R.* 34, 553; Bartlett, "The Trans-Mississippi," 13, 42.
61. General Taylor letter to Major General John Walker, Mansfield, 1:30 [A.M. 9 April 1864] Walker Papers, Southern Historical Collection, Wilson Library, University of North Carolina, Chapel Hill, North Carolina. Hereinafter cited as Walker Letter.

6 The Battle of Pleasant Hill

1. *JCCW*, 77.
2. *O.R.* 34, 392, 422.
3. Scott, *32nd Iowa*, 136–137.
4. Ibid., 136–146.
5. *O.R.* 34, 354.
6. Ibid., 354, 423.
7. Map of the Battle of Pleasant Hill at Mansfield State Historic Site showing the locations of buildings and streets as well as unit dispositions. Map by Col. John Clark, (No. 8) of the Red River Campaign, in the John Clark Collection Cayuga County Museum, Auburn, New York; Venable Map.
8. Pellet, *114th New York*, 193–194; Beecher, *114th New York*, 308; S. F. Benson, "The Battle of Pleasant Hill, Louisiana" in *Annals of Iowa*, 7, (Des Moines,1906), 500; Henry H. Childers, "Reminiscences of the Battle of Pleasant Hill," *Annals of Iowa*, 7, 514–515; *DeSoto Parish History; Sesquicentennial Edition, 1843–1993* (Mansfield, LA: DeSoto Parish Historical Association, 1995),104.
9. Taylor, Walker Letter
10. Blessington, *Walker's Texas Division*, 193.
11. *O.R.* 34, 607.
12. Ibid., 565; Blessington, *Walker's Division*, 194; Hamilton P. Bee, "Battle of Pleasant Hill-An Error Corrected," *Southern Historical Society Papers*, 8 (1880), 184–186.
13. *O.R.* 34, 566, 605.
14. Taylor, *Destruction and Reconstruction*, 166; *O.R.* 34, 566, 605.
15. *O.R.* 34, 566, 605.
16. Ibid., 567.
17. Taylor, *Destruction and Reconstruction*, 167; *O.R.* 34, 602.
18. Taylor, *Destruction and Reconstruction*, 166–169; *O.R.* 34, 567, 608, 617.
19. *O.R.* 34, 567, 608, 617.
20. Taylor, *Destruction and Reconstruction*, 166–169.
21. X. B. Debray, "A Sketch of Debray's Twenty-Sixth Regiment of Texas Cavalry," *Southern Historical Society Papers*, 8 (1885), 158–159.
22. Scott, *32nd Iowa*, 140, 180–183.
23. *O.R.* 34, 430–431; Scott, *32nd Iowa*, 198.
24. *JCCW*, 218.
25. Scott, *32nd Iowa*, 145–147; Taylor, *Destruction and Reconstruction*, 169; *O.R.* 34, 355–356, 361, 363, 366, 369, 423–424.
26. *O.R.* 34, 392–393, 417–418, 423–424.

27. Shorey, *15th Maine*, 85.
28. *O.R.* 34, 341–342, 345–346, 350; Shorey, *15th Maine*, 97.
29. Shorey, *15th Maine*; *O.R.* 34, 317, 328, 350, 373.
30. Taylor, *Destruction and Reconstruction*, 168–169; *O.R.* 34, 605.
31. *O.R.* 34, 309.
32. Johnson, *Red River Expedition*, 163.
33. *JCCW*, 13, 62, 195–196.
34. Ibid., 189.
35. Scott, *32nd Iowa*, 230–235; Hoffman, *Camp, Court and Siege*, 96–97; *O.R.* 34, 309.
36. *O.R.* 34, 309; Scott, *32nd Iowa*, 230–235; Hoffman, *Camp, Court and Siege*, 96–97; Johnson, *Red River Expedition*, 163–164.
37. *O.R.* 34, 309; Scott, *32nd Iowa*, 230–235.
38. Losses calculated from documents at Mansfield State Historic Site, Mansfield, Louisiana.
39. *O.R.* 34, 309; Taylor, *Destruction and Reconstruction*, 167, 171.
40. Ben Van Dyke, "Ben Van Dyke's Escape from the Hospital at Pleasant Hill, Louisiana." Revised by S. F. Benson, *Annals of Iowa* (1906), 524.
41. Shorey, *15th Maine*, 105.
42. Silas T. Grisamore, *The Civil War Reminiscences of Silas T. Grisamore, C.S.A.* Edited by Arthur W. Bergeron, Jr. (Baton Rouge: Louisiana State University Press, 1993), 151. Hereafter cited as *Silas T. Grisamore*; Liz Chrysler, "The Battle of Pleasant Hill-From a Boy's Point of View," *Mansfield Enterprise*, May 17, 1977.
43. Map in the archives of Mansfield State Historic Site, Mansfield, Louisiana.
44. Benson, "The Battle of Pleasant Hill," 503; Shorey, *15th Maine*, 107.
45. Grisamore, *Silas T. Grisamore*, 151; Chrysler, "The Battle of Pleasant Hill-From a Boy's Point of View,"
46. Shorey, *15th Maine*, 107.
47. Benson, "The Battle of Pleasant Hill," 503; Shorey, *15th Maine*, 107; Amos J. Barron, *A History of Pleasant Hill, Louisiana* (N.P., 1969), 4. Barron's work is an unpublished manuscript in the archives of the Mansfield State Historic Site, Mansfield, Louisiana.
48. Heartsill, *Fourteen Hundred and 91 Days*, 211.

7 The Camden Campaign

1. *O.R.* 34, pt. ii, 616.
2. Ibid., 638, 707.
3. Ibid., 704, pt. i, 657, 692.
4. A. F. Sperry, *History of the 33d Iowa Infantry Volunteer Regiment* (Des Moines, IA: Mills and Company, 1866), 61.
5. Ibid.
6. Ibid.
7. Ibid.
8. Ibid.
9. *O.R.* 34, 673.
10. Sperry, *33rd Iowa*, 62–65.
11. Johnson, *The Red River Campaign*, 173.
12. Prushankin, *Crisis in Command*, 114–115.
13. *O.R.* 34, 522.
14. Ibid., 480, 485; Taylor, *Destruction and Reconstruction*, 159.
15. *O.R.* 34, 821.

16. Jerry Ponder, *Major General John S. Marmaduke, C.S.A.* (Mason, TX: Ponder Books, 1999), 134–153; Prushankin, *Crisis in Command*, 115–116.

17. Ibid., 673, 679, 821; pt, iii, 77–78; Sperry, *33rd Iowa*, 66.

18. *O.R.* 34, 821.

19. Ibid., 673, 679; pt. iii, 77–78; Sperry, *33rd Iowa*, 66.

20. *O.R.* 34, 821–822; Sperry, *33rd Iowa*, 66.

21. *O.R.* 34, 821–822.

22. Ibid., 660, 693, 822; pt. iii, 77–78; Sperry, *33rd Iowa*, 67.

23. *O.R.* 34, 660, 823; Sperry, *33rd Iowa*, 67.

24. *O.R.* 34, 552–561.

25. *Ibid.*, 660, 675, 780, 824–825; pt. iii, 77–78.

26. Joiner, *One Damn Blunder*, 45–106, 137–175.

27. Ibid., pt. iii, 77–79.

28. *O.R.* 34, pt. iii, 77–79.

29. Sperry, *33rd Iowa*, 68–72; *O.R.* 34, 675, 687, 780, 824–825.

30. Sperry, *33rd Iowa*, 72; *O.R.* 34, 687, 780, 824–825.

31. *O.R.* 34, 675.

32. *O.R.*.34, 780.

33. Ibid.

34. Johnson, *Red River Campaign*, 180–182.

35. *Ibid.*, 571–572.

36. William Henry King, "A Journal Camp Life as Private Soldier," published as *No Pardons to Ask. nor Apologies to Make*, Gary D. Joiner, Marilyn S. Joiner, and Clifton D. Cardin, eds. (Knoxville: University of Tennessee Press, 2006), 167–174. Hereinafter cited as *No Pardons to Ask.*

37. King, *No Pardons to Ask*, 165.

38. Blessington, *Walker's Texas Division*, 243–244.

39. *O.R.* 34, 486–487, 534, 675, 687; pt. iii, 766.

40. *Ibid.*, 675, 687–688, 695, 781, 825, 838–839.

41. Sperry, *33rd Iowa*, 78–79; *O.R.* 34, pt. iii, 770.

42. Noah Andre Trudeau, *Like Men of War: Black Troops in the Civil War 1862–1865* (Edison, NJ: Castle Books, 2001), 182–200.

43. *O.R.* 34, 661, 668.

44. Williams, *Marmaduke*, 144.

45. *Ibid.*, 848–849.

46. *Ibid.*, 744–745.

47. John M. Harrell, "Arkansas," in Vol. 10 of *Confederate Military History* (Atlanta: Confederate Publishing Company, 1899), 250.

48. *O.R.* 34, 744–745, 791–792, 842, 848.

49. John N. Edwards, *Shelby and His Men: or, The War in the West* (Cincinnati: Miami Printing and Publishing Co., 1867), 276.

50. Harrell, "Arkansas," Vol. 10: 250; Edwards, *Shelby and His Men*, 276.

51. *O.R.* 34, 746.

52. Ibid., 661–662.

53. Ibid., 663.

54. *O.R.* 34, pt. iii, 267–268.

55. *O.R.* 34, 781; Edwin C. Bearss, *Steele's Retreat From Camden & The Battle of Jenkins' Ferry* (Little Rock: Eagle Press of Little Rock, 1966), 49.

56. Bearss, *Steele's Retreat From Camden*, 49.

57. Ibid., 481, 781.
58. Ibid., 781; pt. iii, 267-268; Sperry, *33rd Iowa*, 83.
59. *O.R.* 34, 788.
60. Ibid., 712–713.
61. Ibid.
62. Ibid., 788–789.
63. Ibid.; Daniel E. Sutherland, "1864—'A Strange, Wild Time,'" in Mark K. Christ, *Rugged and Sublime: The Civil War in Arkansas* (Fayettville: University of Arkansas Press, 1994), 118.
64. Ibid., 789, 794, 835–836.
65. Edwards, *Shelby and His Men*, 279; *O.R.* 34, 668.
66. *O.R.* 34, 692, 713–714; Edwards, *Shelby and His Men*, 279
67. *O.R.* 34, 787, 795; Johnson, *Red River Campaign*, 193.
68. *O.R.* 34, 665, 668, 671, 681, 683.
69. Sperry, *33rd Iowa*, 85; O.R. 34, 680.
70. Sperry, *33rd Iowa*, 86–87; *O.R.* 34, 688.
71. *O.R.* 34, 845–846; pt. iii, 794–795, 797–798.
72. *O.R.* 34, 782, 826–827, 829.
73. Ibid., 668–669.
74. Sperry, *33rd Iowa*, 87.
75. *O.R.* 34, 669; Sperry, *33rd Iowa*, 87.
76. *O.R.* 34, 677.
77. Ibid., 782, 799–800.
78. Blessington, *Walker's Division*, 249; Sperry, *33rd Iowa*, 90–91; *O.R.* 34, 782, 800, 802, 809, 815, 817; Harrell, "Arkansas," Vol. 10: 265.
79. *O.R.* 34, 801–802, 829–830.
80. Ibid., 697, 725, 808.
81. Ibid., 556–557, 758, 800, 802–807, 812–813
82. Ibid., 556–557, 677, 725–726, 817; *Compte de Paris [Louis Philippe Albert d'Orléans], History of the Civil War in America*, 4 (Philadelphia: Porter and Coates, 1875–1888), 557.
83. *O.R.* 34, 668, 670, 677, 690.
84. Sperry, *33rd Iowa*, 97, Johnson, *Red River Expedition*, 201–202.
85. Sperry, *33rd Iowa*, 96–98; *O.R.* 34, 393–394.
86. Ibid.
87. Edwards, *Shelby and His Men*, 297; *O.R.* 34, 557, 787–788, 801, 812, 815.
88. *O.R.* 34, 691, 758.
89. Ibid., 770–771, 779–780.
90. Ibid., 684.
91. Johnson, *Red River Campaign*, 203–204.
92. Blessington, *Walker's Division*, 254–260.
93. Ibid., 260; *O.R.* 34, 482.

8 The Navy

1. Silverstone, *Warships of the Civil War Navies*, 149. *O.R.N.* 26, 51, 59–60; *JCCW*, 275–276; Johnson and Buel, eds., *Battles and Leaders*, 4, 366; H. Allen Gosnell, *Guns on the Western Waters: The Story of River Gunboats in the Civil War* (Baton Rouge: Louisiana State University Press, 1949), 15. Hereafter cited as *Guns on the*

Western Waters; Francis T. Miller ed., *The Photographic History of the Civil* War (New York: Review of Reviews Company, 1911), V, 145.

2. Silverstone, *Civil War Navies*, 153.
3. Ibid., 158–159.
4. Ibid., 168.
5. Ibid., 170.
6. Ibid., 183.
7. *O.R.* 34, 168, 179–180.
8. The similarity between the two names confused army and naval officers writing official reports, newspaper reporters covering the campaign, and historians chronicling the campaign. This led to many false reports of Admiral Porter's flagship engaged in actions where it never sailed. Even the Library of Congress and the National Archives have photographs and reports in which the two vessels were interchanged.
9. *O.R.* 34, 168, 179–180.
10. *O.R.N.* 26, 60.
11. *O.R.* 34, 380.
12. *O.R. Atlas*, Plate LII; LaTourette Map (c. 1850). National Archives and Records Administration, Washington, D.C., Records Group 77, folio M72.
13. *O.R.* 34, pt. iii, 98–99; *O.R.N.* 26, 51, 60, 789; *JCCW*, 203.
14. *O.R.* 34, 168, 179–180.
15. Robert L. Kerby, *Kirby Smith's Confederacy: The Trans-Mississippi South, 1863–1865* (Tuscaloosa: University of Alabama Press, 1972), 309; Abstract log of USS *Chillicothe*, March 7, 1864–8 June 8, 1864; *O.R.N.* 26, 777–778.
16. *O.R.* 34, 381.
17. *O.R.N.* 26, 778, 781, 789; *O.R.* 34, 633.
18. *O.R.* 26, 778, 781, 789; *O.R.* 34, 633.
19. Abstract log of USS *Lexington*, March 1, 1864–June 28, 1864, *O.R.N.* 26, 789.
20. Richard Taylor, Walker Letter; *O.R.* 34, 570–571; Anne J. Bailey, "Chasing Banks Out of Louisiana: Parsons' Texas Cavalry in the Red River Campaign," *Civil War Regiments*, 2, no.3: 219.
21. Porter, *Naval History*, 512.
22. Thomas O. Selfridge, *What Finer Tradition: The Memoirs of Thomas O. Selfridge, Jr., Rear Admiral U.S.N.* (Columbia: University of South Carolina Press, 1987), 102; *O.R.N.,* 26, 49.
23. Porter, *Naval History*, 512–513.
24. Selfridge, *What Finer Tradition*, 102.
25. Ibid.
26. *O.R.N.* 26, 49, 55; *O.R.* 34, 172–204, 571, 633.
27. *O.R.* 34, 382.
28. Ibid.
29. Pellet, *114th New York*, 222.
30. *O.R.* 34, 190.
31. Ibid., 505; *O.R.N.* 26, 62.
32. *O.R.N.* 26, 62.
33. Ibid., 78.
34. Ibid., 72–77.
35. Ibid., 74–75, 167, 169, 781–782, 786.

36. Ibid., 75, 81, 83.
37. Ibid., 26, 76; Taylor, *Destruction and Reconstruction*, 218.
38. Porter, *Naval History*, 523–524. Although prone to epic bouts of self-aggrandizement, Admiral Porter's actions were noted by fellow officers.
39. Ibid., 524.
40. *O.R.* 34, 168, 443; pt. iii, 294, 296.
41. Taylor, *Destruction and Reconstruction*, 186; *O.R.N.* 26, 102; *O.R.* 34, 585.
42. Taylor, *Destruction and Reconstruction*, 186.
43. Ibid.; *O.R.N.* 26, 102.
44. *O.R.* 34, 475; Taylor, *Destruction and Reconstruction*, 186.
45. Williams, *56th Ohio*, 73.
46. Ibid.
47. *O.R.N.* 26, 113, 117–118; Williams, *56th Ohio*, 74–78.
48. Ibid.
49. Williams, *56th Ohio*, 74–78; *O.R.N.* 26, 114, 118–119, 134.
50. *O.R.N.* 26, 114, 119, 123, 134; Taylor, *Destruction and Reconstruction*, 185–186; *O.R.* 34, 442, 475, 621, 623.
51. *O.R.N.* 26, 94; *O.R.* 34, pt. iii, 316; Silverstone, *Warships of the Civil War Navies*, 151–153. The actual depth of the keel was six feet on *Cairo* or River Cities class ironclads.
52. *O.R.N.* 26, 94; *O.R.* 34, pt. iii, 316.
53. *JCCW*, 15; Johnson and Buel, eds., *Battles and Leaders*, 4: 358; *O.R.* 34, 402–403.
54. *JCCW*, 15; Tap, *Over Lincoln's Shoulder*, 213–214.
55. *O.R.* 34, 403; pt. iii, 333, 391.
56. Surgeon's certificate and attached correspondence, 30 April 1864, Franklin Papers.
57. *O.R.* 34, 403; pt. iii, 333, 391.
58. E. Cort Williams, "Recollections of the Red River Expedition," *Papers Read before the Ohio Commandery of the Military Order of the Loyal Legion* (Cincinnati: Ohio Commandery of the Military Order of the Loyal Legion, 1888), II: 84. Hereafter cited as *Ohio Commandery*.
59. *O.R.* 34, 403, Johnson and Buel, eds., *Battles and Leaders*, 4: 358.
60. *O.R.N.* 26, 130–31.
61. Ibid.
62. Ibid., 132; *O.R.* 34, 405; Hollandsworth, *Pretense of Glory*, 91.
63. *O.R.* 34, 209, 254; *O.R.N.* 26, 131.
64. Ibid.
65. Porter, *Naval History*, 526.
66. *O.R.* 34, 68, 443, pt. iii, 294, 296.
67. *O.R.N.* 26, 136.
68. Ibid., 132, 149; *O.R.* 34, 255; *JCCW*, 84; Williams, *Ohio Commandery*, 115.
69. *O.R.N.* 26, 132, 149; *O.R.* 34, 255; *JCCW*, 84; Williams, *Ohio Commandery*, 115.
70. *O.R.N.* 26, 132, 149; *O.R.* 34, 255; Johnson and Buel, eds., *Battles and Leaders*, 4: 373.
71. *O.R. Atlas* Plate LIII.
72. For a thorough treatment of the dam, see, Michael C. Robinson, *Gunboats, Low Water, and Yankee Ingenuity: A History of Bailey's Dam* (Baton Rouge: FPHC, 1991).
73. David Dixon Porter letter to his mother dated May 18, 1864, David D. Porter Papers, Division of Manuscripts, Library of Congress; *O.R.N.* 26, 130–135.

9 Union Retreat

1.   John Homans, "The Red River Expedition," in *The Mississippi Valley, Tennessee, Georgia, Alabama, 1861–1864* (Boston: The Military History Society of Massachusetts, 1910) viii; *Papers of the Military Historical Society of Massachusetts* 13 vols. (Boston: The Military Historical Society of Massachusetts, 1895–1913), 1910: 85–86.
2.   Hoffman, *Camp, Court and Siege*, 97; Sprague, *Thirteenth Connecticut*, 190; Edwin B. Lufkin, *History of the Thirteenth Maine Regiment, From Its Organization in 1861 to Its Muster-Out in 1865* (Brighton, ME: H. A. Shorey and Son, 1898), 87. Hereafter cited as *Thirteenth Maine*; George W. Powers, *The Story of the Thirty Eighth Regiment of Massachusetts Volunteers* (Cambridge, MA: Dakin and Metcalf, 1866), 133. Hereafter cited as *38th Massachusetts*.
3.   Map of Grand Ecore Defenses (Union) dated April, 1864, Archives of Jackson Barracks (Louisiana National Guard), New Orleans, Louisiana.
4.   *O.R.* 34, 186.
5.   *O.R.* 34, pt. iii, 128, 592.
6.   Ibid.
7.   *O.R.* 34, 185, 187–188.
8.   *O.R.* 34, pt. iii, 24; *O.R.* 32, pt. iii, 242.
9.   *O.R.* 34, pt. iii, 175, 265–266.
10.   Irwin, *Nineteenth Corps*, 327; Scott, *32nd Iowa*, 230.
11.   *O.R.* 34, pt. iii, 211, 294, 259.
12.   *JCCW*, 17.
13.   Ibid., 193.
14.   *O.R. Atlas*, Plate LII.
15.   *O.R.* 34, 310, 428; pt. iii, 222, 244; Irwin, *Nineteenth Corps*, 328; Sprague, *Thirteenth Connecticut*, 192.
16.   Powers, *38th Massachusetts*, 136–137; Sprague, *Thirteenth Connecticut*, 192; Lubbock, *Six Decades in Texas*, 539.
17.   *O.R.* 34, 310, 428, pt. iii, 222, 244; Irwin, *Nineteenth Corps*, 328; Sprague, *Thirteenth Connecticut*, 192.
18.   *O.R.* 34, 190.
19.   Sprague, *Thirteenth Connecticut*, 193; D.H . Hanaburgh, *History of the One Hundred and Twenty-eighth Regiment, New York Volunteers* (Pokeepsie [sic], NY: Press of the Enterprise Publishing Company, 1894), 103. Hereafter cited as *128th New York*; Williams, *56th Ohio Volunteer Infantry*, 87–88; Lufkin, *Thirteenth Maine*, 87–88.
20.   Lubbock, *Six Decades in Texas*, 540; Pellet, *114th New York*, 229; *O.R.* 34, 581.
21.   *O.R.* 34, 262, 394–395, 460.
22.   Ibid.; Ewer, *3rd Massachusetts Cavalry*, 164.
23.   *O.R.* 34, 580; Taylor, *Destruction and Reconstruction*, 180.
24.   Ibid.
25.   *JCCW*, 15, 34–35.
26.   *O.R.* 34, 262, 460.
27.   Sprague, *Thirteenth Connecticut*, 195; Woods, *96th Ohio*, 74.
28.   *O.R.* 34, 262.
29.   Sprague, *Thirteenth Connecticut*, 195–196.
30.   Ibid., 196–197; *O.R.* 34, 262, 275, 434, 613.
31.   *O.R.* 34, 619.

32. Ibid., 434; Sprague, *Thirteenth Connecticut*, 198–200.
33. *O.R.* 34, 396, 407, 620.
34. Ibid., 611.
35. Lubbock, *Six Decades in Texas*, 539.
36. Clark, *116th New York*, 170; Ewer, *3rd Massachusetts Cavalry*, 166.
37. *O.R.* 34, 63, 580; Ewer, *3rd Massachusetts Cavalry*, 166; Lubbock, *Six Decades in Texas*, 539; Sprague, *Thirteenth Connecticut*, 201.
38. *O.R.* 34, 190, 432–435, 580, 611.
39. Taylor, *Destruction and Reconstruction*, 152.
40. *O.R.* 34, 580, 611–615; Taylor, *Destruction and Reconstruction*, 152.
41. Sprague, *Thirteenth Connecticut*, 201.
42. Ibid.; Ewer, *3rd Massachusetts Cavalry*, 166.
43. *O.R.* 34, pt. iii, 307.
44. *O.R.* 34, 211, 220, 221, 235, 244; pt. iii, 252–253; *O.R.* 32, pt. iii, 407, 420, 422, 437.
45. *O.R.* 34, 11.
46. Ibid., 206.
47. Ibid., 110–11.
48. *O.R.* 34, pt. iii, 190–192.
49. Ibid., 211, 220–221, 235, 244.
50. Ibid.
51. Ibid.
52. Ibid., 252–253.
53. Ibid.
54. Ibid., 278–279.
55. *O.R.N.* 26, 50–54.
56. *O.R.* 34, 181–185; pt. iii, 278–279.
57. *O.R.* 34, pt. iii, 279, 293–294, 306–307.
58. *O.R.* 34, 474.
59. *O.R.* 35, pt. iii, 331–332, 357.
60. Ibid.
61. Ibid., 357–358.
62. Ibid., 409–410.
63. Ibid., 491.
64. Ibid.
65. *O.R.* 34, pt. iii, 521.
66. *Official Report to the Conduct of Federal Troops in Western Louisiana, during the Invasions of 1863 and 1864, Compiled from Sworn Testimony under Direction of Governor Henry Watkins Allen* (Shreveport, LA: Shreveport News Printing Establishment, John Dickinson prop., 1865), 72–73, 99. Hereafter cited as *Report on the Conduct of Federal Troops.*
67. G. P. Whittington, "Rapides Parish, Louisiana—A History," *Louisiana Historical Quarterly*, 18 (1935), 26–28.
68. Ibid.
69. Ibid., 28–30.
70. *JCCW*, 335; Allen, *Report on the Conduct of Federal Troops*, 79; Whittington, "Rapides Parish," 26–28, 31–32, 37.
71. *O.R.* 34, pt. iii, 517, 558–559, 568.
72. Ibid.; Bringhurst and Swigart, *46th, Indiana*, 93.
73. Sprague, *Thirteenth Connecticut*, 207; Beecher, *114th New York*, 347–348.

74. *O.R.* 34, 277, 592–593, 623; Sprague, *Thirteenth Connecticut*, 209–210.

75. *O.R.* 34, 593.

76. Ibid.

77. Scott, *32nd Iowa*, 275; Sprague, *Thirteenth Connecticut*, 212; Ewer, *3rd Massachusetts Cavalry*, 181; Pellet, *114th New York*, 234; Bryner, *47th Illinois*, 114–115; Hanaburgh, *128th New York*, 114, Lufkin, *Thirteenth Maine*, 92; Clark, *116th New York*, 179–180; Shorey, *15th Maine*, 119; Powers, *38th Massachusetts*, 147–148; Beecher, *114th New York*, 349–351; *O.R.* 34, 425.

78. *O.R.* 34, 325, 593; pt. iii, 616; Sprague, *Thirteenth Connecticut*, 212–213; Lubbock, *Six Decades in Texas*, 542–543.

79. Scott, *32nd Iowa*, 275.

80. *O.R.* 34, 443–444; Scott, *32nd Iowa*, 276; Beecher, *114th New York*, 353–354.

81. Taylor, *Destruction and Reconstruction*, 191.

82. *O.R.* 34, 304, 320, 329, 337, 347–348, 357, 364, 367, 370, 467, 594, 624, 631; Taylor, *Destruction and Reconstruction*, 191; Scott, *32nd Iowa*, 259, 277.

83. Johnson and Buel, eds., *Battles and Leaders*, 4: 60.

84. *O.R.* 34, pt. iii, 644; Jones, *22nd Iowa*, 69.

85. Jones, *22nd Iowa*, 69.

86. Irwin *Nineteenth Corps*, 347–348.

87. Harrington, *Fighting Politician*, 163–164.

88. Ibid., 164; Lincoln, *Collected Works of Lincoln*, 8: 121. n.

89. *JCCW*, iii.

90. Harrington, *Fighting Politician*, 167–169.

91. *O.R.* 34, 546–548.

92. Ibid., 540–548.

93. Ibid., 597.

94. *O.R.* 34, 594; Johnson and Buel, eds., *Battles and Leaders*, 4: 360–361.

95. St. Louis *Daily Missouri Republican*, June 10, 1864.

Selected Bibliography

Primary Sources

Banks, Nathaniel Prentiss. Nathaniel Banks to his wife, dated September 22, 1863, Banks Papers, Essex Institute, Salem, Massachusetts. Microfilm copy at University of Texas, Austin, Texas.

Bankston, Mary L. B. *Camp-Fire Stories of the Mississippi Valley Campaign.* New Orleans, Louisiana: L. Graham Company, 1914.

Bartlett, Napier. *Military Record of Louisiana: Including Biographical and Historical Papers Relating to the Military Organization of the State.* New Orleans. L. Graham and Co. 1875.

Bearss, Edwin C. and Willy H. Tunnard. *A Southern Record: The Story of the 3rd Louisiana Infantry, C.S.A.* Dayton, Ohio: Morningside, 1988.

Bee, Hamilton P. Battle of Pleasant Hill—An Error Corrected. *Southern Historical Society Papers,* viii (1880): 184–186.

Beecher, Harris H. *Record of the 114th New York N.Y.S.V. Where It Went, What It Saw, and What It Did.* Norwich, New York: J. F. Hubbard, Jr., 1866.

Belisle, John G. *History of Sabine Parish, Louisiana.* Many, Louisiana: Sabine Banner Press, 1912.

Benson, Solon F. The Battle of Pleasant Hill. *Annals of Iowa.* Des Moines, Iowa: Henry H. English, 1906.

Bering, John A. *History of the Forty Eighth Ohio Veteran Volunteer Infantry Giving a Complete Account of the Regiment.* Hillsboro, Ohio: N. P., 1880.

————. Reminiscences of a Federal Prisoner. *Publications of the Arkansas Historical Association,* Vol. ii, Hillsboro, Ohio: N.P., (1908): 372–378.

Blessington, J. P. *The Campaigns of Walker's Texas Division.* Austin: State House Press, 1994.

Boggs, William R. *Military Reminiscences of Gen. Wm. R. Boggs, C.S.A.* Durham, North Carolina: The Seeman Printery, 1913.

Bringhurst, T. H. and Frank Swigart. *History of the Forty-Sixth Regiment Indiana Volunteer Infantry.* Logansport, Indiana: Wilson Humphreys and Co. Press, 1888.

Butler, Benjamin F. memorandum dated January 19, 1862 in Edwin M. Stanton Papers, Division of Manuscripts, Library of Congress.

Caddo Parish [Louisiana] Records, Conveyance Book N, folio 295.

Carter, Jonathon. Jonathon Carter to the Directors of the Vicksburg, Shreveport and Texas Railroad. Shreveport, Louisiana, February 28, 1863.

Childers, Henry H. Reminiscences of the Battle of Pleasant Hill. *Annals of Iowa.* Des Moines: Henry H. English, 1906.

Clark, Orton S. *The One Hundred and Sixteenth Regiment of New York Volunteers.* Buffalo, New York: Printing House of Matthews and Warren, 1868.

Compte de Paris [Louis Philippe Albert d'Orléans]. *History of the Civil War in America,* 4. Philadelphia, Pennsylvania: Porter and Coates, 1875–1888.

Dearman, Scott. "Statistical Report of Union Troop Strength at the Battle of Mansfield, Louisiana April 8, 1864." Unpublished report at Mansfield State Historic Site, Mansfield, Louisiana.

Dana, Charles A. *Recollections of the Civil War.* New York: D. Appleton and Co., 1898.

Debray, Xavier Blanchard. *A Sketch of the History of Debray's (26th) Regiment of Texas Cavalry.* Austin: Eugene von Boeckmann, 1884; Waco: Village Press, 1961.

————. A Sketch of Debray's Twenty-Sixth Regiment of Texas Cavalry. *Southern Historical Society Papers* Vol. XIII (1885): 153–165.

De Bow's Review, 2 (Revised Series, 1866).

Dimitry, John. "Louisiana" in *Confederate Military History*, X. Atlanta, Georgia: (Confederate Publishing Company, 1899.

Dorsey, Sarah H. *Recollections of Henry Watkins Allen, Brigadier General Confederate State Army, Ex-Governor of Louisiana.* New York: M. Doolady, 1866.

Edwards, John N. *Shelby and His Men: or, The War in the West.* Cincinnati: Miami Printing and Publishing Company, Print, 1867.

Ewer, James K. *The Third Massachusetts Cavalry in the War for the Union.* Maplewood Massachusetts: Historical Committee of the Regimental Association, 1903.

Fearn, Francis, ed. *Diary of a Refugee.* New York: N.P.: 1910.

Flinn, Frank M. *Campaigning With Banks in Louisiana in '63 and '64 and With Sheridan in the Shenandoah Valley in '64 and '65.* Lynn, Massachusetts: Thomas. P. Nichols, 1887.

Fordyce, Dr. Benjamin A. *Dr. Benjamin A. Fordyce Echoes: From the Letters of A Civil War Surgeon.* Edited by Lydia P. Hecht. Bayou Publishing, 1996.

William B. Franklin Papers, Division of Manuscripts, Library of Congress.

Grant, U. S. *Personal Memoirs of U.S. Grant.* New York: Da Capo, 1982.

Grisamore, Silas. *Reminiscences of Uncle Silas: A History of the Eighteenth Louisiana Infantry Regiment.* Edited by Arthur W. Bergeron, Jr. Baton Rouge, Louisiana: *Le Comite des Archives de la Louisiana,* 1981; reprint ed. titled *The Civil War Reminiscences of Major Silas T. Grisamore, CSA.* Baton Rouge: Louisiana State University Press, 1993.

Harrell, J. M. Arkansas. Vol. X. *Confederate Military History.* Atlanta: Confederate Publishing Co., 1899. 12 vols.

Hanaburgh, David H. *History of the One Hundred and Twenty-eighth Regiment, New York Volunteers in the Late Civil War.* Poughkeepsie, New York: Enterprise Publishing Company, 1894.

Heartsill, W. W. *Fourteen Hundred and 91 Days in the Confederate Army: A Journal Kept by W. W. Heartsill for Four Years, One Month, and One Day or, Camp Life; Day by Day, of the W. P. Lane Rangers from April 19th, 1861 to May 20th, 1865,* Bell Irvin Wiley, ed. Wilmington, North Carolina: Broadfoot Publishing Company, 1992.

Hoffman, Wickham. *Camp, Court and Siege, A Narrative of Personal Adventure and Observation during Two Wars 1861–1865, 1870–1871.* New York: Harper and Brothers, 1877.

Homans, John. *History of the Thirteenth Maine Regiment, From Its Organization in 1861 to Its Muster-Out in 1865.* Boston, Massachusetts: The Military History Society of Massachusetts, VIII, 1910.

Howe, M. A. DeWolfe, ed. *Home Letters of General Sherman.* New York: Charles Scribner's Sons, 1909.

Irwin, Richard B. *History of the Nineteenth Army Corps.* Baton Rouge: Elliott's Book Shop Press, 1985.

Johnson, Robert U., and Clarence C. Buel, ed. *Battles and Leaders of the Civil War.* Four vols. Secaucus, New Jersey: Castle, 1986.

Kerby, Robert L. *Kirby Smith's Confederacy: The Trans-Mississippi South, 1863–1865.* Tuscaloosa: University of Alabama Press, 1972.

Lincoln, Abraham. *The Collected Works of Abraham Lincoln,* edited by Roy P. Basler. New Brunswick, New Jersey: The Abraham Lincoln Association, 1953.

Lubbock, Francis R. *Six Decades in Texas.* Austin: Ben C. Jones and Co., 1900.

Lufkin, Edwin B. *History of the Thirteenth Maine Regiment, From Its Organization in 1861 to Its Muster-Out in 1865.* Brighton, Maine: H. A. Shorey and Son, 1898.

Mahan, D. H. *A Treatise on Field Fortifications Containing Instructions on the Methods of Laying Out, Constructing, Defending, and Attacking Intrenchments, With the General Outline Also of the Arrangement, the Attack, and Defense of Permanent Fortifications.* New York: John Wiley, 1863.

Mansfield [Louisiana] State Historic Site. Unpublished casualty lists and reports at Mansfield State Historic Site, Mansfield, Louisiana; Interview with Steve Bounds, Site Manager at Mansfield State Historic Site, Mansfield, Louisiana, September, 15, 2001.

Marshall, Thomas B. *History of the Eighty-Third Ohio Volunteer Infantry, the Greyhound Regiment.* Cincinnati, Ohio: the Eighty-Third Ohio Volunteer Infantry Association, 1913.

Marston, James Family Collection. Unpublished diary in the collection. Shreveport, Louisiana.

Miller, Francis T., ed. *The Photographic History of the Civil War.* New York: Review of Reviews, 1911. 10 vols.

Newsome, Edmund. *Experience in the War of the Rebellion.* Carbondale, Illinois: Author, 1880.

Official Report to the Conduct of Federal Troops in Western Louisiana, during the Invasions of 1863 and 1864, Compiled from Sworn Testimony under Direction of Governor Henry Watkins Allen. Shreveport, Louisiana: State of Louisiana (C.S.A.), 1865.

Olmstead, Frederick L. *A Journey through Texas or, a Saddle-Trip on the Southwestern Frontier; with a Statistical Appendix.* New York: Dix, Edwards, and Company, 1857.

O'Pry, Maude Hearn. *Chronicles of Shreveport and Caddo Parish.* Shreveport, Louisiana: Times Publishing Co., 1928.

Pellet, Elias P. *History of the 114th Regiment, New York State Volunteers.* Norwich, New York: Telegraph and Chronicle Press Print, 1866.

Porter, David Dixon. *Incidents and Anecdotes of the Civil War.* New York: Appleton, 1885.

———. *Naval History of the Civil War.* Secaucus, New Jersey: Castle, 1984.

———. David Dixon Porter letter to his mother dated May 18, 1864, David D. Porter Papers, Division of Manuscripts, Library of Congress.

Powers, George W. T. *The Story of the Thirty Eighth Regiment of Massachusetts Volunteers.* Cambridge, Massachusetts: Dakin and Metcalf, 1866.

Scott, John. *Story of the Thirty Second Iowa Infantry Volunteers.* Nevada, Iowa: Author, 1896.

Scott, Reuben B. *The History of the 67th Regiment Indiana Infantry.* Bedford, Indiana: Herald Book and Job Print, 1892.

———. *The History of the 67th Regiment of Indiana Volunteer Infantry . . . From the Manuscript Prepared by the Late Chaplain John J. Hight.* Princeton: Indiana, 1895.

Selfridge, Thomas O. *What Finer Tradition: The Memoirs of Thomas O. Selfridge, Jr., Rear Admiral U.S.N.* Columbia: University of South Carolina Press, 1987.

Sherman, William T. *Memoirs of Gen. W. T. Sherman Written by Himself.* New York: Charles L. Webster & Co., 1892.

Shorey, Henry Augustus. *The Story of the Maine Fifteenth: Being a Brief Narrative of the More Important Events in the History of the Fifteenth Maine Regiment, Together with a Complete Roster of the Regiment.* Bridgton, Maine: Press of the Bridgton News, 1890.

Smith, Walter G. *Life and Letters of T. Kilby Smith.* New York: G. P. Putnam's Sons, 1898.

Sprague, Homer B. *History of the 13th Infantry Regiment of Connecticut Volunteers, During the Great Rebellion.* Hartford, Connecticut: Case, Lockwood, 1867.

Sperry, Andrew F. *History of the 33d Iowa Infantry Volunteer Regiment.* Des Moines: Mills and Company, 1866. Rept: Fayetteville, Arkansas: University of Arkansas Press, 1999.

Stanyan, John Minot. *A History of the Eighth Regiment of New Hampshire Volunteers, Including Its Service as Infantry, Second N.H. Cavalry, and Veteran Battalion in the Civil War of 1861–1865.* Concord, New Hampshire: Ira C. Evans, 1892.

Taylor, Richard. General Taylor letter to Major General John Walker, Mansfield, 1:30 [a.m. 9 April 1864] Walker Papers, Southern Historical Collection, Wilson Library, University of North Carolina, Chapel Hill, North Carolina.

———. *Destruction and Reconstruction: Personal Experiences in the Civil War.* New York: D. Appleton and Company, 1879.

US Army Corps of Engineers. *Red River Index, ARK.-TEX, to Mississippi River, Index of 1990 Mosaics.* Vicksburg, Mississippi: U.S. Army Engineer District, Vicksburg, Mississippi, 1990.

US Congress, *Report on the Joint Committee on the Conduct of the War, 1863–1866,* Vol 2, *Red River Expedition.* Washington, D.C.: U.S. Government Printing, 1865.

US War Department. *Atlas to Accompany the Official Records of the Union and Confederate Armies.* Washington: U.S. Government Printing Office, 1891–1895.

———. *Official Records of the Union and Confederate Navies in the War of the Rebellion.* 31 vols. Washington, D.C., 1895–1929.

———. *War of the Rebellion: The Official Records of the Union and Confederate Armies.* 128 vols. Washington, 1890–1901.

USS *Chillicothe.* Abstract Log. March 7, 1864–June 8, 1864.

USS *Lexington.* Abstract Log. March 1, 1864–June 28, 1864.

Van Dyke, Ben. Ben Van Dyke's Escape from the Hospital at Pleasant Hill, Louisiana. *Annals of Iowa.* Des Moines: Henry H. English, 1906.

Way, Frederick, Jr. *Way's Packet Directory, 1848–1994.* Rev. Ed. Athens: Ohio University Press, 1994.

Williams, E. Cort. "Recollections of the Red River Expedition," in *Sketches of War History 1861–1865, Papers Read Before the Ohio Commandery of the Military Order of the Loyal Legion of the United States 1886–1888.* Cincinnati: Robert Clarke and Company, 1888.

Williams, Thomas J. *An Historical Sketch of the 56th Ohio Volunteer Infantry.* Columbus, Ohio: The Lawrence Press, 1899.

Maps

John Clark. Map No. 8 of the Red River Campaign (Battle of Pleasant Hill), John Clark Collection, Cayuga County Museum, Auburn, New York.

———. Map of Grand Ecore Defenses (Union) dated April 1864. New Orleans, Louisiana. Jackson Barracks Archives (Louisiana National Guard).

John LaTourette Map (ca. 1850). National Archives and Records Administration, Washington, D.C., Records Group 77, folio M72.

Lavender US Soil Survey map of 1906, the Louisiana State University in Shreveport Archives.

Venable, Maj. Richard, C.S.A. Shreveport and Environs, 1864. Jerome Gilmer Papers, Southern Historical Collection, University of North Carolina, Chapel Hill.

————. Map of the Battlefield at Mansfield, 1864. Jerome Gilmer Papers, Southern Historical Collection, University of North Carolina, Chapel Hill.

————. Map of the Battlefield at Pleasant Hill, 1864. Jerome Gilmer Papers, Southern Historical Collection, University of North Carolina, Chapel Hill.

Newspapers

New York Times, October 30, 1862.

Secondary Sources

Ambrose, Stephen E. *Halleck: Lincoln's Chief of Staff.* Baton Rouge: Louisiana State University Press, 1962.

Bailey, Anne J. "Chasing Banks out of Louisiana: Parsons' Texas Cavalry in the Red River Campaign," *Civil War Regiments*, 3, no.1 (1993), 212–235.

Barron, Amos J. "A History of Pleasant Hill, Louisiana." Unpublished manuscript in the archives of the Mansfield State Historic Site, Mansfield, Louisiana.

Bearss, Edwin C. *Steele's Retreat From Camden & The Battle of Jenkins' Ferry.* Little Rock, Arkansas: Eagle Press of Little Rock, 1966.

Brock, Eric J. "City Geared for Battle That Never Came." Presence of the Past column *Shreveport Journal Page* Nov. 25, 1995.

Brooksher, William Riley. *War along the Bayous: The 1864 Red River Campaign in Louisiana.* Washington: Brassey, 1998.

Chrysler, Liz. "The Battle of Pleasant Hill-From a Boy's Point of View." *Mansfield* [Louisiana] *Enterprise*, May 17, 1977.

Connolly, Thomas L. "Vicksburg: Strategic Point or Propaganda Device?" *Military Affairs* 34 (1970): 49–53.

Edmonds, David C. *Yankee Autumn in Acadiana: A Narrative of the Great Texas Overland Expedition through Southwestern Louisiana October–December 1863.* Lafayette, Louisiana: Center for Louisiana Studies, 1979.

Estaville, Lawrence. *Confederate Neckties: Louisiana Railroads in the Civil War.* Ruston, Louisiana: McGinty Publications, 1989.

Gosnell, H. Allen. *Guns of the Western Waters: The Story of River Gunboats in the Civil War.* Baton Rouge: Louisiana State University Press, 1949.

Harrington, Fred Harvey. *Fighting Politician: Major General N. P. Banks.* Philadelphia: University of Pennsylvania Press, 1948.

Hollandsworth, James G., Jr. *Pretense of Glory: The Life of General Nathaniel P. Banks.* Baton Rouge: Louisiana State University Press, 1998.

Hewitt, Lawrence Lee. *Port Hudson: Confederate Bastion on the Mississippi.* Baton Rouge: Louisiana State University Press, 1987.

Huffstodt, Jim. *Hard Dying Men: The Story of General W. H. L. Wallace, General T. E. G. Ransom, and their "Old Eleventh: Illinois Infantry in the American Civil War (1861–1865).* Bowie, Maryland: Heritage Books, Inc., 1991.

Johnson, Ludwell. *Red River Campaign: Politics and Cotton in the Civil War.* Baltimore: The Johns Hopkins University Press, 1958.

Joiner, Gary D. *40 Archaeological Sites in the Red River Campaign* (1997). Archives of the Division of Archaeology, State of Louisiana, Baton Rouge, Louisiana.

————. *One Damn Blunder from Beginning to End: The Red River Campaign of 1864.* Lanham, Maryland: Scholarly Resources, 2003.

————. *Through the Howling Wilderness: The 1864 Red River Campaign and Union Failure in the West.* Knoxville: University of Tennessee Press, 2006.

————. *Mr. Lincoln's Brown Water Navy: The Mississippi Squadron.* Lanham, Maryland: Scholarly Resources, 2007.

————. "Fred Steele's Dilemma and Kirby Smith's Quest for Glory," in Mark K. Christ, ed. *The Earth Reeled and Trees Trembled: Civil War Arkansas, 1863–1864.* Little Rock, Arkansas: The Old State House Museum, 2007, 90–105.

Joiner, Gary D. and Stephen R. James. *Phase I Cultural Resources Investigation: Harrah's Entertainment Project, City of Shreveport, Caddo Parish, Louisiana* (1997). Archives of the Division of Archaeology, State of Louisiana, Baton Rouge, Louisiana.

Joiner, Gary D., and Charles E. Vetter. The Union Naval Expedition on the Red River, March 12–May 22, 1864. *Civil War Regiments* vol. 4, no. 2 (1994): 26–67.

Joiner, Gary D., Marilyn S. Joiner, and Clifton D. Cardin, eds. *No Pardons to Ask, Nor Apologies to Make.* Knoxville: University of Tennessee Press, 2006. From an unpublished journal by William Henry King, Texas State Archives, Austin, Texas.

Lowe, Richard. *The Texas Overland Expedition of 1863.* Fort Worth: Ryan Place Publishers, 1996.

————. *Walker's Texas Division C.S.A.: Greyhounds of the Trans-Mississippi.* Baton Rouge: Louisiana State University Press, 2004.

Mayeux, Steven M. *Earthen Walls, Iron Men: Fort DeRussy, Louisiana, and the Defense of Red Rive.* Knoxville: University of Tennessee Press, 2007.

McWhiney, Grady. *Cracker Culture: Celtic Ways in the Old South.* Tuscaloosa: University of Alabama Press, 1988.

Mills, Gary B. *Of Men and Rivers: The Story of the Vicksburg District* (1978). Vicksburg District, U.S. Army Corps of Engineers, Vicksburg, Mississippi.

————. *The Forgotten People: Cane River's Creoles of Color.* Baton Rouge: Louisiana State University Press, 1977.

Moore, Waldo. "The Defense of Shreveport—The Confederacy's Last Redoubt." *Military Analysis of the Civil War, An Anthology by the Editors of Military* Affairs. New York: American Military Institute, 1977.

Norris, L. David, James C. Millican, and Odie B. Faulk. *William H. Emory: Soldier-Scientist.* Tucson: University of Arizona Press, 1998.

Ponder, Jerry. *Major General John S. Marmaduke, C.S.A.* Mason, Texas: Ponder Books, 1999.

Prushankin, Jeffery Scott. *A Crisis in Command: Richard Taylor and Edmund Kirby Smith and the Army of the Trans-Mississippi.* Baton Rouge: Louisiana State University Press, 2005.

Ragan, Mark K. *Union and Confederate Submarine Warfare in the Civil War.* Mason City, Iowa: Savas Beattie, 1999.

Robinson, Michael. *Gunboats, Low Water, and Yankee Ingenuity: A History of Bailey's Dam.* Baton Rouge, Louisiana: F. P. H. C., 1991.

Roper, Laura W. "Frederick Law Olmstead and the Western Texas Free-Soil Movement," *American Historical Review,* 56 (1950–1951): 58–64.

Shannon, George W. Jr. Cultural Resources Survey of The Port of Shreveport-Bossier, Caddo and Bossier Parishes, Louisiana. Unpublished report for the Caddo/Bossier Port Commission (1996). Archives of the Division of Archaeology, State of Louisiana, Baton Rouge, Louisiana.

Silverstone, Paul H. *Warships of the Civil War Navies*. Annapolis, Maryland: Naval Institute Press, 1989.

Snyder, Perry Anderson. "Shreveport, Louisiana: 1861–1865: From Secession to Surrender." *Louisiana Studies*, vol. 11, no.1 (Spring 1972): 50–70.

Sutherland, Daniel E. "1864—'A Strange, Wild Time,'" in Mark K. Christ, *Rugged and Sublime: The Civil War in Arkansas*. Fayetteville: University of Arkansas Press, 1994

Tap, Bruce. *Over Lincoln's Shoulder: The Committee on the Conduct of the War*. Lawrence: University of Kansas Press, 1998.

Trudeau, Noah Andre. *Like Men of War: Black Troops in the Civil War 1862–1865*. Edison, New Jersey: Castle Books, 2002.

Warner, Ezra J. *Generals in Blue: Lives of the Union Commanders*. Baton Rouge: Louisiana State University Press, 1993.

———. *Generals in Gray: Lives of the Confederate Commanders*. Baton Rouge: Louisiana State University Press, 1993.

Weddle, Robert S. *Plow-Horse Cavalry: The Caney Creek Boys of the Thirty-Fourth Texas*. Austin: Madrona Press, 1974.

West, Richard S., Jr. *The Second Admiral: A Life of David Dixon Porter*. New York: Coward McCann, 1937.

Whittington, G. P. "Rapides Parish, Louisiana—A History. *Louisiana Historical Quarterly*, vol. XVIII (1935): 26–28.

Williams, Richard Brady. *Chicago's Battery Boys: The Chicago Mercantile Battery in the Civil War's Western Theater*. New York: Savas Beattie, 2005.

Winters, John D. *The Civil War in Louisiana*. Baton Rouge: Louisiana State University Press, 1963.

Zeitlin, Richard H. *Old Abe the War Eagle: A True Story of the Civil War and Reconstruction*. Madison: The State Historical Society of Wisconsin, 1986.

———. *The Eighth Regiment, 1861–1865*. Racine, Wisconsin: Racine County Historical Society, 1984.

Index

abatis, 111, 112

Alexandria, Louisiana, xi, xii, 11, 12, 18, 20, 22, 33, 37, 43, 44, 46, 47, 50–57, 125, 127, 128, 130–136, 138, 139, 144, 145, 147–149, 163, 170

Arkadelphia, Arkansas, xiv, 46, 47, 94, 95, 97, 110

Arkansas, xiii, xiv, 1, 3, 4, 5, 7, 8, 12, 16, 37, 42, 44, 46, 79, 80, 83, 85, 86, 93–96, 98, 101–104, 106–110, 112, 114, 124, 132, 144, 146, 147, 155, 156, 158

Army of the Gulf, 132, 141, 146

Army of the Tennessee, 42, 59, 96, 161

Army of the Trans-Mississippi, xiii, xiv, 157

Army of Western Louisiana, xiii, 103

Army Quartermaster Corps Boats
Black Hawk, 54, 119–122, 167
City Belle, 128, 146, 167
Clara Bell, 123, 167
Emerald, 120, 167
Emma, 128, 167
Iberville, 119, 167
John Warner, 113, 124, 128, 148, 167
Polar Star, 91, 168
Rob Roy, 120, 123, 168

Arnold, Brig. Gen. Richard, 147

Atchafalaya River, 49, 150, 154

Avoyelles Parish, 20

Avoyelles Prairie, 149

Bagby, Col. Arthur P., 74, 84, 159

Bailey, Lt. Col. Joseph, 130–132

Bailey's Dam, 135

Banks, Maj. Gen. Nathaniel P., 2, 8–13, 16–18, 32, 35–42, 46–48, 52–60, 62, 63, 66–68, 70, 71, 77, 79, 80–83, 89–93, 96, 100, 102, 103, 106, 115, 118, 119, 121, 125, 132, 133, 135, 137, 138, 139, 141, 143–151, 154, 155, 159

Baylor, Col. George, 143

Bayou Cotile, 52, 57

Bayou Courtableu, 53

Bayou de Glaize, 33

Bayou Pierre, 23, 56, 57, 92, 119

Bayou Rapides, 52

Bayou Teche, 10, 11, 32, 36, 56, 66, 128

Beard, Col. James H., 67

Bee, Brig. Gen. Hamilton P., 68, 74, 84, 86, 141–144, 157

Benedict, Col Lewis, 82, 87, 89, 92, 141, 142, 160

Benton Road, 103

Berwick Bay, 53

Birge, Brig. Gen. Henry, 141–144

Bisland, Louisiana, 36

Blair's Landing, 79, 82, 84, 90, 120

Blair's Landing Road, 79, 84

Boggs, Brig. Gen. William R., 19–25, 28–30, 56

Boyd, David French, 25, 29, 91

Brashear City, Louisiana, 46, 86

Buchel, Col. Augustus, 84, 86, 159

Butler, Maj. Gen. Benjamin F., 8, 9, 35, 40, 132

Cabell, Brig. Gen. William L., 97, 107, 108

Cabell's Brigade, 97, 107, 108

Caddo Parish, 4, 5, 25, 28, 30

Cairo, Illinois, 124, 125

Calhoun, Arkansas, 104, 106

Camden, Arkansas, 93, 96, 97, 100–104, 106–110

Cameron, Brig. Gen. Robert, 76–79, 142, 159

Camp Ford, 91

Camp Morgan, 23

camphene, 148

Campti, Louisiana, 119, 124

Canby, Maj. Gen. Edward R. S., 10, 16, 59, 66, 96, 146, 155

Carroll's Mill, 62, 66

Chapman's Bayou, 77, 78

Chattanooga, Tennessee, 1, 12

Childers' House, 82

Chisum, Col. Isham, 143, 159

Choctaw Bayou, 148, 149

Churchill, Brig. Gen. Thomas, 80, 83, 86, 87, 103, 107, 112, 158

Churchill's Division, 80, 83, 84, 86, 87, 89, 111, 112, 158

Cloutierville, Louisiana, 141, 143

Coate's Bluff, 25, 28

Confederate gunboats
  Arkansas, 56
  Missouri, 18

Confederate units (Regiments and Batteries)
  Artillery–First (Louisiana) Battery, 127
    Gross Tete (Louisiana) Flying Artillery Battery, 128, 158, 159
  Cavalry–Second Arizona Reg., 143
    Second Louisiana Reg., 52
    Second Texas, 143, 159
    Partisan Rangers, 143, 159
  Engineers–Fourth Confederate Engineer Battalion, Company H., 103
  Infantry–Consolidated Crescent (Louisiana) Reg., 69, 71, 157
    Eighteenth Louisiana Consolidated Reg., 69, 71, 157
    Twenty-Eighth Louisiana Reg., 69, 71, 157

contrabands, 107

Cornay, Capt. Florian O., 107, 158

Corps d'Afrique, 46, 58, 70, 77, 134, 163

Corse, Brig. Gen. John M., 145

Cotile, Louisiana, 52, 57

cotton, 3–5, 7–9, 37, 54, 57, 60, 107, 118, 134, 142

Coushatta, Louisiana, 119

Coushatta Chute, 24, 56, 119, 120

Cross Bayou, 6, 18, 28, 30

Crump's Corners, Louisiana, 61

Daily Missouri Republican, 156

Davis, President Jefferson, 16, 66, 155

Debray, Col. Xavier, 86, 159

Department of Alabama, Mississippi, and East Louisiana, 66, 155

Department of Arkansas, 12, 96

Department of the Gulf, 10, 12, 46, 53, 59, 146, 159

Department of the Trans-Mississippi, 3, 7, 15, 17

DeRussy, Col. L. G., 20

DeSoto Parish, Louisiana, 57, 60

Destruction and Reconstruction, 17, 66

Dickey, Capt. William H., 76

District of Western Louisiana, 17, 36, 66, 157

Dockery, Brig. Gen. Thomas P., 100

Dockery's Brigade, 100

Drake, Lt. Col. Francis, 107, 108

Drake, Lt. Col. George B., 70

Dudley, Col. Nathan A. M., 53, 70, 74, 77, 138, 161

Dunn's Bayou, 128, 129

Dwight, Brig. Gen. William, 81–83, 88–90, 138, 160

Eads, James Buchanan, 44

El Dorado, Arkansas, 93, 107

Elkin's Ferry, Arkansas, 98

Emory, Brig. Gen. William, 77–79, 81, 82, 88–90, 133, 141, 143, 144, 160

Emerson, Col. Frank, 62, 63, 70, 77, 78, 160

Fagan, Brig. Gen. James F., 97, 106–110

Fagan's Cavalry Division, 97, 106–110

Falls, the, 56, 128, 131, 133, 135, 136, 146

Farragut, Adm. David G., 2, 11

Fessenden, Col. Francis, 142, 160

Fincher House, 70

First (Arkansas) Division, 80, 86, 103, 158

First Division, Nineteenth Army Corps, 11, 77, 87, 160

Fort Albert Sidney Johnston, 28

Fort Beauregard, 20

Fort DeRussy, 20–23, 50, 51
Fort Humbug (Avoyelles Parish), 21
Fort Jenkins, 28
Fort Kirby Smith, 29, 30
Fort Scurry, 21
Fort Smith, Arkansas, xiv, 46, 47, 94, 95
Fort Towson Road, 103
Fort Turnbull (Fort Humbug), 25–28, 30, 31
Fourth Division, Thirteenth Army Corps, 62, 69, 79, 160
Franklin, Louisiana, 53
Franklin, Maj. Gen. William B., 11, 36, 53–58, 63, 70, 71, 77, 81, 89, 90, 131, 133, 144, 160
Frontier Division 47, 94, 102

Gano, Brig. Gen. Richard, 99, 158
Gano's Brigade, 99, 158
Gause, Col. Lucien, 86, 158
Gause's Brigade, 86, 158
Gooding, Brig. Gen. Oliver, 58, 62, 147, 161
Grand Coteau, Louisiana, 53
Grand Ecore, Louisiana, 4, 22, 25, 56, 57, 59, 90–92, 100, 103, 106, 117, 119, 120, 124, 125, 130, 137–139, 141, 145, 163
Grant, Lt. Gen. Ulysses S., 1, 2, 6, 12, 13, 22, 37, 38, 40, 42, 55, 72, 85, 96, 108, 131, 133, 138, 144–146
Gray, Col. Henry, 33, 52, 68, 69, 157
Green, Maj. Gen. Tom, 60, 62, 63, 65, 66, 68–70, 73, 74, 79, 83, 86, 120–123, 140, 159
Greene, Col. Colton, 97
Greene's Brigade ,97
Greenwood, Louisiana, 4
Grover, Brig. Gen. Cuvier, 138, 139, 141, 163

Hahn, Michael, 38
Halleck, Maj. Gen. Henry, 6, 10–12, 37–40, 42, 144–146
Harrisonburg, Louisiana, 20, 33, 103
Henderson's Hill, 52, 53, 56, 57

Honeycutt Hill, 63, 65, 67, 68, 71
Hot Springs, Arkansas, 93, 99
Hotchkiss Dam, 23, 56
Houston, Texas, 5, 11, 18, 19, 27
Hunter, Maj. Gen. David, 133, 145

Indian Territory, xiv, 3, 47, 98, 99, 101, 110, 114

Jackson, Lt. Gen. Thomas J., 10, 17, 35, 66
Jefferson, Texas, 5, 18, 99
Jenkins' Ferry, 101, 108, 110
Johnson, President Andrew, 155
Joint Committee on the Conduct of the War, 155

Lake Cannisnia, 57
Landram, Col. William J., 62, 63, 65, 69–71, 76, 77, 79, 160
Lee, Brig. Gen. Albert L., 46, 52, 53, 56–63, 65, 69–71, 73, 79, 89, 138, 139, 161
Liddell, Brig. Gen. St. John R., 141
Lincoln, Abraham, 8–10, 12, 13, 35–37, 42, 83, 132, 145, 146, 155
Little Missouri River, 97, 99
Little Rock, Arkansas, xii, 18, 37, 42, 43, 46, 47, 93–96, 100–102, 106–109, 114
Logansport, Louisiana, 4, 60
Logansport Road, 82
Loggy Bayou, 25, 119
Los Adaes, Louisiana, 60
Louisiana, xi, xii, 1–5, 7, 8, 11, 13, 16, 17, 19, 20, 22, 27, 29, 33, 35–39, 42, 46, 52–54, 60, 66, 68, 72, 74, 75, 83, 93, 96, 100, 102, 103, 110, 115, 124, 132, 133, 144, 155
Louisiana Division, 102, 103
Louisiana Seminary of Learning and Military Institute, 12, 90, 134
Lucas, Col. Thomas J., 62, 70, 161
Lucas' Brigade, 62, 70, 73, 88, 161

Magnolia, Arkansas, 104, 106, 107
Mahan, Dennis Hart, 25
Major, Brig. Gen. James P., 84, 159
Mansura, Louisiana, 149, 163
Mark's Mill, Arkansas, 114
Marksville, Louisiana, 20, 33, 50, 51, 149
Marksville-Fort DeRussy Road, 51
Marmaduke, Brig. Gen. John, 97, 99, 100, 102, 104, 106, 110–112, 165
Marmaduke's Division, 100, 101, 110, 165
Marshall, Texas, 3, 5, 18, 99
Maxey, Brig. Gen. Samuel B., 110, 165
Maxey's Cavalry Division, 101, 110, 165
Maximilian, Emperor of Mexico, 9, 19, 27, 36, 98
McClernand, Maj. Gen. John, 59, 135, 138, 164
McMillan, Brig. Gen. James W., 82, 83, 133, 160
McMillan's Brigade, 82, 87, 160
Meridian Campaign, 8, 32, 38
Military Division of West Mississippi, 147
Mississippi Marine Brigade, 42, 45, 161
Mississippi River, xi, 1, 3–8, 10, 15, 17, 47, 49
Mississippi Squadron, 118, 122
Missouri, xii, 3, 4, 39, 59, 72, 74, 79, 80, 83, 85, 96, 98, 101, 102, 108, 109, 132, 138
Mobile, Alabama, 12, 32, 38, 39, 66, 96, 145, 146
Monett's Ferry, 139, 142
Monroe, Louisiana, 46, 93
Monticello, Arkansas, 97
Moreauville, Louisiana, 150
Moro Swamp, 110
Mouton, Brig. Gen. J. J. A. Alfred, 52, 67–69, 71, 73, 75, 79, 84, 157
Mower, Brig. Gen. Joseph A., 50–53, 150, 154, 162
Mt. Elba, Arkansas, 97, 107

Natchitoches, Louisiana, 20, 57, 60, 68, 80, 91, 103, 138–140, 147
Natchitoches Parish, 4

New England, 3, 8, 9, 13, 15, 37, 146
New Falls City, 24, 25, 56, 119, 125, 171
New Orleans, Louisiana, 4, 8, 9, 11, 17, 23, 32, 36, 38, 41, 46, 52, 53, 118, 132, 138, 146, 155
Nims, Col. Ormand, 70, 73, 74
Nineteenth Army Corps, 11, 36, 41, 46, 52–55, 58, 63, 77, 79–81, 86, 91, 132, 133, 139, 148–150, 160

Old River, 49, 150
Opelousas, Louisiana, xi, 11, 36, 46, 53
Ouachita River, 11, 19, 20, 33, 46, 50, 52, 93, 95, 97, 103, 107, 110

Parsons, Brig. Gen. Mosby M., 80, 84, 85, 88, 103, 107, 158
Parsons' Division, 80, 84, 112, 158
Pass Cavallo, Texas, 138
Pearce Payne College, 82, 90
Phelps, Lt. Cdr. Seth L., 49, 124–127
Pine Bluff, Arkansas, 94, 97, 107, 110, 168
Pine Bluff Road, 107, 110
Pineville, Louisiana, 12, 37, 90, 134
Plain Dealing, Louisiana, 103
Pleasant Grove, 78
Pleasant Hill, Louisiana, 16, 39, 60, 62, 63, 66, 80–83, 89–91, 96, 97, 100, 102, 106, 120, 125, 137, 145
Poison Spring, Arkansas, 101, 104, 105, 109, 114
Polignac, Brig. Gen. Prince Camille A. J. M., 33, 52, 67, 68, 73, 75, 84, 87, 103, 127, 141, 144, 149, 150, 151, 154, 157
pontoon bridges, 30, 100, 103, 110, 111, 149, 154
Porter, Rear Adm. David D., 1, 2, 8, 11, 37, 38, 40–42, 44, 46, 47, 49–51, 54–58, 77, 80, 89, 93, 100, 117–127, 130–136, 145, 146
Prairie d'Ane, Arkansas, 99, 100, 105
Price, Maj. Gen. Sterling, 67, 69, 95, 97, 98, 100–102, 104, 106, 108, 112, 113, 164

Provisional Division, Seventeenth Army
    Corps, 45, 50, 161

raft (Fort DeRussy), 21, 22, 50
raft (Shreveport), 24, 30–32
Randal, Col. Horace, 68, 69, 73, 88, 112,
    113, 115, 157
Ransom, Brig. Gen. Thomas E. G., 62, 63,
    71–74, 76, 77, 91, 138, 159
Red River, xi, 1, 3–5, 11–13, 15, 17–25,
    28, 30, 33, 37, 40, 42, 44, 46, 47, 49,
    50, 54, 55, 57, 63, 94, 97, 98, 101,
    103, 118, 127, 128, 132, 136, 138,
    141, 154
Red River Campaign, xi, xii, 1, 2, 6, 8, 10,
    12, 13, 16, 19, 27, 38, 39, 55, 59, 63,
    74, 75, 96, 108, 122, 124, 132, 155
Red River Valley, 3, 4, 5, 15, 20, 23, 37,
    54, 120
Reynolds, Maj. Gen. John M., 146
Rio Grande River, 5, 6, 145
Rockport, Arkansas, 95
Rocky Mount, Louisiana, 103

Sabine Crossroads, 63
Sabine Pass, 11
Sabine River, 11, 13, 36, 60
Salomon, Brig. Gen. Frederick, 110, 167
Saline River, 97, 107, 110, 111, 114
San Antonio, Texas, 18
Scopini Island, 23, 25
Scopini's Cut Off, 56
Scott, R. B., 73, 74
Scurry, Brig. Gen. William R., 21, 68,
    113–115, 157
Scurry's Brigade, 88, 157
Second (Missouri) Division, 103, 166
Second Indian Brigade of Choctaws, 101,
    106
Selfridge, Jr., Lt. Cdr. Thomas O., 51,
    121, 122
Seventh Army Corps, 47, 94, 167
Shaw, Col. William, 82, 83, 85–87, 162
Shelby, Brig. Gen. Joseph, 97, 99, 100,
    106, 108, 165

Shelby's Brigade, 99, 106, 108, 165
Sherman, Maj. Gen. William T., 2, 3, 8,
    12, 13, 17, 32, 37–41, 44, 47–49, 54,
    66, 72, 90, 96, 106, 133, 134, 138,
    145, 146, 155
Shongaloo, Louisiana, 103
Shreveport, Louisiana, xi, xii, 2–6, 13,
    16–18, 20, 22–25, 28–31, 40–43, 46,
    47, 51, 54–57, 67, 68, 79, 88, 90, 91,
    93, 94, 102, 103, 106, 107, 109, 117,
    132, 138, 145
Shreveport defenses (Batteries)
    Battery I, 27
    Battery II, 28
    Battery III, 28
    Battery IV, 28
    Battery V, 28
    Battery VI, 28
    Battery VII, 28
    Battery VIII, 28
    Battery IX, 28
    Battery X, 28
    Battery XI, 28
    Battery XII, 28
    Battery Ewell, 27
    Battery Price, 30
    Battery Walker, 30
Shreveport navy yard, 18
Simmesport, Louisiana, 21, 33, 50, 147,
    150, 155
Sixteenth Army Corps, 39, 45, 50, 58, 72,
    81, 82, 88, 89, 148, 161
Smith, Brig. Gen. Andrew Jackson, 39–41,
    45–47, 49, 50, 56–58, 80–82, 86–89,
    118, 138–141, 144, 146–148, 150,
    161, 162
Smith, Lt. Gen. Edmund Kirby, 16–22, 24,
    29, 32, 33, 35, 56, 65–67, 78, 95–98,
    102–104, 106, 107, 109, 110, 112,
    113, 115, 144, 145, 155–157
Smith, Brig. Gen. Thomas K., 50, 58,
    118–120, 124, 125, 131, 162
Southern Pacific Railroad, 18, 46, 94
Spanish Royal Road (El Camino Real), 60
Sperry, A. F., 95

Springfield Landing, 57, 80
Stanton, Edwin M., 145
Steele, Maj. Gen. Frederick, 12, 16, 37, 39, 42, 46, 47, 74, 93–104, 107, 109–114, 138, 144, 145, 167
Stone, Brig. Gen. Charles P., 138
St. Landry Parish, 11
St. Mary Parish, 11, 36, 53
submarines, 18, 30, 171
Summer Road, 23

Tappan, Brig. Gen. James, 85, 88, 103, 158
Tappan's Brigade, 85, 158
Taylor, Maj. Gen. Richard, xii, 16–18, 20–23, 25, 27, 32, 33, 35, 36, 50–52, 54, 60, 63, 65–69, 71, 73–75, 78–80, 83–85, 87–91, 95–97, 102, 103, 115, 123, 128, 131, 137, 139–141, 144, 147–150, 154–157
Taylor, Gen. Zachary, 22
Ten Mile Bayou, 63, 77, 78
Texas, xi, xii, 3–13, 16–19, 21, 22, 27, 33, 35–37, 41, 50, 52, 53, 60, 68, 74, 83, 98, 102, 115, 132, 135, 145
Texas Trail, 4, 5, 6
"Thanks of Congress," 10, 132, 136
Thayer, Brig. Gen. John M., 94, 95, 97, 99, 100, 102, 168
Thirteenth Army Corps, 41, 46, 53, 58, 59, 62, 69, 72, 79, 81, 82, 89, 138, 139, 142, 146, 148, 159
Thomas, Lt. Col. Lorenzo, 77
Tone's (Tones) Bayou, 17, 23–26, 56, 91, 119
Toxie Creek (Cox Creek), 112
Trinity, Louisiana, 20, 33, 50, 52
turpentine, 148
Tyler, Texas, 5, 18, 90

Union spies, 18
Union units (Regiments and Batteries)
    Artillery–Chicago Mercantile Battery, 70, 76, 160
        First Indiana Battery, 70, 168
        Nims' Battery, 70, 73, 74

Cavalry–Fourteenth New York Cavalry, 119, 161
    Third Massachusetts Cavalry, 74, 77, 161
Infantry–Eighty-Third Ohio Regiment, 74
    Fifty-Sixth Ohio Regiment, 128, 129, 160
    Fifty-Eighth Illinois Regiment, 88
    First Kansas Volunteer (Colored) Regiment, 104, 106, 168
    Sixty-Seventh Indiana Regiment, 73, 74, 160
    Thirty-Second Iowa Regiment, 85–87, 158
    Thirty-Third Iowa Regiment, 95
    Twenty-Third Wisconsin Regiment, 74, 160
Union gunboats and support vessels
    Benefit (supply transport), 117, 120, 169
    Benton, 44, 124, 129
    Black Hawk, 45, 54, 119, 169
    Carondelet, 45, 131, 169
    Champion No. 3 (pump boat), 126, 127, 169
    Champion No. 5 (pump boat), 125–127, 169
    Chillicothe, 45, 58, 117, 120, 131, 133, 169
    Choctaw, 44, 169
    Cricket, 45, 58, 117, 125–127, 169
    Covington, 45, 128–130, 149, 169
    Dahlia (tug), 117, 133, 169
    Eastport, 45, 49, 51, 56, 57, 117, 124–126, 131, 169
    Essex, 44, 169
    Forest Rose, 45, 169
    Fort Hindman, 45, 58, 117, 125–127, 131, 133, 134, 169
    Gazelle, 45, 169
    General Sterling Price, 45, 169

Juliet, 45, 126, 127, 169
Lafayette, 45, 169
Lexington, 45, 58, 117, 120, 122, 124, 131, 134, 169
Louisville, 45, 131, 169
Mound City, 45, 131, 169
Neosho, 45, 58, 117, 130, 131, 134, 169
Osage, 45, 51, 58, 117, 120–123, 131, 134, 169
Ouachita, 45, 169
Ozark, 45, 131, 133, 169
Pittsburg, 45, 131, 169
Signal, 45, 128–130, 149, 169
St. Clair, 45, 169
Tallahatchie, 45, 169
William H. Brown (dispatch vessel), 117, 169
"Upper Cotton Kingdom," 5

Vance, Col. Joseph W., 63, 77, 160
Venable, Maj. Richard M., 21, 24, 29, 30, 76

Vicksburg, Mississippi, 1, 3, 6, 8–10, 16, 17, 32, 35, 37, 39, 40, 44, 49, 59, 61, 69, 96, 118, 122

W. P. Lane Rangers, 91
Wade, Ben, 155
Wade Committee, 155
Walker, Maj. Gen. John G., 8
Walker's Texas Division, 8, 166
Walker, Col. Tandy, 101, 165
Washington, Arkansas, 173
Washington, D.C., 74
Waul, Brig. Gen. Thomas, 68, 88, 157, 166
Welles, Gideon, 131, 144
West, Capt. John A., 128, 158
Wharton, Maj. Gen. John, 140, 141, 144, 149, 150
Williams, Col. James, 104
Wilson's Farm, 62, 91, 173
Withenbury, Wellington W., 57

Yellow Bayou, 150–152, 154
Yellow Bayou forts, 21

CPSIA information can be obtained at www.ICGtesting.com
Printed in the USA
LVOW06s0018190614

390655LV00004B/5/P